THE ULTIMATE
DOLL BOOK

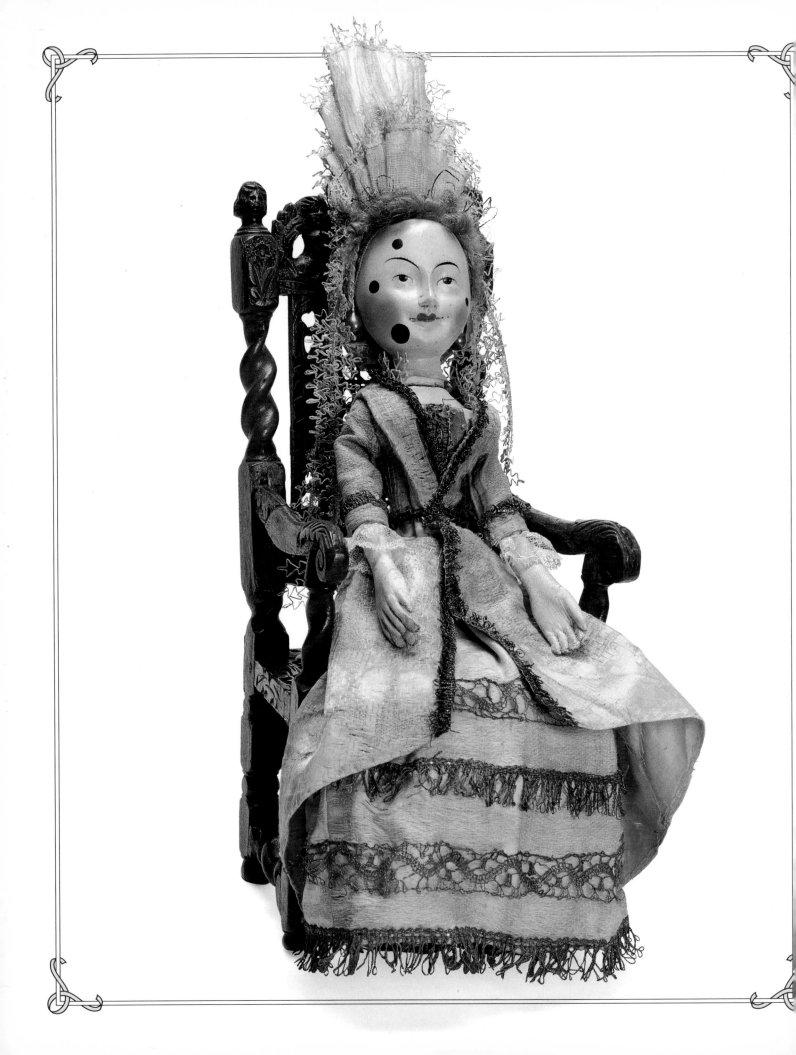

THE ULTIMATE DOLL BOOK

Caroline Goodfellow

Foreword by
Dorothy and Evelyn Jane Coleman

Photography by
Matthew Ward

DORLING KINDERSLEY
London · New York · Stuttgart

A DORLING KINDERSLEY BOOK

Project Editor Gillian Roberts
Art Editor Kevin Ryan
Assisting Editor Polly Boyd
Production Meryl Silbert

Managing Editor Mary-Clare Jerram
Managing Art Editor Gill Della Casa
Consultant Faith Eaton

First published in Great Britain in 1993
by Dorling Kindersley Limited,
9 Henrietta Street, London WC2E 8PS

A CIP catalogue record for this book
is available from the British Library

ISBN 0 8628 8327 X

Computer page make-up by
Cooling Brown Partnership, Great Britain

Text film output by The Right Type, Great Britain

Reproduced by Colourscan, Singapore

A description of the dolls **on these pages**
can be found *on these pages* of the book:
page 1 *"Solid Comfort"*, page 88; **page 2** *"Old
Pretender"*, page 13; **page 3** *Patterned Shoulder Head*,
page 49; **page 4** *Harry The Hawk*, page 103;
page 5 top *Mandarin with Long Fingers*, page 135.

Contents

PORCELAIN PARADE (BELOW) This selection of nine bisque and untinted bisque dolls illustrates the fine craftsmanship of French and German doll-makers in the late 19th and early 20th centuries.

Foreword

Dorothy and Evelyn Jane Coleman

GLAZED CHINA DOLL
(BELOW) This fine example from the Coleman Collection was made in Germany between 1865 and 1870, and has the typically classical look that was so fashionable at that time. The shoulder plate has a moulded, decorated design. The body is of stuffed cloth, with kid lower arms. Ht: 50cm (20in)

EVEN IN THE DAYS of the early Greeks, dolls were part of domestic life, and since then they have played a significant role in almost every civilization. Today, collecting dolls is a prominent, popular pursuit worldwide: everywhere, dolls are objects of great interest and desirability.

It has been our good fortune to visit numerous museums and private collections of dolls throughout the world. What a thrill it is to see the early native dolls in Alaska, the dolls in the many American countries, the Australian dolls, and of course, the dolls in Europe. Recently, we revisited Thuringia, in Germany, where the majority of the dolls in our collection were originally produced. Sadly, its once-prosperous doll-making industry has almost ceased to exist, but the antique dolls themselves live on in public displays and individual collections.

Looking at Dolls

In 1992, during our second visit to Australia, we gave many talks on dolls, including a programme of lectures at the Powerhouse Museum in Sydney. Some of the people attending had travelled long distances just to be there. While we were at the museum, the curator showed us some of the dolls that had been brought to Australia in the distant past. Most had never been seen before by the public, and not even by doll collectors in Australia. We were not certain which gave them the greater pleasure: was it the very special privilege of seeing these dolls that had come to Australia long ago, or the rare opportunity of viewing our colour slides of different and exciting dolls from around the world?
Fortunately, one does not always have to travel a great distance in order to see pictures of beautiful dolls. Readers of *The Ultimate Doll Book* can look at, study, and enjoy some of the dolls that belong to

"LADY BETTY MODISH"
(ABOVE) This elegant, c.1902 Kestner bisque-headed doll (see pages 74–75) is one of the major exhibits at the Wenham Museum. Ht: 45cm (17½in)

major private collections such as Faith Eaton's, in England, and our own, in the United States: both of these have been decades in the making. *The Ultimate Doll Book* also provides wonderful photographs of dolls from London's Bethnal Green Museum of Childhood (a branch of the Victoria & Albert Museum) and the Wenham Historical Association and Museum, near Boston in the United States. These two famous museums have outstanding collections of dolls; some of the dolls date back many years, or even centuries.

The World of the Collector

Once you buy a doll, hopefully you may live with it for a good many years; as you learn more about it, your doll may become an even greater treasure. Seek dolls in as original condition as possible, not ones that have been repaired or altered. Be sure the clothes are of about the same period as the doll, too. Examine and familiarize yourself with the marks and every detail of their heads, bodies, and clothes, especially the shoes. This can tell you a considerable amount about your dolls, such as who made them, and where – and perhaps, when – they were made.

Dissemblers and Fakes

Dolls are often put together at various stages of their lives, for example, the head could be purchased and the rest of the doll made at home; parts may have been replaced at a doll hospital; or dealers today can put parts of different ages together to create a doll. If a doll that appeals to you has been altered and wears recently made clothes, wait until you can find a similar doll, but in its original condition, including the wig and the costume.

Future Preservation

Millions upon millions of dolls with bisque heads were made in the nineteenth and early twentieth centuries, yet few have survived intact. Their modern, porcelain relatives – now often produced as collectors' dolls rather than playthings – do not have to suffer the same harsh treatment; instead, they are handled with care, so that they will be available for years to come. Now, many of the dolls of old are being given similar consideration. At least a few surviving old dolls, as well as some newer ones, can be enjoyed in *The Ultimate Doll Book*, and thus provide pleasure for this and future generations.

WAX-OVER-COMPOSITION (*ABOVE*) *Made in the mid-19th century in England or Germany, this doll from the Faith Eaton Collection has a wax-over-papier mâché shoulder head, cloth body and upper arms and legs, and kid lower arms. Ht: 80cm (31in)*

WATERCOLOUR MINIATURE (*ABOVE*) *One of a group of miniatures, "The Four Whitmore Children", by 18th-century artist, Paul-Peter Lens, shows a girl holding a contemporary doll.*

PIEROTTI DOLL (*BELOW*) *Made by Pierotti in England in the early 20th century, this lady is exhibited at the Bethnal Green Museum of Childhood. It has a poured wax shoulder head, and lower arms and legs. The skill of the maker is evident in the fine modelling and graceful pose of the doll's hands. Ht: 41cm (16in)*

Introducing Dolls

ASK TEN DIFFERENT PEOPLE "What is a doll?", and you will probably get as many different answers, each one qualified by the period, culture, and society that have formed and shaped that person's singular perception of the world. Yet, crossing all barriers of individual perspective and time, race, and class, we discover the generally accepted idea of what a doll is: an inanimate object that represents a human being in miniature.

〜 In *The Ultimate Doll Book*, we have chosen to include a majority of dolls used as playthings. Of course, there are many other types of doll: dolls' house dolls and paper dolls, marionettes and puppets, to name just a few. All of these are quite separate subjects in their own right. Vying for attention with the playdolls featured in this book, they would not have received the closely detailed pictorial and textual commentary they deserve.

〜 Although all the dolls illustrated and described in these pages were made within the last three hundred years, our knowledge of ancient civilizations leads us to the correct assumption that dolls did not suddenly appear in the seventeenth century, but had evolved to that point over thousands of years. A swift trip through *The Ultimate Doll Book* reveals a continuing ebb and flow to this process of gradual evolution, as new materials and innovative manufacturing techniques have changed the course of doll-making history.

GIRL WITH A DOLL (*ABOVE*) *This oil on canvas painting, entitled "Portrait of Lilly, Daughter of J. Noble, Esq.", is the work of English artist, Sir John Everett Millais, who lived between 1826 and 1896. The figure held by the child shows an example of the gorgeously dressed lady dolls that were made in France in the later years of this period.*

C.1915 CHARCOAL SELLER (*BELOW*) *Created in the United States by one of the New Orleans' Vargus family, this wax doll portrays a "Cry" of the same city. Cries represent familiar trades and occupations, and are usually seen as pictures, rather than as three-dimensional objects. Ht: 18cm (7in)*

Dolls as Playthings

The use to which dolls have been put over the years has varied enormously, from religious offerings at one end of the spectrum to playthings at the other. But the majority of the dolls produced between 1680 and the 1990s – the time period covered by our book – were almost certainly intended to be used as children's playthings. Many were designed for a particular age group: in the eighteenth century, simple rag dolls, stitched and stuffed by mothers using any readily available household materials, were generally made as comfort toys for young babies and children under five.

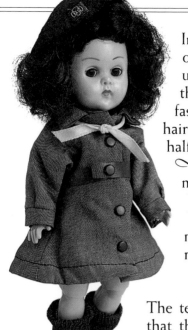

In England, older middle-class children had "Sunday only" dolls, which were taken out to be played with under strict adult supervision for an hour or two in the afternoon. The elegantly attired, bisque-headed fashion dolls and those with elaborately moulded hairstyles, made in France and Germany in the latter half of the nineteenth century, fall into this category.

～ Since the 1930s, more and more dolls have been mass-produced, particularly in the United States. Faced with rising costs and the whims of a must-have buying public, manufacturers target niche markets as a matter of survival, ensuring a good return on their capital outlay and investment.

Chronology and Order

The ten sections of *The Ultimate Doll Book* are arranged so that the materials from which dolls have been made are described, as they were first used for this purpose, in a loosely knit chronology. History is not so neatly ordered, however, that one section begins where the previous section came to an end: doll-makers did not stop using one material simply because another became available.

～ Some materials, such as wood, have stepped backward in their "evolution". Others, for example bisque, have been superseded by newer ones. Even within the bounds of this scenario, a material can be rediscovered, perhaps in a novel form. Individual doll-makers are now using a ceramic-like art clay called Sculpey, formulated in the United States, to create doll heads with the look of fine bisque porcelain.

～ Manufacturing innovations have played their part in the story as well. Realistically modelled plastic dolls would scarcely be possible without the techniques of injection moulding that were developed in the 1940s. For some, such technology allows realism to be carried to unpalatable extremes: Villy Nielsen's Judith "Mother and Baby" – a doll with a spring-loaded abdominal cavity that "gives birth" to a tiny baby – or Effe's male-sexed *Bimbovero* are not to everyone's taste.

The Language of Dolls

Remember, as you read *The Ultimate Doll Book*, that unfamiliar words, or familiar words used in unfamiliar ways, are just a means of identifying the different types of doll. Transported into nineteenth-century France, "doll" becomes *bébé* (baby) for dolls representing young children as well as babies, and *poupée* (doll) for older child and adult dolls – confusing stuff for newcomers who might assume that a French *bébé Jumeau* is a Jumeau baby doll. But learning the special language of dolls is all part of the fun of discovering this fascinating subject.

GIRL SCOUT OF AMERICA *(ABOVE) This 1950s' Vogue Dolls, Inc. Ginny is typical of the hard plastic dolls made after World War II. Ht: 18cm (7in)* Vogue Dolls® is a registered trademark of Dakin, Inc. All Vogue Dolls designs © 1993 Dakin, Inc., Woodland Hills, California, USA, reproduced here courtesy of Dakin.

RUSSIAN NESTING DOLL, YELTSIN *(BELOW) The correct term for these brightly painted wooden dolls is Matryoshka. The dolls fit inside each other, and are usually made in series of between six and ten figures. Ht: 11cm (4¼in)*

BÉBÉ JUMEAU *(ABOVE) Large, bulbous eyes are a feature of early Jumeau dolls. This one is described in extensive detail on page 58. Doll ht: 55cm (22in)*

1980S' GERMAN DOLL *(BELOW) The original wrist tag bears the legend "Stupsi, your lovable cuddly companion". A bendable soft vinyl doll, Stupsi is made soft and friendly with a stockinet cover. Ht: 43cm (17in)*

Wooden Dolls

Cheap and readily available, wood has always been used for making dolls. Wooden dolls with any accurately documented history date from c. 1680, although they were, of course, made before this time. A few figures have been found in ancient burial sites, yet genuine examples of very early dolls have all but disappeared – destroyed, perhaps during times of religious conflict as idolatrous images, or simply deemed not worth keeping.

RECORDS ATTESTING TO DOLL-MAKING activities tell us that of the dolls surviving from the 1600s and 1700s, the majority – or even all – are English. Most are made of pine, a timber that was in plentiful supply, easy to carve or turn on a lathe, but also able to withstand rough treatment. As with other types of doll, a great number of wooden dolls were made by parents for their children, but the most accomplished examples are almost certainly the work of professional carvers, making dolls for sale.

  In Europe, the toy-making industry (which also produced dolls) evolved over more than two hundred years. By the 1600s, it was established as an organized craft guild alongside other guilds that embraced similarly traditional skills. This indicates that doll-making existed in Europe long before the end of the eighteenth century, when dolls attributed to European makers came onto the market. In the Grödener Tal region of Austria (now a part of Italy) and in Oberammergau, Berchtesgaden, and Sonneberg, three small German towns, rich forests of pine provided abundant raw materials for making dolls. The town of Erzgebirge, near Dresden, was another energetic centre of wooden toy-making.

Early Dolls

The early wooden dolls – those made between 1680 and 1720 – are considered to be carefully crafted. Each has the head and torso carved as one, and shows a distinctly individual facial expression, with painted or inset glass eyes, and noses, mouths, and ears which are well defined. Their limbs are attached by various pinning and jointing methods, according to the material. The upper arms are most usually made of bound

LADY AND LORD CLAPHAM (*LEFT & RIGHT*) *These two carved wooden dolls wear "Fashionable Undress" – costumes so typical of the late 17th-century English upper class that they date the pair c. 1690. The similarity between the dolls suggests that they are probably the work of a single maker. Both are entirely painted over a gesso base, and have painted eyes and facial features. Ht: 48cm (19in)*

PEG WOODENS POSTCARD (*RIGHT*) *During the 1890s, Bertha Upton wrote a series of children's books, illustrated by her daughter, Florence. The series inspired a range of merchandise, including card games and postcards. The adventures of two peg wooden dolls (and their friend, Golliwogg) were some of the most popular of their stories.*

GRÖDENER TAL SHOULDER HEADS (*ABOVE & RIGHT*) *Sometimes known as Wooden Bettys, and now rather uncommon, heads such as these cheap 1930s' designs were mass-produced from 1880 to 1940, mainly for export. They are quite crudely carved and painted, and are usually attached to coarse cloth bodies. Ht: 10cm (4in)*

linen, while the lower parts are made of carved wood. Fingers and thumbs are separate and many examples display finger-nail detail. Wood was usually used for the upper and lower legs. The feet tend to be skilfully made, with well carved toes and toe-nails. The whole body was covered with a base layer of gesso first, then delicately painted, and finally varnished. The finished dolls were dressed in stylish period costumes.

A Retrograde Development

After 1720, wooden dolls deteriorated, rather than improved, in quality. A more stylized, less individual appearance is conveyed in the dolls' flattened faces and facial features. The painstaking carving of the earlier doll bodies gave way to a crudely fashioned torso and limbs, although the narrow-waisted, broad-hipped shape was retained. As before, the wooden limbs and knee joints were attached to the torso with pegged tongue and groove joints. When all-wooden arms had replaced the earlier linen-and-wooden type, tongue and groove joints were also applied to the shoulders and elbows. Despite the relatively unrefined workmanship, the joints themselves are surprisingly efficient, allowing easy mobility for the arms and legs. Ball joints were used for some 1800s' dolls, giving them the look of an artist's manikin or lay figure, and providing their limbs with even greater freedom of movement than the tongue and groove joints.

Finishing techniques were also less sophisticated than those of earlier dolls. The gesso base layer was still used, but paint was applied only on the face and upper torso – areas that were meant to resemble naked "flesh" – while the rest of the body was left white. Towards the end of the 1700s, even the gesso layer was abandoned, and doll bodies were unpainted, showing the bare wood.

The overall decline in the quality of wooden dolls continued into the nineteenth and twentieth centuries. They were generally considered cheap, throw-away items, and their appearance helped only to support this view. However, some dolls did once again exhibit the individual personality of the 1680s' dolls, as we can observe in the work of such fine craftsmen as the innovative American doll-makers, Joel Ellis (see page 14) and Albert Schoenhut (see page 15).

LUCKY MASCOT (*LEFT*) *Small wooden dolls were once peddled at the Derby – a classic fixture of the English flat-racing season – and worn in the hatband for good luck. Sir John Everett Millais' pen and ink drawing of 1853 pokes fun at a couple's despair after losing a bet.*

Early Dolls
· 1680s to 1820s ·

MOST EARLY WOODEN DOLLS were made in England, probably in London and the surrounding area, by a number of different makers. Fewer than thirty seventeenth-century English wooden dolls have survived. Female dolls far outnumber males, which have the same shape, but are dressed in masculine attire. The formal appearance and fashionable clothing of both types suggests that they were made for adults, rather than as children's toys.
⌒ Dolls of this period are often called "Queen Anne" dolls, a misnomer, because most were made either before 1702 or after 1714, the years of her reign. Dating these rare, virtually priceless dolls is difficult. The clothes, usually sewn to the body, do not allow examination of the naked figure, which is likely to reveal clues to the doll's age.

Head and torso made from one block of wood, turned on a lathe, and carved

Dark brown glass eyes, embedded in slots cut in the face

Torso has a rounded chest, narrow waist, flat back, and broad, squarish hips

Curly human hair wig, nailed to head

Lathe-turned head and torso are painted in flesh tones over a gesso base

Linen upper arms

Separate, carved fingers are often broken off or damaged

Wooden lower arms

Wooden peg

Legs and lower torso are painted white over a gesso base

Tongue-and-groove joints, with wooden pegs, at knees and hips

HT: 41cm (16in)

Roughly shaped feet have no toes

Sleeves conceal linen upper arms, stitched to torso through holes drilled in shoulders

Silk damask winter dress with lace trim

Carved, separate flat fingers and thumbs on wooden lower arms

Lower arms are covered with kid gloves

Dress conceals linen, wool-embroidered petticoat and linen undergarments

AUGUSTA MARIANNA (ABOVE) *This c.1780 lady is typical of dolls made after 1760. It lacks the finely modelled features of earlier dolls, an example of which can be seen on the right.* Ht: 48cm (19in)
1745 DOLL (RIGHT) *The well-defined nose, mouth, lozenge-shaped eyes, and brows and lashes indicated with dots of paint, give this figure a definite personality.*

Bulbous glass eyes, slotted into face

Head and narrow-waisted torso carved from one piece of wood

Well-defined nose, ears, and mouth

Shaped and painted breasts

Original linen upper arms have been rebound and nailed to the shoulders

Finely carved hands show rounded fingers with finger-nails

Hips are carved either side to house tongues from leg joints

Wide-hipped lower torso, shaped at back to suggest buttocks

Carved, but not separate, toes

Lower legs have fine calves and ankles

EUROPEAN RIVAL, C.1820 (RIGHT) From the end of the 18th century, cheaper German dolls competed with the expensive English models. They were painted directly onto the wood, on areas that would show: the costly gesso base layer was omitted. Ht: 22cm (8½in)

Painted hair, eyes, and mouth

Wedge, inserted into face, forms nose

Limbs are attached to torso with wooden pegs

UNCLOTHED MODEL (ABOVE) This doll, made between 1700 and 1720, is remarkable in its relatively close resemblance to the human form. Its unclothed state provides a rare opportunity to study the maker's craftsmanship. Ht: 48cm (19in)

1680s' carved walnut and cane chair, styled after full-sized chairs in Holyroodhouse

Head and body, carved from separate pieces of wood, are gessoed and painted

Painted eyes, a feature of many early dolls

Black beauty patches were the height of fashion

"FASHIONABLE UNDRESS FOR SPRING 1755" (RIGHT) In the mid-1700s, a young English girl, Laetitia Clark Powell, created doll costumes based on dresses she had once worn herself. This costume, made when she was 13, is worn by a typical, stylized wooden doll. Ht: 28cm (11in)

Human hair wig

Brown glass eyes

Painted facial features

Kid-covered hands appear large, but are in proportion to head

Cloth covers wooden lower arms, to look like gloves

Informal "at-home" costume, made of silk brocade

"OLD PRETENDER" (ABOVE) The attire, face patches, and known history of this doll suggest it was made c.1680. It is said that it belonged to the court of King James II at Holyroodhouse in Edinburgh, Scotland. Ht: 53cm (21in)

Dolls from the New World

· 1850s to 1930s ·

IN THE UNITED STATES, New England was the creative centre for toys and dolls in the mid-nineteenth century. Many American makers were already established producers of wooden toys, but their doll designs, though innovative, were often unsuccessful: the buying public – composed largely of recently settled Europeans – found dolls of the familiar European style and type more to its taste (see pages 18–19).

Some early American dolls were the work of individuals, made in their spare time; other makers progressed to form companies that manufactured dolls on a grander scale. By the twentieth century, makers were very often immigrants who had worked with toys or dolls in their native land, and doll-making had spread beyond New England to other parts of the country.

Head and neck are painted to resemble skin

Mortise and tenon joints at shoulders give full articulation

Upper torso painted yellow

Mortise and tenon joints at elbows

Mortise and tenon joints at hips

Hands and wrists are made of cast lead, painted cream

A metal pin secures each mortise and tenon joint

Flesh-toned paint on lower legs

Cast lead feet and ankles, painted to resemble boots

Hair is usually brownish black; blonde hair is rare

Moulded facial features are hand painted

Dowel post attaches rigid head to body

Stiffened cotton apron, with printed "embroidery" in a traditional design

Hand-painted drawstring purse, tied to wrist

Bloomers trimmed with intricate cotton tatting

JOEL ELLIS, 1873 PATENTED DOLL *The Co-operative Manufacturing Co. produced these dolls for the Vermont Novelty Works, founded in 1858 by Joel Ellis, Rodney Britton, and Ellis Eaton in Springfield, Massachusetts. Ellis's doll has a rock maple head, steamed and shaped in a hydraulic press, and lead hands and feet.*

HT: 38cm (15in)

KENTUCKY MOUNTAIN PAIR

(RIGHT) Dating from the 1930s, this pair is thought to be the work of one person making dolls as a hobby, rather than a company. The male figure is distinguished from the female essentially by its clothes, and in small details such as the hair and body padding. Ht: 25cm (10in)

Brown, poor-quality mohair wig, stuck to head

Solid wood head, with roughly carved facial features

Cheeks and chin are stained with pink ink or water-based paint

Cloth-over-wood, padded upper torso

Wooden lower and upper arms

Suit conceals stuffed cloth upper legs and lower torso

Wooden lower legs, with blue ink- or paint-stained feet

Eyes, lashes, and brows are defined with pencil

Female figure has no padding

Dress conceals feet, which are almost identical to the man's

Both dolls have a handwritten ink mark on the upper back that reads "Hall", probably the name of the maker.

SCHOENHUT ALL-WOOD PERFECTION ART DOLL

(BELOW) Albert Schoenhut, a German emigrant, started trading in Philadelphia, Pennsylvania in 1872. In 1911, his company was awarded a patent for an all-wood doll with metal spring joints. The unique flexible jointing system allows much movement, but is rigid enough for the doll to be posed without falling over. Ht: 40cm (16in)

Solid wood head

Joints at elbows, neck, shoulders, wrists, hips, knees, and ankles

The mark is impressed into the upper back of the doll. This model was made until 1939.

Oblique hole allows doll to hold foot in tip-toe position

Straight hole allows doll to hold the foot resting flat

Hair is moulded with the head and painted yellowish blonde

Head turns through 360°

Mortise and tenon joints, with wooden pegs, at shoulders and hips

Rock maple body, unpainted on parts likely to be clothed

Ball and socket joints at knees and elbows

Cast lead feet, painted blue to represent boots

JOINTED DOLL COMPANY

(LEFT) This doll has ball and socket joints patented by George W. Sanders, and a composition-over-wood head, patented by Charles C. Johnson. It was produced and distributed by the Jointed Doll Co., Vermont, c.1880. Ht: 30cm (12in)

Poupards and Simple Dolls

· 1800s to the present day ·

NOT ALL OF THE EARLIEST DOLLS were as sophisticated as the elegant individuals shown on pages 12 and 13. Stump Dolls (simple, one-piece figures, carved from a single block of wood) were produced at the same period in England and Germany. The majority were quite roughly made, although some had intricate, painted decoration that showed the type of clothing worn by fashionable ladies. Poupards succeeded stump dolls, and came mainly from the Erzgebirge region of Germany. These had no legs (although they did sometimes have arms), were crudely carved or turned on a lathe, and painted in bright colours. Poupards usually represent babies in swaddling clothes, or men and women. Twentieth-century versions sometimes have the added refinement of jointed heads and arms or sound mechanisms. Other types of simple dolls are those made from wooden spoons or old-fashioned, straight clothes pegs, materials that remain firm favourites with makers even today.

Carved grooves give texture to painted hair

Nose is a triangular wedge of wood, inserted into a slit in the face

Crudely painted mouth

Painted hair continues around back of doll's head

Doll's name and origin, handwritten in pencil in German script, "Thÿmiane/die Düftende/geboren zu/Sterzing/20. Juli 1926" (Thÿmiane/the Aromatic One/born in/Sterzing/20 July 1926)

Painted wavy line around neck, suggesting lace trim to the swaddling

Doll is roughly carved from one piece of wood, with smoother finish on head and torso

Painted floral decoration is applied over the body base colour

Flat back has been left unpainted

Lower part of inscription is illegible

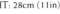

HT: 28cm (11in)

THE "AROMATIC ONE" *Thÿmiane die Düftende is the female half of a pair of large poupards. According to the pencil inscriptions on their backs, the doll and its male companion, the "Awkward One" – Schnattissimo der Rüpel – were "born" in the German village of Sterzing on 20 July 1926. Both figures are painted, on the front only, to represent young babies swaddled, or wrapped, in cloth strips, in the traditional fashion.*

Front of figure is painted with flesh tones, now faded to cream

Face and upper torso are painted in flesh tones

Unjointed wooden arms, pegged to torso at shoulders

Painted lower arms are unvarnished

Legs end in roughly shaped, painted shoes

1920s' PEG WOODEN (ABOVE)
Quantities of cheap dolls were produced in Grödener Tal throughout the 1800s. The 20th-century version shown here differs from them only in its "flapper" costume. Ht: 15cm (6in)

WOMAN WITH HAT (BELOW)
Poupards with arms usually represent adults. This German doll was made between 1900 and 1930, but is based on an old design. Ht: 15cm (6in)

Arms, carved as wide sleeves, are of a piece with the body

Lathe-turned doll, made in 1983

Sides of bobbed hair are shaped as part of the head, and defined with paint

HAPPY DAYS Regd
MADE IN ENGLAND

The mark is screen-printed on the back of the head, over the painted hair.

Metal rivets join limbs to torso

HAPPY DAYS GIRL (LEFT)
This 1930s' English doll is made from flat pieces of wood, painted and varnished to show facial features, hair, and feet. The simple fixings at the shoulders and hips hold the arms and legs in place, and provide an effective, if basic, jointing system. Ht: 20cm (8in)

Legs and arms have limited sideways and up-and-down movement

CLOTHES PEG DOLL (RIGHT) The straight, old-fashioned clothes pegs were often transformed by mothers into improvised playthings. The raffia hair of this c.1955 doll is ingeniously bound to fall either side of its neck, so that the plaits form the doll's arms. Ht: 11.5cm (4½in)

Mouth and eyes are drawn with ballpoint pen

Clothes are made from rag-bag scraps of cotton material

Wood has been neither painted nor varnished

1920s' FLAPPER (BELOW) This wooden spoon shows how household equipment can be transformed with a little imagination. Painted in black on white, with touches of red and gold, it is a stylish impression of a flapper. Ht: 30cm (12in)

Original poupard design, reinterpreted by a modern maker

Pencilled eyes, nostrils, and mouth

Carved nose

Slots in body sides allow arms to be raised and lowered

Convex sides of spoons form feet

1991 POUPARD (ABOVE) This fine piece of wood-turning is the work of doll artist, Elizabeth Pongratz. Ht: 14cm (5½in)

BAVARIAN BABY (LEFT) A small doll has been decorated with oil-based paints. Ht: 9cm (3½in)

Dress, made of black nylon upholstery fringe, "dances" when spoon handle is twirled

TOMMY SPOONER (ABOVE) This character, made in the United States c.1896, is constructed from five wooden spoons, attached to a carved, hollowed-out body. The legend on its back – "Pack carefully, do not handle" – may have been added at a later date. Ht: 30cm (12in)

Peg Woodens
· 1790s to the present day ·

JOINTED WOODEN DOLLS made after 1790 are usually called Dutch Dolls or Peg Woodens. The first term may be a corruption of *deutsch*, meaning German – indicating their country of origin – or a reference to the Dutch ports through which they were exported from Germany to England. The second refers to the use of pegs in the jointing and the fact that the dolls resemble straight, old-fashioned clothes pegs. Regardless of terminology, these dolls are united in being relatively simple, turned and carved figures, which were usually painted only on the parts that were unclothed.
~ Although World War II created a hiatus in the mass-scale production of peg woodens, a recent awakening of interest in the old techniques, together with improved machinery and paints, has given this inexpensive type of doll a new lease of life today.

The printed label, sewn into the dress, indicates that this doll was made in 1963 as a favour to mark the annual Convention of the United Federation of Doll Clubs, held in the United States.

Head and torso are carved as one unit

High, carved comb on top of head

Head and chest area are finished with flesh-toned paint

Painted hair and facial features

Joints are neater than those of similar 19th-century dolls

Simply carved hands have thumbs but no fingers

Torso is shaped into broad, flat hips and a narrow waist

Straight, unshaped thighs

Doll wears a dress in the style of a young lady of the late 19th century

Lower legs have rounded calves and trim ankles

Mortise and tenon joints attach limbs to torso and give movement to lower legs and arms

Dainty black slippers are painted onto the feet

Lower legs are painted to show white stockings

TUCKCOMB DOLL, "ANGELITA" *Hand-crafted in the United States by S. Smith, this fully jointed peg wooden is a modern version of an 1850s' German doll. The high comb, often painted yellow, was a fashionable hair ornament of that period. It is carved as one with the head, and is a special feature of early 19th-century wooden dolls.*

HT: 16.5cm (6½in)

Ht: 43cm (17in)

Largest doll has ball joints at shoulders and hips

PEG WOODEN PARADE (LEFT)
This set was produced in the Grödener Tal region of Austria between 1925 and 1940. The largest figure has a relatively sophisticated jointing system, and even the tiniest of the nine has peg joints at the shoulders and hips.

PONYTAIL PEG DOLL (RIGHT)
The decorative tuckcomb, a feature of early 19th-century, Grödener Tal-made peg woodens, has been reinterpreted in this c.1960 version and updated as a carved ponytail. It was made by English collector, Faith Eaton. Ht: 13cm (5in)

Facial features and hair are painted over base of flesh-coloured oils

Ht: 30cm (12in)

All dolls have painted black hair, blue eyes, and red mouths

Ht: 25cm (10in)

Clothing conceals torso, carved from same piece of wood as the head

Noses of three largest dolls made of wooden wedge, slotted into the face

Ht: 17cm (6¾in)

Mortise and tenon joints at hips, shoulders, elbows, and knees

Noses of middle-sized dolls are painted; smaller dolls have no noses

Ht: 11cm (4¼in)

Ht: 8cm (3¼in)

Ht: 4.5cm (1¾in)

Ht: 2.5cm (1in)

Ht: 1.5cm (⅝in)

Lower legs are stick like, but still have painted shoe detail

Feet are always painted to represent shoes

DOLL MOUNTED AS AN ORNAMENTAL PIN (ABOVE) This early 1960s' miniature peg wooden was made by S. Smith in the United States. It has a carved comb on top of the head and a safety pin on the back of the frame. Ht: 2.5cm (1in)

Fully jointed doll is encased in glass-fronted wooden frame

1820s' PEG WOODEN (BELOW)
Peasants in the Grödener Tal carved dolls like this one during the harsh winter months, when they could not work in the forests. Though made in quantity, each doll has its own special features. Ht: 9cm (3½in)

Original coarse cotton dress, shawl, and apron

Rounded head, with an elongated neck

DOLL DRESSED AS A NUN
(RIGHT) Many of these cheap dolls were clothed to represent figures from everyday life. In 1920s' rural Austria, nuns were very much part of the Catholic communities. Ht: 15cm (6in)

Hand-painted facial features

Woollen wimple and habit

Glass rosary beads, with a metal crucifix

Flat arms have simple peg joints at the elbows

Composition Dolls

The collective term "composition" is used to describe a variety of pulped wood- or paper-based mixtures from which doll heads and bodies are made. Originally introduced as a cheaper alternative to wood, composition also had the advantage of being a more malleable material. Towards the end of the eighteenth century, exciting experiments took place in the development of papier mâché – the doll industry's most favoured type of composition.

FROM THE START, manufacturers found that the papier mâché mixture could be pressed into moulds for shaping. The revolutionary idea – which sprang to life in the 1800s, and had far-reaching effects for doll-making – was to mould the mixture *under pressure*. Treated in this way, papier mâché was found to be a strong, durable material that lent itself to cheap mass-production by machine. This versatility could now be exploited to fashion a wide range of products other than doll parts, including ornaments, boxes, and furniture. After moulding, a glutinous wash called size was applied to the objects. This eliminated the need for the expensive gesso layer that was used with wood (see page 11), and prepared an even ground for paint.

Manufacturers took great pride in developing their own especially formulated papier mâché mixtures, and kept the recipes a close secret. A variety of rather bizarre ingredients might be added to the basic pulp – rags, bread, crushed eggshells, or ground animal bones or bone ash, for example – that increased the strength of the moulded material while reducing its raw cost. As most recipes were neither recorded nor patented, the precise formulation of the composition used for a particular doll is invariably unknown, and can be determined only by expensive chemical analysis.

Getting the Formula Right

Other types of composition, still based on wood or paper, were developed from the mid-nineteenth century. The increased use of additives such as glue, flour, boiled sawdust, plaster, and almost anything that was cheap and to hand, did not always produce a result that was as indestructible as the manufacturers claimed. Composition containing edible ingredients attracted rodents and insects; other mixtures were affected by temperature and humidity, and would swell or shrink according to changes in the weather.

❦ Papier mâché was the unrivalled success of all the experimentation, and became the most widely used type of composition for doll heads and, somewhat later, bodies. Its first practical application was in the making of shoulder heads; papier mâché socket heads followed, introduced from the third quarter of the nineteenth century. But, papier mâché composition really came into its own with the development of

COTTAGE INDUSTRY (*LEFT*)
The processes required to finish machine-made composition heads and limbs were usually carried out as piece-work by families in their own homes. In this engraving, the man is painting the heads, while the woman is dressing the completed doll.

1850S' GIRL *(RIGHT)*
Most wax-over-composition dolls were made in Germany. This model has a wax-over-papier mâché shoulder head and lower limbs, with a stuffed cloth torso and upper limbs. With its auburn mohair wig, sleeping glass eyes, and period costume, the doll is a fine example of its type. Ht: 30cm (12in)

of the original colour tones changes, and the surface is left exposed and vulnerable to damage.

∽ From the turn of the twentieth century onwards, the material that had started out as a cheap substitute for wood and then bisque increased in popularity with manufacturers in both France and Germany. And in the United States – a country that had no tradition of making bisque dolls – composition was used for almost all dolls until it was superseded by modern plastics, such as polyethylene and vinyl, in the 1940s.

Wax-over-composition

The process of coating composition heads with a layer of wax to enhance the appearance of the doll heads evolved almost as soon as manufacturers realized the potential of machine-moulding papier mâché mixtures. The technique was used with other types of composition and also with other materials, but was found to be most successful when applied to papier mâché composition. Unfortunately, one principal disadvantage of wax-over-composition was soon revealed: an unsightly deterioration in the smooth surface of the wax. Caused by the different rates at which the two layers of composition and wax expanded and contracted, this produced faults ranging from fine-line crazing to wide cracks. Manufacturers

doll bodies, in particular those with jointed limbs. Its strength, durability, and lightness, as well as suitability for moulding, allowed manufacturers to make a range of different body types. Thin wooden slats provided additional support for the parts that received the greatest degree of stress: at the joints, and as stays within the torso itself.

∽ The whole surface was painted with water-based, flesh-coloured tones after sizing, and varnished. This thin finishing layer of clear varnish tended to discolour with age, giving many old composition dolls a faint yellowish cast. Attempts to wash off the varnish can damage the doll, as the appearance

were not able to find a solution to this problem, and the production of wax-over-composition doll parts ceased altogether during the first decade of the twentieth century.

BABY-WALKER DOLL *(LEFT) The all-composition construction of this c. 1860s' German doll extends even to its dress. The shoulder head is coated with a layer of wax. The doll's semi-mechanical movement allows its legs to move back and forth as the baby walker is wheeled along. Ht: 15cm (6in)*

KÄTHE KRUSE GIRL AND BOY *(RIGHT) These 1930s' figures were designed by Käthe Kruse, a famous German maker who is most usually associated with pressed felt dolls. Their composition socket heads were probably based on designs for cloth heads, made at an earlier period. Ht: 48cm (19in)*

Greiner and German Dolls

· 1840s to 1900s ·

ONE OF THE FOREMOST manufacturers of composition doll heads in the United States was Ludwig Greiner, based in Philadelphia. It was run by Greiner himself from 1840 to 1874. Thereafter, the company operated as Greiner Bros., in care of his sons, until 1883. Greiner was granted his first patent for a reinforced papier mâché shoulder head in 1858. The patented recipe consisted of 480g (1lb) each of pulped white paper, dry Spanish whiting, and rye flour; 25g (1oz) glue; and linen, which reinforced the heads. These were formed by pouring the mixture into plaster moulds, and were then painted and varnished.

The large size of the heads dictated the use of correspondingly large bodies: most dolls with Greiner heads are over 33cm (13in) in height. The stuffed bodies were either handmade by individuals, or were produced commercially by another company.

GREINER'S IMPROVED PATENT HEADS. Pat. March 30th '58

Early Greiner dolls bear a label on the back of the shoulder plate, marked "PATENT HEADS". Later models include the patent extension date, 1872.

Moulded wavy hair has corkscrew curls at the back of the head and centre parting

Head and shoulder plate cast as one unit and painted

Moulded and painted facial features

Shoulder plate is glued onto the top of the torso

Well-defined, closed mouth

Stuffed cloth upper arms, torso, and legs

Kid lower arms

Hands have separate, stitched fingers and thumbs

Seam at hip line allows doll to sit

"Seam" lines at knees, formed by age and handling

Lawn cotton dress covers four layers of petticoats and pantaloons with eyelet lace trim

Damage to shoe reveals toes, formed by stitching

GREINER PATENT HEAD *This naked lady clearly demonstrates an interesting convention that applies to most dolls: the head is proportionately larger than any other part of the body. The reason for this is that the head is intended to embody and convey the doll's individual "personality".*

HT: 60cm (24in)

Open mouth shows bamboo teeth

FINE MASS-PRODUCED DOLL
(LEFT) Sonneberg, in Germany, produced many composition dolls for export. This 19th-century model has a wig added over the usual painted hair of the papier mâché shoulder head, and a gusseted kid body: both are signs of a better quality product. Ht: 50cm (20in)

Gracefully modelled kid hands

Toes are stitched, but not separate

THE CHEAPER END OF THE MARKET
(RIGHT) This papier mâché shoulder head was also made in Sonneberg, in the 1820s–1830s. The stuffed cloth torso lacks shape, while the legs end in stubby feet, without toes. The arms are unjointed and made of kid. Ht: 65cm (26in)

Painted hair, with brushstroke "curls"; no wig

Kid arms are stitched to resemble gloves

Simply styled hair is moulded and painted

Painted facial features

Papier mâché shoulder head, glued onto torso

Upper limbs and torso are tightly stuffed with sawdust

Carved wooden lower arms and legs

Blue paper bands conceal joins; bands can also be red or green

Papier mâché shoulder head; moulded and painted hair

Painted hazel eyes, with black pupils

Closed mouth, painted red

Holes for sewing head onto cloth body

1840s' PRE-GREINER DOLL
(BELOW) This doll closely resembles a Greiner, and does indeed have its origin in the United States. The papier mâché shoulder head has moulded and painted hair that suggests a small boy's style; the head could also be that of a girl. Ht: 102cm (40in)

Inset brown glass eyes; no pupils

Open/closed mouth with moulded teeth

HOLZ-MASSE HEAD
(ABOVE) The German firm Cuno & Otto Dressel registered "Holz-Masse", meaning wood pulp, as a trademark in 1875. The mark was applied to heads of papier mâché, composition, or wax-over-composition. This shoulder head, made c. 1890, is stamped with the symbol of a helmet with wings, which appeared as part of the original trademark. Ht: 15cm (6in)

LADY WITH PAINTED ORANGE SLIPPERS
(LEFT) Made in the 1830s, this doll is a typical Sonneberg export. The bands of blue paper at the elbows and knees cover and neaten the joins between the stuffed kid of the upper arms and legs and the carved wood of the lower limbs. Ht: 25cm (10in)

Real baby shoes, made of leather, date from 1869

Developments in Composition

· 1850s to 1930s ·

WHILE LENDING ITSELF ADMIRABLY to the construction of heads and large jointed bodies, composition proved to have two features that made it an unsatisfactory material for entire dolls: it was easily damaged; and its surface texture was subject to crazing, giving the dolls a worn appearance after only a short time. Yet some of the manufacturers found that composition had its advantages. Like bisque, it could be moulded and painted – but unlike bisque, it did not need to be fired. From 1900, many companies were established, predominantly in Germany and the United States, manufacturing a wide range of inexpensive, all-composition dolls, as well as those with stuffed cloth or kid bodies. One such company was Stephan Schilling, which operated in the town of Sonneberg, in Germany, from 1878 to 1928.

Two lace-trimmed "tails", called lappets, at back of cap

Blonde mohair wig, pinned in curls

Sleeping glass eyes, with heavily painted lashes and brows

Closed, painted mouth

Composition shoulder head, glued onto torso

Starched white cotton oversleeves

Stuffed cloth upper arms

Composition lower arms

Scissors and bone-handled penknife on silver-plated chatelaine

Spread-fingered hands; fingers and nails defined with red-painted lines

Back of the right thigh is stamped with Schilling's winged angel head trademark, registered in 1895

Stuffed cloth upper legs

Original period costume

Well-shaped composition lower legs

Toes are moulded, but not separate

Dress conceals undergarments, including green-and-white striped stays with elastic suspenders and black stockings

C.1900 SCHILLING DOLL *The English nanny who gave this doll to her charge in 1904 dressed it in an exact replica of her own uniform. Although it is of good quality for its type, the relative cheapness of the doll is indicated by the body, which is straw filled; more expensive dolls were stuffed with animal hair or other soft fibres.*

HT: 60cm (24in)

Tufts of woollen hair and earrings suggest "ethnic" appearance

Composition socket head

Composition bent arms

Accessories include a stork-shaped hanger, swan's-down powder puff, a bristle brush, mirror, and combs

DOLL IN CANE BASKET

(RIGHT) This German 1930s' doll has a composition flange neck head, an open mouth, showing two bottom teeth, and sleeping glass eyes with metal eyelids. The stuffed stockinet torso and limbs are stitch-jointed at the shoulders and hips. Ht: 30cm (12in)

Composition bent legs

"TOPSY" (ABOVE) Black dolls,

representing babies and toddlers, grew in popularity during the 1920s and 1930s. As this c.1935 American example shows, the heads were often cast from the same moulds as those used for Caucasian dolls. Ht: 30cm (12in)

Ribbed silk skullcap, with yellow silk braid-and-tassel trim

Reverse socket head

Inset glass eyes; no pupils

"SUSAN" (BELOW) Versatile composition

could be tinted to produce a range of colours: dolls designed to represent ethnic children usually had hair painted black in contrast to a brown skin tone. No attempt has been made to disguise this doll's Caucasian features. Ht: 46cm (18in)

c.1855 TODDLER DOLL (RIGHT)

Made in Sonneberg, Germany, this black doll has realistic, moulded, non-Caucasian features. A bellows squeaker is housed within the torso of its fully jointed, papier mâché, Mottschmann-type body. Ht: 20cm (8in)

Shiny light brown glaze indicates that this is a good-quality doll

All-composition construction, jointed at shoulders and hips, with bent limbs

The mark on the back of the neck clearly identifies this model.

Gown conceals stuffed cloth torso

Composition head, with sleeping, flirty glass eyes

Lower legs are jointed at ankles

Unjointed, bent limbs made of composition

SINGER SEWING MACHINE DOLL

(LEFT) This doll and its clothing, which shows examples of machine stitching, were used as a window display in one of Singer's London stores during World War II. It was made in the late 1930s by Seyfarth & Reinhardt of Germany, which operated from 1922 into the 1930s. Ht: 46cm (18in)

Original organdie dress

Long gown, coat, and bonnet are decorated with machine-quilting

Alexander Doll Company

· 1926 to the present day ·

IN 1926, SISTERS ROSE AND BERTHA ALEXANDER, who later changed her name to Beatrice, founded the Alexander Doll Company of New York. This firm is known even today for its quality products. Many of its early dolls were inspired by living or fictional characters, such as Shirley Temple or the glamorous heroine of *Gone With The Wind*, Scarlett O'Hara. On 28 May 1934, five little girls were born to the Dionne family in Montreal, Canada. These babies quickly became media personalities, and many doll manufacturers eagerly grasped the marketing opportunity presented by such an unusual event. However, only the Alexander Doll Co. was granted the right to register the Dionne Quintuplets as a trademark in 1936 in the United States. This set of dolls formed part of the firm's highly collectable Madame Alexander range.

Moulded and painted hair

Sleeping brown eyes

Human hair upper lashes; painted lower lashes and brows

Composition doll, jointed with elastic stringing at neck, shoulders, and hips

Open/closed painted mouth

Arms are bent, but straighter than those of the babies

Chubby torso and limbs

Straight legs allow doll to stand unaided

Flat feet, with dimpled toes

Green trimmings are exclusive to Cecile

Doll's name is engraved on a medal pinned to its dress

White cotton socks

Cloth, ankle-strap shoes, with metal buckles on toes and snap fastenings

DIONNE TODDLER DOLLS *In 1937, two years after the creation of the baby dolls, the Dionne toddlers were produced so that the range kept pace with the development of the real-life quins. All five dolls are identical, and are distinguished only by the different colours of clothes and accessories: Annette wears yellow; Marie, blue; Yvonne, pink; Cecile, green; and Emelie, lavender.*

HT: 29cm (11½in)

PHYSICIAN AND NURSE (LEFT) Dr. Allan Roy Dafoe and the nurse, Louise De Kirilene, who had attended the birth of the Dionne babies, were also part of the Dionne Quintuplets set. Made of composition, the dolls are jointed at the shoulders and hips, and have mohair wigs. The physician's features are all painted, whereas the nurse has sleeping glass eyes. Ht: Physician 34cm (13½in); Nurse 33cm (13in)

Wrist tag is identical to that of the physician; the reverse side is shown

TODDLER AND BABY DOLLS (BELOW) The first generation of Madame Alexander Dionne Quintuplet babies were issued in Spring 1935. Their bent legs allow the dolls to sit but not stand, unlike the toddlers, which stand unaided. Ht: 18cm (7in)

Original wrist tag of the Alexander Doll Co.

DOLL MARKS

Most dolls have the name "ALEXANDER" moulded on the back of the neck or back of the torso. Other variations include "Mme. Alexander" or "ALEX".

The reverse of this gold wrist tag reads "AN/ ALEXANDER/ PRODUCT/ SUPREME/ QUALITY/ AND/ DESIGN".

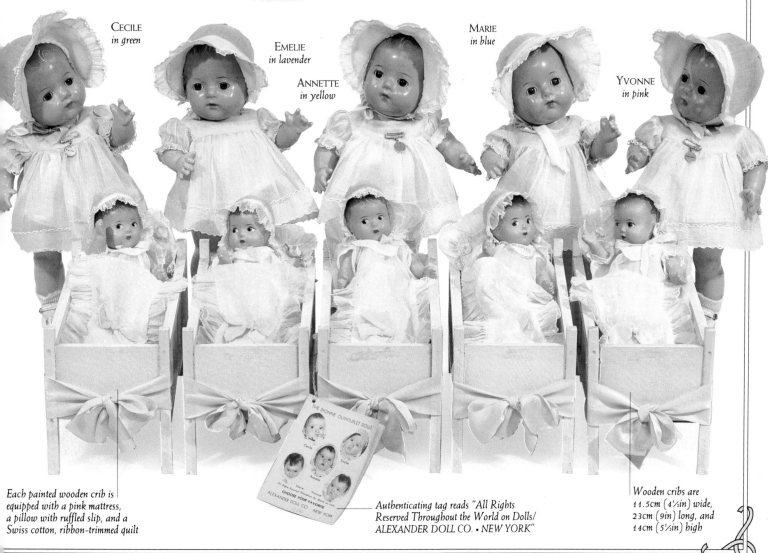

CECILE *in green*

EMELIE *in lavender*

ANNETTE *in yellow*

MARIE *in blue*

YVONNE *in pink*

Each painted wooden crib is equipped with a pink mattress, a pillow with ruffled slip, and a Swiss cotton, ribbon-trimmed quilt

Authenticating tag reads "All Rights Reserved Throughout the World on Dolls/ ALEXANDER DOLL CO. • NEW YORK"

Wooden cribs are 11.5cm (4½in) wide, 23cm (9in) long, and 14cm (5½in) high

Wax-over-composition Dolls

· 1830s to 1900s ·

THE IDEA OF ENHANCING composition with wax was realized by many German doll-head makers from c.1830. Between 1870 and 1900, a small number of English companies working in London also manufactured wax-over-composition heads; these were attached to stuffed cloth bodies. The English dolls are usually very well marked with body stamps; if there are no markings, wax-over-composition dolls are usually assumed to be of German origin.

The manufacturing process involved applying a thin layer of wax over heads and also limbs made of composition, to give the surface a smoother and more natural appearance. Wax-over-composition dolls looked better than those made of composition alone; they also had the advantage of being significantly cheaper – both to manufacture and to buy – than their poured-wax relatives (see pages 30–41).

Velvet, silk-lined hat is tied with lace-trimmed organdie ribbons and secured with blue, glass-headed hat pins

Curled auburn mohair wig

Moulded and painted mouth shows two rows of small teeth

Inset blue-grey glass eyes

Cape is made of silk and poplin

Finely modelled shoulder head has a thin, tinted layer of wax over its composition base

Wax-over-composition arms

Starched cotton apron over a button-fronted cotton bodice and skirt

Glazed cotton upper legs and torso are stuffed with straw

Composition lower legs

Feet are moulded and painted to show stylish, side-buttoning, heeled boots

C.1900 GERMAN DOLL

The young owner who dubbed this pretty lady "Nurse Cross" could hardly have chosen a less apt name, for the doll's half-smiling expression radiates anything but displeasure. The costume is a detailed replica of the uniform worn by a child's nanny in England c.1900.

HT: 43cm (17in)

Penny-toy bought from street vendor on Ludgate Hill, London

Shoulder head is made of plaster

C.1830 BAGMAN'S BABY (LEFT)
Cheap German-made dolls were once a common item of merchandise for pedlars, often referred to in England at the time as "Bagmen". The method of inserting the wig into the head through a vertical groove cut in the crown also gives these dolls the name of "slit-head". Ht: 68cm (27in)

Pink kid arms; separate fingers and thumbs

Dress conceals stuffed cloth torso and legs

Costume conceals hard, stuffed cloth upper legs and torso, stitched at hips

Beneath dress, a wire protruding through the base of the lower torso opens and closes the glass eyes

Elaborate, felt-topped head-dress, made of black animal fur and secured with a "gold" chain chinstrap

Auburn mohair wig

Open mouth shows three teeth

Sleeves hide unjointed composition arms

Hands have separate thumbs and joined fingers, delineated with painted red lines

SCOTTISH COSTUME DOLL (LEFT) *Typical of dolls produced in Germany and exported throughout Europe, this finely dressed 1890s' model has a wax-over-composition shoulder head, and unjointed arms and lower legs of composition. The inset blue glass eyes have light irises and darker pupils, and are an advance on the pupilless eyes of many earlier models. Ht: 35cm (14in)*

Handmade Highland Regimental costume

C.1860 GERMAN DOLL WITH ALICE BAND (RIGHT)
Fashionable hairstyles, sometimes accessorized, as shown in this example, were moulded with the head and painted before the application of the wax coating. Dolls with moulded and painted hair tended to be less expensive than those with either human hair or mohair wigs.
Ht: 46cm (18in)

Lead-weighted sleeping eyes, with metal eyelids

Dress conceals body, made in the 1850s, which pre-dates the doll's c.1860s' head

LATE 19TH-CENTURY GIRL
(RIGHT) Thick wax covers the composition of this German shoulder head, and a lead-weight mechanism operates the sleeping glass eyes. The hands are well modelled, yet the maker has not cleaned up the casting lines at the ends of the fingers. Ht: 45cm (17½in)

Ash blonde mohair wig

Wooden lower arms with spoon-shaped hands

Printed cotton dress is older than the doll

Composition lower arms and legs

Wooden lower legs, painted to show flat-heeled bootees

Poured Wax Dolls

*One of the original uses for wax was in the making of religious effigies and votive offerings.
This practice, widespread in Roman Catholic parts of Europe, but much less customary
in Protestant communities, gave many makers their first experience of wax-modelling. Seeking
new expression for their creativity, they carried their skills to London where, by
the nineteenth century, they had established an unrivalled tradition of wax doll-making.*

SOME OF THE most inspired of European doll-makers worked in England between 1850 and 1930. Their originality was matched by their choice of material: translucent, luminous, and warm to the touch, wax is perfectly suited to creating dolls, in particular portrait dolls, which rely for their realism on the faithful reproduction of facial features and skin tones.

Casting the Head

All nineteenth-century wax modellers followed the same technical, yet simple, process to create their doll heads. The first stage involved the skilled modelling of the head in wax or clay. From this, a cast was produced in the form of a two- or three-part plaster mould. The molten wax mixture – a blend of colouring, bleached beeswax, and numerous other additives, was poured into the mould and allowed only a very brief setting period before the excess mixture was poured out. Some heads were made with a single pouring; others were built up using multiple layers of wax, which produced a stronger head with a more translucent, skin-like texture. In either case, the final thickness of the wax was no more than 3mm (⅛in). After the wax had cooled and solidified, the casting was lifted from the mould, and any traces of the casting lines were removed from the sides of the head.

∽ It was the finishing processes that determined whether or not the head was a good one. Blown or moulded glass eyes, set into the cut-out and shaped eye sockets, were fixed either with a small extra amount of wax, or by warming the socket to melt the surrounding wax. Sleeping eyes are rarely found in poured wax heads, but where they are used, they are normally placed on a push–pull wire. The lead-weight mechanism type can damage the head if it knocks about inside. The hair of the doll

1806 ENGLISH DOLL (*LEFT*) *This small, beady-eyed figure shows the special feature of early dolls: a shoulder head and lower limbs moulded entirely from solid wax. Its feet have been cast and dipped in green-coloured wax to resemble shoes. The torso and upper limbs are made of stuffed cloth. Ht: 13cm (6in)*

PLASTER MOULD (*RIGHT*) *Cast wax doll heads are always hollow, and made in a mould of three or, as here, two parts. The two lugs at the top fit snugly into correspondingly positioned holes on the other half of the mould, which forms the back of the head.*

This engraving, reproduced in the 26 November 1887 edition of The Queen, The Lady's Newspaper, *illustrates the following eight steps, showing how a wax-headed doll was created and finished: 1. Making the Model; 2. Joining the Head; 3. Setting the Eyes; 4. Waxing the Head; 5. Painting the Face; 6. Dressing the Hair; 7. Fixing the Head; 8. Dressing the Finished Doll.*

MONTANARI MARK (ABOVE)
Wax heads are rarely signed, but their cloth bodies may carry the maker's name. Mme. Montanari's handwritten signatures sometimes include her business address, as here.

rarely sawdust. To ensure an exact colour match, heads and limbs for complete sets of dolls were produced during the same casting session. Most poured wax arms were cast to above the elbow joint, and legs to above the knee. These, too, had grommets embedded into the wax, and were fixed to the upper stuffed cloth limbs in the same way as was the head to the torso.

In what was still largely a home-based business, each one of these steps in the finishing process was assigned to a particular member of the family. Enduring very poor conditions, and dealing with dangerous materials, many of the workers paid a high price for their occupation. Molten wax, which was poured at extremely high temperatures, often caused severe burns; the materials with which the bodies were stuffed contained tiny particles of dust that, if inhaled, could lead to breathing difficulties; but perhaps the most hazardous of all was the white lead used to colour the wax, which proved to be an insidious – and in some instances deadly – poison.

was applied next, inserted either as single strands or as small clumps into fine cuts or pin-holes in the head. (Hair eyelashes were similarly inset.) Done in this way, the hair seems to "grow" from the scalp; it has more natural movement than can be achieved with a wig; and enhances the realistic appearance of the head itself. Makers used both human hair and mohair, and sometimes combined the two. Buyers could even choose to have snippings of their own child's hair inset at almost no additional cost. Finally, colouring was applied to the mouth and the whole surface was dusted with fine pumice to remove the shine.

Completing the Doll

Poured wax heads usually have deep shoulder plates. The head is sewn to the body through a hole at each of the lower corners of the front and back plates. In better quality dolls, grommets or metal eyelets reinforce the holes and protect them from wear and tear. The cloth bodies are mostly of a rather clumsy, inelegant shape. They are made of calico and stuffed with cow or other animal hair, or woolly fibres, but

1980S' PORTRAIT DOLL
(RIGHT) *Mrs. Peggy Nisbet is doll number 4001 in a limited-edition series of 5000 collectors' pieces. The dolls were designed by the House of Nisbet in consultation with Faith Eaton – a well-known English doll authority – to commemorate the company's founder. Ht: 46cm (18in)*

Early Dolls
· 1750s to 1850s ·

THE MAJORITY OF WAX-HEADED DOLLS that have survived date from the last two centuries. Even the earliest dolls show the skill of the wax-modeller. Most were expensive to buy, so it is quite unlikely that they were ever treated as throw-away items. The fact that few were made seems a more satisfactory explanation for their relative scarcity now, than questions of quality.

〜 Many wax dolls appear almost exact copies of each other. However, their similarity merely reflects contemporary style and fashion, as with modern-day favourites like Barbie or Action Man. For example, wax doll heads made between 1750 and 1850 are modelled to show a high forehead. In Georgian England, this was a visible sign of good breeding and refined sensibility.

〜 Inset glass eyes, another common feature, are pupilless and black in pre-1820s' dolls. By the 1830s, makers could choose coloured eyes, which were usually blue glass with a black pupil, to give their dolls a more realistic expression.

Wax shoulder head, with inset pupilless black glass eyes

Moulded and painted facial features

Satin stole is a later addition

Painted brownish black, curly hair shows a typical style of the period

Sleeves conceal stuffed cloth upper arms

Lower arms to above elbow joint are made of wax

Ears are simple shapes, set close to the sides of the head

Dress conceals stuffed upper legs and torso, made of striped mattress ticking

Shoulder plate is very deep

Off-white, very fine cotton muslin dress, with petticoat and bloomers beneath

1812 HEIRLOOM DOLL, "BESSIE"
The essence of any doll is conveyed in its head, and this fine example of early wax modelling suggests an accomplished maker. Lovely "Bessie" was the homecoming gift of Captain Nathaniel Osgood – a young shipmaster living in the Atlantic seaboard town of Salem, Massachusetts, in the United States – to his small daughter, Elizabeth.

HT: 50cm (20in)

Inset auburn human hair

Wax head to base of neck; upper torso made of calico painted in flesh tones

Upper arms, torso, and legs are made of stuffed calico

Wax lower arms

Beneath the dress, doll wears a complete set of linen undergarments

1758 COSTUME DOLL (ABOVE)
Young English lady Laetitia Clark designed and made this splendid silk outfit, which she called "A Long Robe Coat Dress for a Lady of Sixteen". The doll itself is nicely modelled, but owes its fame entirely to its clothes and their maker. Ht: 33cm (13in)

Wooden cradle decorated with Regency-patterned paper and bead finials

Inset mohair and painted facial features on all three dolls

Red-painted shoes are hollow and very fragile

SHADOWBOX TRIO (ABOVE) All-wax, hollow dolls are usually quite small, because of their fragility. Made in England and Germany from 1790 to 1820, they were popular ornaments, and were often displayed in a glass-fronted case. Ht: 4–6cm (1½–2½in)

Pale wax shoulder head

Dress conceals stuffed calico upper arms, torso, and legs

Wax shoulder head

Poured wax lower arms to above elbow joint

Inset bright blue glass eyes, with pupils

Dress conceals stuffed cloth legs and torso stitched at hips

Red, moulded wax shoes

1757 "PARTY DRESS" DOLL
(ABOVE) This simple costume was also designed and sewn by Laetitia Clark (see top left). Red was widely used for doll footwear at this period. By the end of the 1790s, green was the favoured colour. Ht: 20cm (8in)

TWIN SISTERS (LEFT) Made in England c.1838 and representing twins, these dolls are identical — something of a rarity — down to their lace-trimmed pantelettes. The fading of the shoulder heads to pale beige is due to natural changes in the wax. Ht: 50cm (20in)

Hand-stitched leather shoes

Original, fine cotton clothing

~ English Makers ~

· 1850s to 1930s ·

TOWARDS THE MIDDLE of the nineteenth century, wax became an increasingly popular material for creating doll heads and limbs. By far the greatest exponents of the craft were the English-born and emigré, often Italian, makers who were based in London. During the next 50 years, wax doll-making reached its zenith, particularly with the achievements of such virtuosi as the Pierottis (see pages 36–39) and Montanaris. Examples of their work were displayed and won prizes at international exhibitions.

~ The Great Exhibition of 1851, held at the Crystal Palace in London's Hyde Park, helped to establish the reputations of many makers. Madame Augusta Montanari won her first medal at this event. A great number of her dolls were portraits, some of which represented Queen Victoria's children. Perhaps it was this, rather than the medal she won, that earned her the patronage of the queen.

Blue glass eyes, set into sockets

Two grommets, for sewing head to torso

Poured wax lower arms, cast to include the elbow joints

Chubby baby hands and wrists

Hip seams attach legs to stuffed calico torso, and allow doll to sit

Legs can bend at seamed knees

Poured wax lower legs; feet have well-defined toes showing toe-nails

Quilted and ruched silk bonnet, tied with satin ribbons

Blonde hair is set into the head in small clumps

Three-tiered carrying cape

Lavish silk tassel and braid trimming

Long lawn robe is everyday late 19th-century baby attire

HT: 65cm (26in)

MONTANARI DOLL

A usual practice among makers of this time was to team baby heads and limbs with adult bodies. True baby-doll bodies had shapeless torsos, but because the body was intended to be covered up, its form scarcely mattered. This 1870s' Montanari baby doll is dressed in period Edwardian clothing.

Inset human hair

Wax shoulder head, coloured in pink tones

Very full head of inset human hair

Sleeves cover stuffed calico upper arms

Inset auburn human hair

Wax shoulder head; modelled facial features represent those of a young girl

Meech's southeast London workshop address is stamped on the doll's thigh.

Wire-operated, sleeping brown glass eyes

Wood-handled silk parasol, opens and closes

Dress conceals stuffed calico upper legs and torso

LUCY PECK HEAD (ABOVE)
A high proportion of beeswax used in the casting gives this c.1900 shoulder head its dark flesh tone. Ht: 68cm (27in)

Lower arms to above elbow are made of wax

BY ROYAL APPOINTMENT
(ABOVE) *This 1883 shoulder head shows the talent of Londoner Herbert John Meech, who worked between 1865 and 1917. Royal patronage entitled him to use the crest that he included with many of his body stamps. Ht: 58cm (23in)*

"C. C." incised on the sole is the mark of an unidentified maker

Pale wax lower legs and arms

LUCY PECK GIRL (ABOVE) *From 1891 to 1930, Lucy Peck made dolls and ran a repair service. She designed and created this 1890s' example, but the dolls she repaired would often also bear her firm's mark. Ht: 50cm (20in)*

The ink stamp appears on the back of the doll's torso.

1880S' SOHO BAZAAR DOLL
(RIGHT) *Charles Marsh came from a famous family of doll-makers and repairers, and worked between 1878 and 1895. His dolls are wax-over-composition, wax-over-papier mâché, or poured wax, as here. Ht: 46cm (18in)*

Human hair from the future owner was often inset into the doll's head

Inset glass eyes; human hair lashes and brows

The stamp on the doll's torso clearly identifies the maker.

The Pierotti Family

· 1770s to 1935 ·

THE PIEROTTIS WERE NOT SIMPLY doll-makers. They were, and called themselves, wax-modellers. The business was founded by Domenico Pierotti, an Italian who married an English girl and learned the basic skills of plaster mould-making and wax-casting and modelling from her family. One of their 12 children, Anerico Cephas, born 1809, carried the wax-modelling business forward, and perfected the poured wax method for the production of heads. His son, Charles William, was also an innovative wax-modeller. Many of the designs created by these two were adapted by later members of the family. In 1935, with the retirement of Charles Ernest, Charles William's son, four generations of family trading came to an end.

Straw boater is contemporary, but not original to doll

Inset violet blue glass eyes

Long titian mohair inserted into the wax

Eyebrows and lashes of mohair, match that of hair

Clothing belonged to a real child and dates from 1872

Stuffed cloth upper arms are sewn to torso under the shoulder plate

Threads, waxed with resin, attach the shoulder head to the torso

Hands have dimpled knuckles and short, stubby fingers

Upper legs, made separately from the torso, attached with seams at hips

Calico torso, stuffed with cowhair

Lower limbs are secured to upper limbs by thread through the grommets

Lower legs have shaped calves, and feet showing insteps

Hem of dress is decorated with pattern of trailing vine leaves

Socks and shoes are made of silk

HENRY PIEROTTI, GIRL *Anerico Cephas Pierotti is usually known by the anglicized name, Henry. This doll, which he made c.1870, represents a young girl. Its wax shoulder head and lower limbs are coloured peach, rather than the standard pink. The doll's straw boater, cotton dress, and silk socks and shoes belonged to a child, and date from 1872.*

HT: 60cm (24in)

1920s' FORTUNE TELLER
(LEFT) Charles Ernest Pierotti made this unique doll to raise money at a Masonic bazaar. It has a legless body fitted onto a wooden stick handle. As the stick was twirled, streamers with fortunes flew out, like the ribbons of a maypole. The shoulder head and limbs are made of darkly coloured wax, which gives the doll an exotic and gypsy-like appeararance. Ht: 68cm (27in)

Inset brown glass eyes

Black hair is a combination of inset human hair and mohair

Costume, made by Eleanor Bessie Pierotti, cannot be removed

Hands have slender, delicate fingers and thumbs

Gracefully modelled wax lower arms

Skirt would have had cloth and paper streamers attached to the waistband

Wooden stick is joined to doll's stuffed cloth torso

Head made of thin, single layer of wax

Portrait head of an unknown old man

Portrait head of young woman; finished portrait heads were discarded if not true likenesses

Blown glass eyes are rounded and bulbous

Blue, grey, or brown eyes used for portrait dolls, depending on colour of person's eyes

Moulded glass eyes are lozenge shaped

Crown is set with "pearls" and encrusted with coloured glass "gems"

Inset blue glass eyes, with pupils

Blue velvet Cap of Estate, inside the crown, is edged with miniver

Inset human hair, plaited and coiled around head

Pale wax shoulder head

Fur tippet is draped over top of cloak

Darker wax arms, cast to above elbow joint

Fur-trimmed velvet cloak covers the naked back of the doll

Crown shows "scar" where head was cut to insert eyes and then repaired

Silk and net, sequinned gown extends only to doll's sides

Titian mohair, wound around sticks, is curled into ringlets

Wooden sticks, joined with strips of linen gauze

C.1840 QUEEN VICTORIA
(ABOVE) Henry Pierotti was an especially gifted wax-modeller, and created many of the portrait dolls for which the family became famous. The strong resemblance of this model to the young queen is a testament to his ability. Ht: 48cm (19in)

PROTOTYPES AND PARTS
(LEFT) Experiments formed a vital element of the Pierottis' work, and not all resulted in viable products. Prototype heads, like these of an old man and young woman, were made of a single layer of very thin and fragile wax. The eyes and hair were particularly important features, helping to give the dolls expression and personality.

Pierotti Portrait Dolls

· 1900s to 1930s ·

WAX-MODELLERS were quick to discover that the material offered unique possibilities for rendering highly realistic portrait heads. Members of royal families, soldiers, and statesmen were all popular subjects. Henry Pierotti was one of a few wax portrait modellers who created dolls representing Queen Victoria (see page 37) and Lord Roberts (see below). Other dolls have no known sitter, but are clearly portraits – perhaps of friends or family – to judge by their idiosyncratic facial features and expressions.

 Carrying the realism further, the Pierottis introduced three styles of body that corresponded to the age and gender of the person the doll was to represent. The standard shape – chubby shoulders, a narrow waist, and broad hips – was used for most of the dolls, except those portraying babies and men.

White mohair, inset to show a receding hairline

Blown glass eyes, with mohair brows and upper lashes

Mohair moustache and goatee

Brownish patina often forms as the wax ages

Long, stuffed cloth arms, typical feature of male dolls

Full dress uniform, decorated with gold braid, brass buttons, ceremonial medals, and rank insignia

Shoulder head is secured to torso by thread through grommets

Large poured wax hands, cast to above wrist joint, typical feature of male dolls

Sleeve slash and stripe denote rank of Commander-in-Chief

Hamley Bros.' tag: the Regent Street, London toyshop was formerly located at 812 Oxford Street

Lower half of stuffed cloth torso extends to form the upper legs, typical feature of male dolls

White kid breeches

Poured wax lower legs; only one style was made

Black leather gaiters and black leather shoes, made to represent boots

Sword, sheathed in a leather scabbard

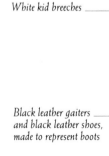

LORD ROBERTS AND MALE DOLL BODY
This tribute to Lord Roberts – Commander-in-Chief of the British Army during the Boer War – was modelled by Charles Ernest Pierotti c. 1900, adapted from an earlier model created by Charles William Pierotti. The naked doll shows the characteristics of the male body style.

HT: 50cm (20in)

STANDARD BABY HEAD

(RIGHT) Pierotti non-portrait baby dolls have one style of head. The eyes are of inset blue glass, with blonde mohair lashes and brows; the hair also is inset blonde mohair. A delicate pursing of the lips gives the mouth a bowed, slightly open shape. Ht: 50cm (20in)

Shoulder head has a short, thick neck and plump chest

Mohair is set into the head in small clumps

Child-like nose, with broad bridge

Moulded, closed mouth, painted red

c.1900 PORTRAIT BABY HEAD

(LEFT) Charles Ernest Pierotti produced this portrait of his only child, Patrick Enrico, who died when still very young. The fragile beauty of the infant is evident in the subtle pink colouring of the wax, the large pale blue glass eyes, and the gold-blond mohair curled over the forehead and around the sides of the face. Ht: 55cm (22in)

Lace-trimmed silk robe, adorned with cream satin ribbons and French knots

Inset mohair or human hair

Standard poured wax baby shoulder head

Blue eyes were usual; buyers could choose other colours

No grommets in sew holes on cheaper models

Joined fingers and separate thumbs

Small feet are in proportion to the hands

Inset blue glass eyes, with painted facial features

Well-defined chin and jaw-line

HEAD PROFILE (ABOVE)

The elegant curves of this young woman's head and shoulders contrast with the chubby, fleshy modelling of the neck and shoulders of the Pierotti baby dolls.

Inset long strawberry-blonde mohair, caught up at back of head into a loose plait

Pale wax shoulder head has a slim neck

Elaborate leg-o'-mutton dress sleeves, with stitched knife-pleating

Fingerless lace mittens have half-thumbs

C.1905 BABY DOLL (ABOVE)

The stuffed calico or glazed cotton torso of the stylized baby body is waistless, and usually extends to the upper legs, unless the doll is large. The upper arms, of the same fabric, are sewn to the torso under the shoulder plate. The poured wax lower arms are cast to above the bent elbow joint. Ht: 30cm (12in)

COSTUME DISPLAY DOLL

(RIGHT) In the early 20th century, fashionable London shops and dress designers enticed would-be clients with miniature versions of their latest creations, exhibited on doll models. This c.1910 portrait of a young lady displays its modest cleavage in an off-the-shoulder, striped silk taffeta evening gown. The fine shoulder head is teamed with the narrow-waisted, stuffed cloth body that was used for all dolls except babies and men. Ht: 40cm (16in)

"Princess Daisy"

· 1890s ·

SEEN IN THE LIGHT of their quirky history, some otherwise rather unremarkable dolls can acquire great charm. In 1894, when Miss Twiss, living in Amsterdam, Holland, purchased a rather plain English wax doll, the city was preparing to host the International Exposition that was to be held the following year. Miss Twiss had the idea of commissioning Dutch craftsmen to make clothes and accessories for the doll, which would be used as a model to display their work at the exposition.

The display was purchased by a group of English ladies, who presented the doll, "Princess Daisy", and her extensive trousseau, to Princess Mary of Teck (later queen to George V, King of England) as a christening gift for her daughter Mary, born in 1897.

Inset very pale blonde mohair

Poured wax shoulder head

Rosettes and streamers, attached to waist ribbon, match those on the bonnet

Sleeping blue glass eyes; mohair eyebrows and upper lashes

Wide band of cream moiré silk ribbon, tied in a bow, secures the doll to its cushion

Poured wax lower arms, cast to above elbow joint

Stuffed calico upper limbs and torso

Buttoned, padded drawers, worn over nappy

Darker bands of calico cover the joins

Poured wax lower legs, cast to above knee joint

Muslin christening robe, inset with broderie anglaise

HT: 46cm (18in)

CEREMONIAL PRESENTATION "Princess Daisy" is displayed lying on her own christening cushion, as was the custom in late 19th-century England when babies were presented for baptism. The cotton lawn cushion is padded with eiderdown feathers, and has a slip-cover of silk-embroidered, lace-edged muslin. The doll wears a lace bonnet, trimmed with silk ribbon rosettes, and a traditional christening robe over a satin underdress and linen undergarments.

Handmade brass clothes stands are part of the doll's accessories

Satin travelling cloak, with lace-trimmed cape and elaborate lace collar

Decorative pink satin bows on shoulders of dress

Pink ribbon sash matches the satin bows on the shoulders

Afternoon dress, made of cotton lawn and embroidered with daisies

Large satin bows and rosettes decorate almost every item

Satin and lace bonnet hangs on its own brass hat stand

ROYAL APPAREL (LEFT) Miss Twiss provided an inventory, listing each piece of clothing in "Princess Daisy's" wardrobe. Every item uses only the finest natural materials — muslin, silk, satin, and wool — and is embroidered with either the initial "D" or the doll's name, "Daisy", depending on its size.

CANOPIED CRADLE (BELOW) The specially commissioned accessories include a wrought-iron stand, with curlicued stretchers and legs, which allows the metal cradle to swing gently to and fro; six top and bottom sheets, pillowslips, and blankets; and an ivory cross with winged cherub, to ensure "Princess Daisy" sweet dreams.

LAYETTE BASKET AND CHRISTENING GIFTS (BELOW)

The satin-lined basket contains myriad accessories, including a real sponge in an oiled silk bag, tiny safety pins, soaps, and a silver bed-warmer. Only the rubber teats for the feeding bottles and the box of special biscuits have perished with time.

Wooden sock hangers

Two-layered canopy, made of Swiss dot cotton over satin

Padded satin quilt

Basket stands on four plaited wicker feet

Hallmarked silver spoons and fork set

Real gold "Daisy" name-pin and bracelet

Real pearl necklace, with a pavé diamond clasp

Forged iron cradle and stand, painted white, with gold paint edging and trim

Porcelain Dolls

One of the most fascinating aspects of language is that individual words — which have precise definitions — can become easily translated in everyday speech into a variety of imprecise meanings. The word "porcelain", for example, seems to take on different meanings when used by different people. As a term in our special doll language, however, porcelain describes with a single word three types of doll head: glazed china; untinted bisque; and bisque.

THE PRODUCTION OF porcelain doll heads was rarely the principal output of any manufacturer, so it is useful to understand the development of porcelain as a doll-making material in its historical context. This very fine grade of ceramic ware is fired in a kiln at not less than 1300°C (2372°F). Few clays are able to withstand such extreme temperatures: feldspathic china clay or kaolin and china stone are two that can.

The discovery of these clays in parts of Germany at the beginning of the eighteenth century led to the establishment of the Meissen factory, near Dresden, in 1709. In the southwest of England, Cornish clay-pits revealed sufficient reserves for the first manufacture of porcelain items in 1770. Extensive deposits of these naturally occurring clays were mined throughout Germany, especially in the region of Thuringia. The porcelain industry flourished there, with a number of factories churning out inexpensive figurines and decorative ornaments, as well as the exquisite domestic tableware that was their stock-in-trade. For many manufacturers, the production of doll heads was nothing more than a lucrative sideline.

Mouldings and Castings

From the start of the nineteenth century, porcelain began to enjoy increasing favour with the doll-head manufacturers. This popularity lasted for the next hundred years or so, when porcelain was supplanted by the new, more versatile compositions and plastics introduced in the first quarter of the twentieth century. All the porcelain doll heads that were manufactured in

GLAZED CHINA DOLLS *(LEFT) In the United States, all three of these dolls are called Frozen Charlottes. In Britain, the larger figures are known as Bath Dolls. The smaller ones were often hidden as good-luck charms inside Christmas plum puddings, giving them the name of Pudding Dolls. Ht: Largest 46cm (18in); smallest 2.5cm (1in)*

UNTINTED BISQUE SHOULDER HEAD *(RIGHT) Dolls made in the late 1860s' classical style owe much to the ideas of Ancient Greece and Rome. The typical formality of the style, shown in the modelling of this German doll's head, is echoed in the Greek key pattern that decorates its pretty cotton dress. Ht: 40cm (16in)*

the nineteenth century were produced in moulds. Like those used in poured wax castings (see pages 30–31), these were made of plaster and in two or three parts. In the early days, a porcelain mixture with a malleable, dough-like consistency was pressed into the moulds for shaping. Refining their production techniques, manufacturers introduced a wetter, fluid mixture that could be poured rather than pressed into the moulds.

Glazing and Finishing

The heads were usually given three separate firings and two layers of glaze. The initial firing produced biscuit ware or bisque, so called because of its close, brittle texture. The second and third firings fused the painted decorations and glazes. After the firings, the appearance of the heads identifies each of the three different types: glazed china heads are those with a shiny overglaze; untinted bisque heads have a matt finish and are usually white; bisque heads are tinted with a tinge of colour. Manufacturers produced both shoulder and socket heads, and achieved equally good results with pressed and poured porcelain. From the outside, pressed heads cannot be distinguished from poured ones, and give no clue to the casting method

C.1860 GLAZED CHINA HEAD

"THE DAY BEFORE MARRIAGE"
c.1838 George Baxter Aquatint

C.1850 GLAZED CHINA HEAD

C.1840 GLAZED CHINA HEAD

GLAZED CHINA SHOULDER HEAD (*LEFT*) *Similarities between this doll and the untinted bisque lady at far left are no coincidence, as both were made in Germany* c.1865. *Likenesses include the hairstyles and facial features; pierced ears; the shoulder plate, which displays a moulded blouse with a bow; and the stuffed cloth body with kid arms. Ht: 53cm (21in)*

LIFE RECREATED AS ART (*ABOVE*) *Wonderfully detailed hairstyles, moulded and painted as braided buns, ringlets, curls, or even done up in net snoods, are the special feature of porcelain doll heads. The young lady depicted in the aquatint "The Day before Marriage" (top right) shows how faithfully these styles were modelled on those of real people. The three glazed china heads (above) are described on page 45.*

used. However, there are some differences that can be seen from examination of the inside of the head. A pressed head is likely to be found to have a rough inner surface and will be uneven in thickness; the insides of poured heads, on the other hand, are smooth and consistently even.

~ The fine texture of porcelain enabled the delicate moulding of much ornamental detail. Many porcelain doll heads were cast to show the fashionable hairstyles of the period, and these usually also have moulded and painted eyes. Other heads were left plain: the crown was cut away so that glass eyes could be inserted, and a wig was attached as part of the finishing process.

~ Moulded hairstyles were largely replaced by hair wigs after 1870, as they were considered to be more natural. The introduction of porcelain character dolls in the early twentieth century saw a revival in moulded and painted hair, but the extremely decorative styles of the mid-nineteenth century were never repeated.

Fancy Glazed China Heads

· 1830s to 1880s ·

WHEN GERMAN MAKERS introduced the first porcelain doll heads with moulded hairstyles in the 1830s, a variety of quality dolls came onto the market. These early shoulder heads are called glazed chinas because they are overglazed – a finish that makes them glossy while retaining the whiteness of the porcelain. The colouring of the cheeks and facial features is fixed in the underglaze, but it is quite rare for such heads to be tinted overall with flesh tones.

Reflecting real-life trends, the styling and adornment of the dolls' hair closely followed contemporary fashions. The clothing that was designed for the finished glazed china dolls was equally modish, and usually shows the most up-to-the-minute outfits as worn by the young ladies of the period.

Hair is styled with a central parting that has been left white

Moulded side bows, with touches of gold paint, are a special feature

Hair is held in a snood at the back of the head

Eyebrows and upper lids are finely detailed in black paint

Shoulder head is sewn to body through holes in front and back of shoulder plate

Stitched seams form joints at shoulders

Stuffed cloth arms

Overlarge hands: this body type was used to teach girls about human anatomy

Torso is hand-seamed at the left side

Stitched seams at knees and hips allow limited movement

Cotton skirt and bodice, with frilled peplum at waist

Feet have no toes

C.1865 GERMAN DOLL WITH MARY HEAD *The wearing of gilded hair bows was such a popular style with Mary Todd Lincoln – wife of the United States' President – that doll heads showing her favourite coiffure are often named after her.*

HT: 58cm (23in)

C.1840 GERMAN HEAD

(LEFT) The high quality of this shoulder head is indicated in the delicately moulded facial features; a fine red line that describes the curve of each eye socket; and the even blackness of the hair.
Doll ht: 38cm (15in)

Layers of overglaze give a deep, smooth sheen

PRESSED PORCELAIN

(LEFT) This c.1840 German shoulder head is unusual in its flesh-pink colouring. The hair, which shows rounded side panels covering the ears, and a tightly knotted bun at the back of the head, is modelled after a style associated with the young English Queen Victoria. Head ht: 23cm (9in)

Entire head is covered with a tinted underglaze

Front shoulder plate is slightly shaped to form a rounded bosom

Uneven thickness of the material indicates a pressed head

Untinted head, with brightly painted, "rouged" cheeks

Wavy hair falls in loose curls and ringlets

Brush-marked hair detail at sides of face

Painted eyes, with black upper lids and brick red shadow-line above

Sloping shoulder plate is sewn to a stuffed cloth torso

ONE OF A PAIR (ABOVE)

Although styled in the same way, the black colouring of this c.1865 German lady's hair gives the doll a different appearance from that of its companion, shown rear view below.
Doll ht: 45cm (17½in)

REAR VIEW (ABOVE)

As the 19th century progressed, plain hairstyles soon gave way to more elaborate models. These ringlets and braided, coiled bun belong to the c.1850 German doll at right.
Ht: 10cm (4in)

Different shades of colour suggest fine hair texture

Tassels are adorned with a layer of lustrous gold paint

Hair is held loosely tucked up at the back of the head

GILDED SNOOD (LEFT)

Popular in the 1860s and 1870s, snoods neatly dressed long hair and decorated a lady's head at the same time. This one, displayed on a c.1865 head, contains hair of a golden brown colour, also known as café au lait.
Doll ht: 32cm (12½in)

C.1850 DRAPED HAIRSTYLE WITH RINGLETS (ABOVE)

Changing tastes softened the 1840s' sculptural "Queen Victoria" look into less severe styles. Few other changes were made to the whole doll, which still had the shoulder head attached by strong thread to a cloth body, often with kid arms. Ht: 40cm (16in)

Plain Glazed China Heads

· 1840s to 1870s ·

SOME PORCELAIN DOLL HEADS are marked, but the maker is not known; others are unmarked. Where a mark exists, it often appears on the inside of the shoulder plate. Many of these heads are still sewn to their original bodies and cannot be examined, as damaging the threads to remove the head from the body would divest the doll of much of its historical and collectable value. Occasionally, a porcelain head is found that has never been used with a body. As so few makers have been identified, the information that can be gleaned from such heads makes them as valuable as complete dolls. Not all doll heads were designed to show the ornate, elaborate hairstyles of fashionable ladies. Some have quite simply modelled hair, with moulded curls and painted feathering. These dolls with less decorative hairstyles generally portray either children or babies.

Moulded and painted hair, with side parting

Fine lines indicate upper eyelid and eye socket detail

Underglaze painted facial features

Closed mouth, coloured orange, with darker shading between lips

Tape sewn around upper arms reinforces and hides the joins

Sleeves conceal glazed china arms, cast to above elbow

Oval blue ink stamp reads "Fr.H & Co]/Patent"

Binding around middle gives definition to the unshaped torso

Hands have moulded, joined fingers and separate thumbs

Stitched seams at hips allow doll to sit securely on its rump

Clothing is from the doll's original wardrobe, part of which was bought at Izzard, a London toyshop

Painted pink garter band, tied in a bow

Feet are shaped and painted to represent flat-heeled black ankle-boots

Glazed china lower legs; left leg is a replacement of a slightly different size

Hound's-tooth check tweed trousers, with buttoned fly front

"ALLAN ALBERT" This c.1861 glazed china shoulder head is sewn to a Fischer, Naumann & Co. stuffed cloth body. The front of the torso bears the ink stamp of Franz Haas & Co. Haas was probably the sales agent in London for the German company, Fischer, Naumann and in 1860 applied for a British patent for a cloth body that – like this one – enabled the doll to sit.

HT: 46cm (18in)

The ink stamp, used c.1850, appears inside the shoulder plate. It shows a spread eagle encircled with the words "KOENIGL. PORZELLAN MANUFACTUR".

Very small head; hairstyle is that of a young man

Shoulder head is attached to a stuffed cloth torso and legs

High quality pressed head is finely moulded

Moulded hair, with feathered painting around the face

Flesh-coloured tint covers the whole head

Droopy, sloping shoulders

HEAD OF A YOUTH

(ABOVE) *The Königliche Porzellan Manufaktur is one of the few known makers of porcelain heads. This example of its design for a youth's head, made in the 1850s, is unfinished because of a firing flaw. Head ht: 13cm (5in)*

BOY WITH LONG LEGS

(LEFT) *With its elongated limbs and shoulder head measuring a mere 7.5cm (3in) high, this 1860s' German doll has an odd, but rather endearing appearance. The kid arms have hands shaped as fists, with no fingers or thumbs. Ht: 40cm (16in)*

FLESH-TINTED HEAD (ABOVE)

Sometimes the same heads were used for dolls representing babies and older children. This c.1850 German head of an infant or child is marked with an "R" on the inside of the shoulder plate. Head ht: 8cm (3¼in)

Painted cobalt blue eyes, with black pupils

Pressed shoulder head

RARE HEAD (ABOVE) *It is the colouring that makes this head unusual: it has purple rose shadings above the eyes, below the mouth and at its corners, and on the ears; and the hair and eyebrows are dark brown — more common from the 1860s, but still less usual than black. It was made in the 1860s to late 1870s, probably in France. Doll ht: 23cm (9in)*

Informal smoking jacket, with wing-collared shirt and silk cravat

C.1865 GERMAN FLANGE NECK HEAD (RIGHT) *Relatively few flange neck heads were made: the majority of glazed china heads have shoulder plates. This example has moulded blonde curls rather than the usual head of dark hair. Its face is modelled to show the facial features of a baby. Ht: 16cm (6¼in)*

Painted pale blue eyes

Cleft, slightly double, chin

Stuffed cloth upper limbs and torso

Glazed china lower arms; fingers are curved towards palms

Hands are fists, with stitched fingers; stiff leather body

Doll wears its original clothes

Glazed china lower legs

Feet are moulded to show joined toes

MINIATURE DOLL (RIGHT) *This diminutive figure of a young man, made in Germany c.1850s–1860s, has a flesh-tinted glazed china shoulder head. It is possibly a dolls' house doll. Underglaze painting gives the doll delicately rosy cheeks, violet blue and black eyes, and wispy locks of brown hair. Ht: 13cm (5in)*

Fancy Untinted Bisque Heads
· 1860s to 1880s ·

BY 1860, A MATT PORCELAIN called untinted bisque began to replace glazed china. These later heads are sometimes also known as "parian", particularly in the United States, where the term has been used ever since the 1930s. "Parian" in fact refers to a variety of porcelain that was developed in the late 1840s by two English pottery factories, Minton and Copeland. This new porcelain, whose special properties gave it the luminous quality of white Parian marble, was probably never used for making doll heads, as it was so expensive to produce. However, the word "parian" appeared in many advertisements, perhaps as a sales ploy.

Untinted bisque heads lack the glossy finish of the glazed chinas, but are otherwise quite similar. They are usually white, except for the colouring of the facial features, and represent either ladies or men and children, according to the style of the moulded hair.

Blue bead decoration is moulded with the hair

Painted eyes, with black pupils and fine line below blue irises

Darker line between lips gives mouth slightly down-turned corners

Blonde hair is moulded into high braids around head

Moulded bead decoration accentuates horseshoe shape above

Bead earrings, threaded on wire through pierced ears

Seersucker cotton blouse, with lace trim at neck and cuffs

Stuffed cloth upper arms

Two sew holes in back and front of shoulder plate

Hands have rounded, stuffed palms

Simply shaped hands; lines of stitching show fingers and thumbs

Leather lower arms

Cloth torso, shaped and stuffed to make a rounded sitting rump and narrow waist

Stuffed cloth upper legs

Stout lower legs, made to resemble blue stockings

Velvet-trimmed plum wool skirt

Heeled boots of maroon leather, with buttoned fastening at sides

Box-pleated hem, decorated with silk velvet ribbons

C.1890 GERMAN LADY *The mark of Alt, Beck & Gottschalck – a company founded near Ohrdruf, Germany in 1856 – is incised on the back of this fine untinted bisque shoulder head. The cloth body with leather arms is very similar to a type patented in 1878 by Mary Steuber of Philadelphia, Pennsylvania, United States.*

HT: 50cm (20in)

Inset blue glass eyes, with black lashes and feathered blonde brows

Pearl and gold bead earrings through pierced ears

Hair is moulded to show looped curls

Copper lustre finish on plume, giving it a metallic shine

1870S' GERMAN GIRL (LEFT)
With its head marked "4 L 7", this doll is thought to be the work of C.F. Kling & Co. of Ohrdruf, Germany. The deep shoulder plate is sewn by three holes on either side to a stuffed cloth body. Ht: 48cm (19in)

Leather lower arms; separate stitched fingers and thumbs

Hair is crimped into waves over forehead and curled and set in coils at back of head

UNTINTED BISQUE HEAD WITH MOULDED HAT (LEFT)
The chic moulded hairstyles of lady doll heads were often adorned with trimmings, such as bows, or more elaborate confections. This 1860s' German doll wears an elegant hat tipped low over a head of luxuriant blonde hair. Doll ht: 25cm (10in)

Shoulder head is sewn to a stuffed cloth body, with bisque lower limbs; lower legs are moulded to show flat-heeled boots

GERMAN HEAD WITH TIARA (LEFT)
Lustreware — porcelain with lustre decoration — was greatly admired during the second half of the 19th century. Its popularity is reflected in the headdress of this delicately featured untinted bisque shoulder head, made c.1860. Head ht: 14cm (5½in)

Gold earrings are painted onto ears

Moulded black bow

Feathered eyebrows and painted lashes

Blonde moulded hair

Dress conceals stuffed cloth upper limbs and torso

Leather boots sewn to checked stockings form the lower legs

Unmarked German head, made late 1870s to early 1880s

STYLISH REAR VIEW (RIGHT)
The back of a hairstyle can be almost more decorative than the front, as this immaculately presented 1870s' coiffure shows. The German doll to which it belongs has an untinted bisque shoulder head on a cloth body. Doll ht: 30cm (12in)

Regional costume is handsewn

Pierced ears, with rosy lobes and gold earrings

Shoulders are tinted flesh pink

PATTERNED SHOULDER HEAD (LEFT)
This impressive example of porcelain moulding and painting has thick braids of blonde hair set high on the crown of the head, and two tiny kiss-curls to soften the forehead. Around the doll's throat is a black "velvet" neckband with drop pendant. The tucked bodice sports ribbons, bows, and lace. Ht: 60cm (24in)

SIMON & HALBIG LADY (RIGHT)
The mark "S 0 H" on the front of the shoulder plate identifies this head as one made by this famous firm. Inset glass eyes and bisque lower limbs, with the lower legs moulded to show boots with heels and blue garter ribbons, all date the doll c.1870s. Ht: 30cm (12in)

Plain Untinted Bisque Heads

· 1860s to 1880s ·

UNTINTED BISQUE DOLL HEADS made around the end of the 1860s were often designed to show neat, flat hairstyles that were usually moulded quite close to the crown, with a central parting. Popularly known as flat-topped heads, most portray children or older boys. Heads that represent ladies were still produced, but in smaller quantities. Like the heads of the children and boys, the lady heads also show hairstyles that are far simpler than the crimped waves, exuberant curls, and coiled braids of the earlier models.

A noteworthy feature of the later dolls is the increasing use of bisque for the lower limbs, which are modelled in a fairly convincing manner. Particular attention was given to the legs, with the tiny feet moulded and then painted to show fashionable boots.

Central parting is faintly indicated; no indent or white line

Painted blue eyes, with black pupils; light brown painted brows

Painted red mouth, with darker crossline and full lower lip

Inner eye corners and nostrils are highlighted with red dots of paint

Head is modelled to show a short, child-like neck and dimples beneath the collarbone

Two sew holes in front and back of shoulder plate

Doll wears a striped jacket over a coarse cotton undershirt

Hands have separate thumbs and inward-curving fingers

Cloth upper arms

Bisque lower arms; thumbs show vertical casting lines

Stitching at joins between upper cloth and lower bisque legs allows the limbs to bend

Cloth upper legs and torso, shaped at waist; internal wire frame and sawdust stuffing

Bisque lower legs are short and chunky, but well shaped

Breeches match the jacket

Painted boots on male dolls can have "elastic" at sides or "laced" fronts

Small heels — a post-1860 fashion style — help to date the doll

Decorative lower legs

Painted pink garter ribbons

Purple-coloured copper lustre finish on ankle-boots

UNTINTED BISQUE HEAD WITH BISQUE LOWER LIMBS *The flowing blond curls of this c.1865 German shoulder head are typical of styles worn by young boys in the second half of the 19th century, when male children had long hair well beyond babyhood. The lower legs end in minute feet, shaped and decorated as fashionable heeled boots.*

HT: 25cm (10in)

Eyes lack socket lines and dots at corners

Poor-quality untinted bisque shoulder head

1860S' BOY WITH FLAT BOOTS (LEFT)
Poorer quality porcelain heads have a slightly grainy appearance, and are sometimes described as "stoneware". The example shown here was made in Germany. Boots without heels were a popular style of footwear for both sexes before 1860. Ht: 23cm (9in)

Stuffed cloth upper limbs and torso

Curls extend around back of head

INTAGLIO EYES (RIGHT)
The usual practice of moulding painted eyes as convex shapes is reversed for intaglio eyes, which are concave – a style that was inherited from statuary carvings. Although intaglio eyes are a common feature of the later Gebrüder Heubach character heads, no other features of this German C.1870 untinted bisque shoulder head suggest that this famous firm was the maker. Doll ht: 38cm (15in)

Deep curls and ringlets

Eye sockets are heavily shadowed

Shoulder plate is moulded as a blouse

1860S' GERMAN HEAD (LEFT)
A slight irregularity in the facial features adds a charming naivety to this untinted bisque shoulder head. Its mouth is finely modelled, with the somewhat down-turned corners of a child's face in repose. Doll ht: 43cm (17in)

SCOTSBOY (BELOW)
With its moulded hair painted brown, this costume doll possibly dates between 1870 and 1875: hair coloured either brown or blond may indicate a later head. The eyes are moulded to show heavy lids over large black pupils and pale blue irises. Ht: 22cm (8½in)

Bisque lower arms; hands are simply modelled

Shoulders slope sharply away from the neck

Feathered, light brown eyebrows

Pale red mouth, with darker highlights

C.1875 SWIVEL HEAD (RIGHT)
Representing a young girl, this swivel head was probably made by the famous German doll manufacturer, Simon & Halbig. It has especially striking, luminous dark blue painted eyes, framed by black lashes and feathered eyebrows. The full, orange-red lips, separated by a crimson crossline, appear almost to smile. Doll ht: 23cm (9in)

Painted flat-heeled boots

Ceramic lower legs, cast to above knees

Feathered eyebrows follow the shape of the eye sockets

Painted black upper and lower eyelashes

Inset blue glass eyes

Rosebud mouth

Neck fits into the separately cast shoulder plate, allowing head to turn

Hands have stitched fingers and separate thumbs

LADY WITH GLASS EYES (RIGHT)
The hair of this C.1870s' shoulder head is styled into rows of ringlets and deep fronds over the forehead that provide a nice balance to the head's square jaw. Delicately painted facial features complement the doll's deep blue glass eyes. Doll ht: 30cm (12in)

Moulded and painted tassel

Heel and boot upper are painted to look like leather

BISQUE DETAIL (LEFT)
The Lady with Glass Eyes at left has a stuffed cloth torso and upper limbs, and lower limbs of bisque. The lower legs are moulded and painted to show gaiter-type boots, with a scalloped side-button fastening. Worn by young women of the smart set, they have toes designed to fit only the daintiest of fashionably small feet.

Sporran is made of horse or deer hair

Bisque Dolls

Doll language gives the name "bisque" to a type of porcelain that has been fired twice, with colour added — both as an overall tint and as detailed highlights — before the second firing. The difference between bisque heads and other porcelain types lies in the finish: though glazed, bisque does not have the glossy sheen of the glazed chinas; neither has it the matt texture and marble-like whiteness of most untinted bisque heads.

BISQUE BECAME AN INCREASINGLY POPULAR material for doll heads from the mid-nineteenth century, and remained so until the 1930s. Bisque heads were expensive to make, but if produced in large quantities, could be cost-effective. Many of the German factories that produced bisque heads, limbs, and complete dolls were already manufacturing porcelain or earthenware household items. Some were almost cottage industries, with only a single kiln. Others were much larger, having workshops covering several hectares. Most were in Thuringia, a region in eastern Germany furnished with great supplies of raw clay and wood. Cheap labour was available too.

To make a bisque head, a clay mixture was cast in a two- or three-part, usually plaster, mould. The moulds were carefully scrutinized prior to the casting, as any flaws would be reproduced in the castings. Each mould was used only 40 or 50 times before it was discarded. Early heads were made of a stiff clay "paste" pressed into the moulds; later, a pourable, semi-liquid clay slip was perfected. This slip produced heads with a smoother surface, and allowed greater refinement in the modelling of facial features than was possible with the pressed material.

When firmly set, the doll head or other part (known in its pre-fired state as greenware) was removed from the mould. The casting lines were cleaned, it was fired, coloured, and then fired again. The heads needed special supports while in the kilns, because

C.1880 BÉBÉ JUMEAU (*LEFT*)
Finding a famous-name, marked doll, with its original clothing and packaging, is a real joy. This bébé has a pressed bisque head and a composition and wood body, stamped "BÉBÉ JUMEAU Bte. S.G.D.G. DÉPOSÉ". Ht: 80cm (31in)

POST-1910 INDIAN GIRL (*RIGHT*) *This charming figure is one of Simon & Halbig's "Dolls of Four Races". Its bisque socket head, composition body, flirty glass eyes, and human hair wig are all coloured to represent an Indian girl. Ht: 30cm (12in)*

WALTERSHAUSEN WORKSHOP
(LEFT) *Kämmer & Reinhardt was founded in 1886 by doll-designer, Ernst Kämmer and salesman, Franz Reinhardt. The left-hand side of the photograph at left shows the painting of doll heads at one of its workshops in Waltershausen, Germany, using a new technique developed by the company. The right-hand side of the photograph shows the making up of human hair eyelashes. This was also a Kämmer & Reinhardt innovation.*

ASSEMBLING THE DOLLS
(LEFT) *Another photograph taken in one of Kämmer & Reinhardt's Waltershausen workshops shows a selection of bisque heads and composition bodies, ready to be put together. The finishing of the dolls was always done in the factory, but outworkers were hired for other parts of the production process, such as the making of the blown glass eyes. Kämmer & Reinhardt produced numerous doll designs, including a successful range of character dolls.*

C.1897 GIRL (ABOVE) *This J.D. Kestner doll has what is known as a "bald head". Beneath the wig, the pate has not been cut away for the insertion of the eyes. Ht: 46cm (18in)*

they were liable to sag on their necks as water in the porcelain slip evaporated during the initial firing.

∽ The first heads made had moulded hair and eyes, and closed mouths. Later heads have glass eyes, either inset, or of the lead-weighted sleeping or flirty type, and for these, the eye sockets were cut out and shaped at the greenware stage. Moulded ears, teeth, and tongues were usually designed as part of the mould, but inset teeth (produced in quantity by the Simon & Halbig company) were made separately, and glued into the mouth before the final dressing of the head.

Investigating the Facts

Today, there is a good deal of confusion about where and when bisque doll heads were made, and by whom. Many of the incised marks on bisque heads are unclear, and some trademarks, too, are often very similar to each other, making it hard to identify the true maker. What *is* known is that far more bisque doll heads were produced in Thuringia than anywhere else. The production of some French factories, for example Jumeau and Steiner, is also well documented; and it is probable that German firms occasionally met the production needs of French factories whose output was oversubscribed. Large numbers of bisque heads

were exported, and attached to their "foreign" bodies at a later date: a German head on a French body, dressed in England, for example, is still classed as an original doll. Nowadays, a doll's country of origin is given as the country in which its head was made, as it is in the head that the doll's "personality" is conveyed.

∽ France and Germany undoubtedly dominated the international market for bisque doll heads, limbs, and complete dolls until 1914, when World War I interrupted their manufacture. In England, stoneware rather than porcelain doll parts were produced, usually of a poor quality; and dolls from Japan, though made of porcelain, fell far below the very high standards set by France and Germany.

1920s' ENGLISH STONEWARE HEAD (RIGHT) *Glass eyes were usually inserted into ceramic heads by cutting away the crown, fixing the eyes, and then replacing the cut section with a piece of cork – a very neat operation that was completely concealed beneath the doll's wig. Head ht: 10cm (4in)*

Fashionable Lady Dolls

· 1860s to 1890s ·

FASHION DOLLS – stylish representations of elegant young ladies in haute couture – were at their most popular from 1860 until 1890. Although the majority came from France, many were merely assembled there, using swivel heads or shoulder heads imported from German porcelain makers on French-made bodies. While many heads are unmarked, and others bear marks that are not identified as those of any known maker, it is thought that some well-known French factories, such as Jumeau and Bru, did produce bisque heads.

Dolls of this type usually have inset (rarely sleeping) oval or almond-shaped glass eyes. Their stuffed kid bodies are skillfully pieced together in sections to re-create the undulating curves of a young woman wearing a tightly laced, boned corset.

Ash blond mohair wig (a modern replacement) is pinned to the original cork pate

Painted eyebrows and lashes

Inset glass eyes are pale blue, with a darker outer rim

Pierced ears

Closed mouth

Sleeves conceal shoulder plate, marked "4" on the edge

Original strawberry blond mohair wig

Pale bisque swivel head, with typically long face and full cheeks

Inset brown glass eyes are a striking feature; blue eyes are usual

Elbows have V-shaped gussets so that arms can bend

Stuffed kid arms, torso, and legs, in excellent condition

Top of kid torso is glued over the bisque shoulder plate

Arms, legs, and torso are made of firmly stuffed kid

Thumbs and fingers are separate

Hands have separate fingers and thumbs

On back of doll: large gussets between rump and upper thighs allow limited movement

Stockings, pinned to legs, cover gussets at backs of knees

Sawdust-stuffed body; internal wire frame gives support

Striped silk dress, with heavy velvet collar and sleeve trim

Sewn-on shoes hide simply shaped feet

C.1875 FRENCH LADIES
At 13in (33cm) high, the undressed doll shown here is somewhat shorter than its dressed companion, though the two are quite similar otherwise. Their bisque swivel heads have socket necks set into the bisque shoulder plates; this allows the heads to be angled attractively.

HT: 18in (46cm)

Inset large blue-grey glass eyes

Closed mouth

SUMMER OUTFIT (LEFT) The rounded face and sweetly innocent facial expression of this c.1875 French Belton-type shoulder head indicate that the doll was intended to represent a young girl rather than a lady. It sports the pierced ears – here threaded with blue bead earrings – seen on most of the fashion dolls. Ht: 38cm (15in)

UNDERGARMENTS A LA MODE (RIGHT) Attributed to Margueritte Frène of Caen, France, this bisque shoulder head dates from the late 1870s. The doll has two rare features: the vibrant colouring of the cheeks; and the closed, upturned "smiling" mouth. Ht: 65cm (26in)

Chestnut brown human hair wig

Painted chin highlights echo those of the cheeks

Stuffed kid arms, with gussets at elbows

Gusseted kid arms, torso, and legs

Separate fingers and thumbs

Simple cotton outfit, with a flower-trimmed straw hat atop, suits the doll's childlike appearance

Period undergarments cover the stuffed kid body and legs; gussets at hips and knees

Flat-soled feet have separate toes

FOOTWEAR FOR LADIES (BELOW) The fine accessories of fashion dolls were hand-crafted with as much attention to detail as the real-life items they copied. These tiny leather shoes are for cloth or kid feet. Dolls with bisque lower legs have moulded and painted feet to suggest boots.

Post-1875 pink-tinted bisque shoulder head

Inset blue glass eyes; fine lines radiate from pupils to edges of irises

Ostrich feathers, dyed blue to match stripes in dress

TEA ON THE LAWN (RIGHT) Dolls with heads that turn and movable limbs have great appeal. This 1870s' French lady has a bisque swivel head. The hips and knees have V-shaped gussets that allow the limbs to be placed in a variety of positions. Ht: 32cm (12½in)

c.1875 leather shoe, with high back and buttoned ankle-strap

Moulded bisque gaiter-type boot, with tassel top: foot detail of lady at right

Silk and lace parasol, with brass fittings

Inset blue glass eyes have very large pupils

Pale pink bisque lower arms

Promenade dress, made of net woven with stripes of blue satin

Dress conceals sawdust-filled cotton body

Bisque lower arms; hands have joined fingers and separate thumbs

GIRL WITH PAINTED BOOTS (RIGHT) Made in France after 1875, this doll is thought to have been created by doll-maker, Huret. The short dress indicates that the doll represents a girl rather than a lady. A detail of the doll's bisque lower leg is shown in close-up above. Ht: 48cm (19in)

Close-up of boot is shown above

Developments in Body Types

· 1860s to 1880s ·

THE 20 YEARS BETWEEN 1860 and 1880 were halcyon days for the fashionably dressed dolls of France and Germany, and manufacturers ensured their continuing popularity by making increasingly realistic bodies for the dolls' fine bisque heads. Bisque lower arms and sometimes legs replaced stuffed kid limbs, and though early models seem clumsy opposed to the delicately stitched kid limbs, later castings are more refined. The articulation of doll bodies was a new challenge, and it was here that the greatest advances were made. ∾ The French firm, Gesland, operated in Paris from 1860 to 1928. The jointed metal frame of its padded stockinet body allowed the limbs and torso to assume and retain a variety of positions, and was a major innovation of this particular period.

Swivel head can be turned on its shoulder plate

Light blonde mohair wig

Pierced ears

Beneath padding, left side of shoulder plate bears Gaultier's mark "F.G."

Doll wears a contemporary walking outfit of white silk; collar trimmed with broderie anglaise forms a shoulder-cape

Padded arms conceal wire frame, which allows elbows to bend

Back of torso is stamped with Gesland's mark

Bisque hands, cast to just above wrist joints

Upper legs, torso, and arms made of stockinet, padded with wool fibre, over a wire frame

Deep border of broderie anglaise on French cuffs

Shapely lower legs, made of bisque

Flat feet, with moulded toes

Eight mother-of-pearl buttons fasten the coat

Petticoat and undergarments are made of matching broderie anglaise

GESLAND BODY WITH GAULTIER HEAD

Cooperative agreements were a common practice within the doll industry, especially where parts made of different materials were teamed together. This c.1880 lady has a bisque swivel head, hands, and lower legs made by Gaultier of Paris and a Gesland padded stockinet body over a wire armature.

High-heeled, laced black leather boots, with brown leather facings and soles

HT: 60cm (24in)

White mohair wig

Long, waisted jacket of purple silk, with square scallop detail at hem

Kid hands have well-shaped, separate fingers and thumbs

Original striped silk skirt, showing damage by ultraviolet light

BISQUE-HEADED TWINS (RIGHT) Probably of German origin, this pair was made towards the end of the 1870s. The naked figure is a fine example of a kid doll body of the late 1800s. Other materials were also available, but high-quality bodies were usually of kid. Ht: 46cm (18in)

Torso, upper arms, and legs are made of wood covered with kid

Inset blue glass eyes, with painted lashes and brows

Bisque lower arms

Tenon joints at elbows and waist

Joints at hips, so doll can sit easily

Joints at ankles and knees, for optimum movement

Bisque swivel head

Promenade costume, made of silk

Thick mohair wig, dressed in braids, pinned to a cork pate

Close-fitting, short-waisted jacket, with flared sleeves

Bustle and train at back of skirt

Flat-fronted skirt: a late 1870s' style

C.1866 "MANUELITA" (ABOVE) This elegant French lady doll has a body of stuffed kid and a pale bisque swivel head, with inset, almond-shaped dark blue glass eyes, and a mohair wig. Ht: 38cm (15in)

Brown mohair wig over a cork pate

Shoulder plate is moulded to show a high bosom

V-shaped gussets at elbows

Finely made kid hands, with long fingers

Elaborate, two-tiered train, edged with chequered quilting and lace

Lower eye sockets have dark painted rims

THE BRIDE (LEFT) Fashion dolls are unrivalled in displaying the styles of the period. Here, a doll with a French or German bisque shoulder head and kid body models an 1880s' bridal gown. Ht: 35cm (14in)

C.1870 BARROIS LADY (RIGHT) The mark "E. Déposé B.", which is incised on this doll's front shoulder plate, is that of E. Barrois. Porcelain factories in both France and Germany produced heads for this famous Parisian company between 1844 and 1877. Ht: 32cm (12½in)

Lace-trimmed, cream satin gown, with pleats, bows, and flounces

Arched feet have toes indicated with lines of stitching

Satin-trimmed muslin skirt over a hooped crinoline

Bisque shoulder head

Blonde fleece wig, with skin backing

Closed mouth

Inset azure blue glass eyes

Dress conceals stuffed kid upper arms, torso, and legs

Bisque lower arms, with moulded fingers and thumbs

Jumeau Dolls

· 1842 to 1958 ·

PIERRE FRANÇOIS JUMEAU established his company in Paris in 1842, originally making wood or kid doll bodies and doll clothes. In 1867, his son, Emile, joined the firm, bringing a fresh spirit of commercial enterprise. The company expanded, and in 1873 began to make bisque doll heads, cast at its factory outside Paris in Montreuil-sous-Bois. Soon after, Emile introduced the *bébés Jumeau* – dolls with fine bisque heads, jointed composition bodies, and an innocent expression, whose quality and appeal did much to establish Jumeau's reputation. Faced with increasing competition from German doll-makers, Jumeau amalgamated in 1899 with other French companies to form the *Société Française de Fabrication de Bébés et Jouets* (S.F.B.J.). Both name and company survived within the *Société* until trading came to an end in 1958.

En suite *velvet bonnet, trimmed with dyed ostrich feathers*

Inset *pale blue glass eyes; fine lines radiating from pupils give life-like effect*

Lower eyelashes are detailed with precise brushstrokes

Dark blonde *mohair wig, curled into corkscrews over forehead*

Bisque *socket head*

Rosebud mouth, deeply indented; darker highlights accentuate the fine moulding of the lips

Long silk tunic dress, *with silk checked collar*

Wood and composition arms, ball-jointed at elbows and shoulders

Marked *composition torso, moulded to show a rounded belly and chest*

Childlike, chubby hands, with short fingers and thumbs

Doll wears its original outfit, a tunic dress; front facings form two false pockets at hem

Composition *legs, with ball joints at knees and hips*

Whole body is varnished over five layers of flesh-tone paint

Pleated silk "skirt", trimmed with lace

Petticoat is edged with handmade lace

Long toes are *moulded together, but still well defined*

BÉBÉ JUMEAU *The inspiration for the bébés Jumeau is said to have come from a portrait of Henri IV of France, aged four. Whatever the source, their insouciant charm has won the hearts of buyers and collectors since the first doll was sold. This example dates from between 1880 and 1885, and shows the exceptionally fine quality of Jumeau dolls manufactured before 1899.*

HT: 55cm (22in)

Faded maroon leather *shoes are stamped on soles "EJUMEAU/ MED OR/ 1876/ PARIS/DÉPOSÉ"*

Machine-knitted *socks, made of mercerized cotton*

Silk rosettes *match the rest of the doll's outfit*

Strawberry blonde
mohair wig

Pierced ears

Large inset blue
glass eyes

White line suggests
a row of teeth

Cork pate fits
snugly into
head cavity

Glass eyes
inserted
through
cut section

Socket head
turns easily
to either side

DOLL MARKS

These ink stamps are from
the doll "Florence"; they are
usually found together.

Patented head details include
the size: "14" indicates a
height of 75cm (30in).

DÉPOSÉ
TÊTE JUMEAU
B⁫ˢ S.G.D.G.
14

Body mark refers to the 1885
Paris Exhibition – the doll
was awarded the gold medal.

JUMEAU
MÉDAILLE D'OR
PARIS

"FLORENCE" (RIGHT)

Named by her original
child owner, "Florence" is a
large bébé of late 1880s'
or early 1890s' vintage.
Like all the bébés, the
doll has a bisque socket
head and a papier mâché
composition body, jointed
at the shoulders, elbows,
hips, and knees so that
the limbs can be moved
into various positions.
The head and body
are both marked (see
Doll Marks, right).
Ht: 75cm (30in)

Salmon pink velvet dress
is a later purchase; dolls
were often sold unclothed

HEAD PROFILE (ABOVE)

Carefully removing the mohair wig
from the head of "Florence" reveals
the cork pate to which it was pinned
– a method of fixing hair that was
used for most Jumeau dolls. The
profile also shows two other features:
the realistic modelling of the moulded
ears; and the bulbous, luminous
blown glass eyes (sometimes called
paperweight eyes).

Blonde mohair
wig, styled
in ringlets

Inset pale blue
glass eyes

Fingers of
right hand are
curved to hold
a parasol

FRENCH NURSEMAID (LEFT)

This mechanical doll has an
unmarked bisque swivel head,
probably made by Jumeau between
1880 and 1890. Inside its body is
a Roullet & Decamps clockwork
mechanism, which is wound with a
key projecting from the doll's right
hip. The nursemaid and mailcart –
the vehicle holding the baby – are
fixed together, allowing the entire
ensemble to move forward as the
doll "walks". Ht: 30cm (12in)

Fringed silk canopy,
now very worn

Baby is all-bisque, jointed
at shoulders and hips

Bent arms, with
hands shaped as fists

Metal mailcart – a
type of pushchair

Bisque lower
legs, moulded
and painted
to show
heeled boots

C.1875 FASHION DOLL (LEFT)

Though unmarked, this doll is of a
type also associated with Jumeau. Its
bisque swivel head, with inset glass
eyes, pierced ears, and blonde
mohair wig, and gusseted,
stuffed kid, internally wired
body are common features
of fashion dolls made from
1860 to 1880. The doll
wears a silk walking
outfit and side-
buttoning leather
boots in period style.
Ht: 35cm (14in)

PARIS
DÉPOSÉ

The bee trade-
mark, stamped on
the soles of some
doll shoes made
by Jumeau, was
registered in 1891.

Stockings conceal
bisque lower legs

Bru Dolls

· 1866 to 1950s ·

IN 1866, THE FRENCH FIRM, Bru Jne. & Cie., appeared as a strong contender for supremacy in the bisque doll marketplace, seriously rivalling the products of the other up-and-coming manufacturer in France, Jumeau (see pages 58–59). Casimir Bru Jeune (junior) was the firm's first proprietor, followed by H. Chevrot in 1883, and Paul Eugène Girard seven years later. In 1899, Bru became a member of the new *Société Française de Fabrication de Bébés et Jouets* (S.F.B.J.), which produced dolls using original Bru moulds until the 1950s.

Both before and after joining the *Société*, Bru produced a host of different models, among them mechanical dolls, such as its own type of *bébé baiser* or kiss-throwing doll. Most Brus have swivel, socket, or shoulder heads made of bisque; fleece, mohair, or human hair wigs; glass eyes; and pierced ears.

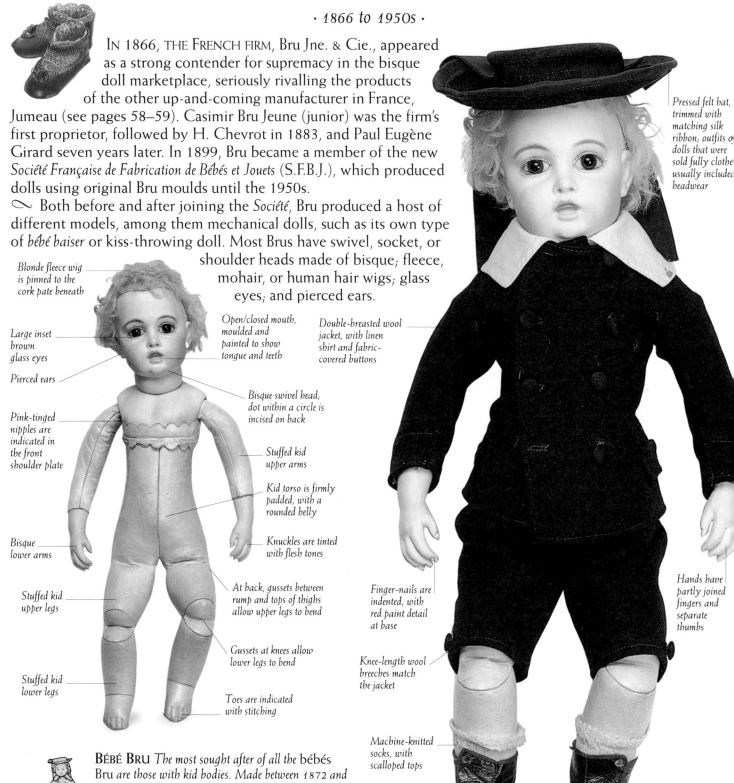

Pressed felt hat, trimmed with matching silk ribbon; outfits o dolls that were sold fully clothe usually included headwear

Blonde fleece wig is pinned to the cork pate beneath

Large inset brown glass eyes

Pierced ears

Open/closed mouth, moulded and painted to show tongue and teeth

Double-breasted wool jacket, with linen shirt and fabric-covered buttons

Pink-tinged nipples are indicated in the front shoulder plate

Bisque swivel head; dot within a circle is incised on back

Stuffed kid upper arms

Kid torso is firmly padded, with a rounded belly

Bisque lower arms

Knuckles are tinted with flesh tones

Stuffed kid upper legs

At back, gussets between rump and tops of thighs allow upper legs to bend

Finger-nails are indented, with red paint detail at base

Hands have partly joined fingers and separate thumbs

Gussets at knees allow lower legs to bend

Stuffed kid lower legs

Toes are indicated with stitching

Knee-length wool breeches match the jacket

Machine-knitted socks, with scalloped tops

Glacé leather, flat-heeled boots

BÉBÉ BRU *The most sought after of all the bébés Bru are those with kid bodies. Made between 1872 and 1954, the bébés could be purchased naked; partly dressed, in chemise and drawers; or fully clothed. This c.1880 doll wears the costume of a sailor boy, but could equally well represent a girl child, as two dresses and petticoats form part of its original wardrobe.*

HT: 38cm (15in)

New mohair wig, pinned to the original cork pate

Open/closed mouth

Finely modelled right hand

Glass eyes may have been reset

Ball joints at shoulders

C.1890 BRU GIRL (LEFT)
Illustrating another style of body designed by Bru, this doll has a bisque swivel head and shoulder plate incised "BRU JNE/8". Heads on kid-and-composition bodies often bear this type of mark, which may be found also on heads used with gusseted kid bodies. Ht: 55cm (22in)

Upper arms of kid over wood-and-composition

Hinged elbow joints

Bisque lower arms

Hidden mortise and tenon joints at hips

Kid over wood-and-composition upper legs and torso

DOLL MARKS
Swivel heads have corresponding marks incised on the neck and shoulder plate.

BRU. Jᴺᴱ R 12

Leather boots and shoes made for Bru dolls may be stamped with the maker's name inside an oval.

BRU J PARIS

Heavily painted eyebrows, a special Bru feature

Titian mohair wig

Inset blue glass eyes

Bisque swivel head, incised on nape of neck "Bru Jne/6"

Lower legs made of painted composition

1880S' GIRL CHILD (LEFT)
This pert-faced bébé Bru has the same head and body as the sailor boy opposite, with a mohair, rather than fleece, wig. The practice of replacing wigs was once quite common among collectors who did not like the makers' original designs. Ht: 46cm (18in)

Silk costume is in period style but not original to doll

Delicate bisque lower arms, a feature of Bru dolls

C.1890 "SERENA"
(RIGHT) The owner of this Bru girl has kept the doll intact, with its original eyes and wig. It has a bisque swivel head and shoulder plate, large inset brown glass eyes, and a long ash blonde mohair wig. The lace that borders the dress and decorates its skirt was handmade by a nanny in Ayrshire, Scotland. Ht: 50cm (20in)

HEAD PROFILE (ABOVE)
Along with other makers of the period, Bru made its own style of lady doll between 1866 and 1870s. These dolls have bisque shoulder or – as here – swivel heads, usually teamed with stuffed kid bodies. They may also be called "smilers", after their main feature: a small mouth, with the lips pursed into a tight smile. Ht: 40cm (16in)

Clothes cover a kid over wood-and-composition body and composition legs

Bronze leather ankle-strap shoes, with matching ribbon bows on toes

Lady with Wooden Body

· 1870s ·

A VARIETY OF DIFFERENT STYLES OF DOLL were made during the 1870s, as companies vied with each other to produce the very best models showing the most innovative designs. Dolls that could walk, talk, throw kisses, or even do all three at once, found eager buyers; but against all the competition, a model of enduring popularity emerged: the doll with a fine bisque swivel head and matching shoulder plate attached to a shapely body. Many attempts were made to create the ideal body – an objective that proved elusive until the development of fully jointed types. ∽ In 1872, Bru Jne. & Cie. issued a product catalogue listing doll bodies made of stuffed kid or a combination of kid and wood. It also included a marvellous new design – an all-wooden lady doll body (quite similar to the one shown here) resembling an artist's lay figure, which used two different varieties of joint to provide optimum movement to the limbs.

Reddish blonde human hair wig

Closed mouth, darker paint detail highlights bow of the lips

Bisque swivel head, lightly tinted to resemble fine white skin

Neck socket is lined with kid, to prevent chafing as head turns

Inset blue glass eyes

Mortise and tenon joints at shoulders

Band of kid covers the join between bisque shoulder plate and wooden torso

Cotton chemise top; front fastens with cotton-covered buttons

Flange joints allow lower arms to rotate

Mortise and tenon joints at elbows

Wooden parts are painted flesh pink and varnished

Wooden torso, carved to show narrow waist, buxom hips, and flattened bosom

Mortise and tenon joints at hips

Flaking paint exposes bare wood beneath

Ball and socket joints at wrists

Boned cotton twill corset, shaped to the doll's torso

Longish, nicely rounded thighs

Flange joints at mid-upper legs, so lower legs can rotate

Mortise and tenon joints at knees

Bottoms of feet are arched between ankles and toes

Split drawers with open crotch, made in one piece with the chemise

HT: 55cm (22in)

C.1870 ARTICULATED LADY *This elegant, carved wooden body, designed specifically for lady dolls, recreates the "ideal" look of the 1870s, when a rounded body with small waist was considered the most becoming female shape. Compared to the curvaceous torso, the doll's limbs appear rather unrefined, though the feet are surprisingly detailed.*

Deep notches separate the toes

Delicately modelled feet

Rounded lid provides extra space for topmost items packed inside

Parchment paper and "ivory" fan, painted with white edelweiss

Lace-trimmed satin peignoir – a type of dressing gown

TRAVELLING BOX (LEFT) The lady's wardrobe of fashionable outfits, undergarments, and accessories is housed conveniently inside a Saratoga trunk – a round-lidded case used particularly by ladies when travelling. This miniature replica of a full-sized trunk is made of wood, covered in leather cloth, with leather bindings and metal fittings. A removable tray (see below) fits snugly within the body of the trunk. The lining paper is printed with coloured candy-stripes – a favourite late 19th-century design.

Feather-stitching attaches the lace trim

Pretty short-sleeved summer frock, made of printed muslin

Strap secured to lid and base

Metal carrying handles at sides

Back view of doll's corset, with laced eyelet fastening

Wicker jewellery box; base is lined with cotton

Embossed "silver" pendant necklet

"Pearl" and "jet" necklaces

Pink and black bead necklace, with bead drops

LIFT-OUT TRAY (BELOW) The more fragile items and those that might damage the clothing are kept in the trunk's removable tray. Stored in the front section are (left to right) two pairs of leather walking boots; stoppered glass bottles for scent and toilet waters; a leather purse; "diamanté" jewellery on a satin reticule; and a mirror with filigree back.

Straw hat, with braided brim and chiffon trim

Black lace and ribbon trim

Bonnet with ostrich feathers and ruched silk

LADY AT LEISURE (BELOW) Writing letters was a popular pastime of wealthy young ladies in the 19th century. They would correspond about society, clothes, music, dancing, their travels, families, and their latest "beaux".

Bone-handled umbrella, with cotton cover and metal fittings

Elbow-length kid gloves

Handmade writing paper

Matching envelopes, tied with original silk ribbon

Mirror-backed wooden hairbrush

Kid gloves

Cotton parasol, with wooden handle

Tortoiseshell lorgnette

French miniature pocket watch

Wooden hairbrush, with real bristles

Tortoiseshell comb

Steiner Dolls

· 1855 to 1908 ·

JULES NICHOLAS STEINER is probably better remembered for his company's wonderful mechanical dolls than for their intricate clockwork movements, which he also designed. A former clockmaker, Steiner founded the Steiner Société (also known as Steiner Cie.), in 1855. The company survived his death in 1891, and continued to trade until 1908, yet it was undoubtedly Steiner who provided the creative impetus for this Parisian business; during his leadership, the firm won several prizes. ~ Alongside the complex, expensive mechanical dolls, the Steiner Société also produced simpler models and non-mechanical play dolls. All have bisque heads, which are thought to have been made in French porcelain factories, although the heads of the mechanical dolls rarely bear any company's mark.

Lace-trimmed silk bonnet, tied with silk velvet ribbons

Inset deep blue glass eyes

Open mouth, showing four teeth at top and bottom

White silk floss wig, pinned to a cork pate

Unmarked pale bisque shoulder head

Heavy metal armature at shoulders, for moving the arms

Upper arms of kid stretched over pressed card

Kid-covered wooden torso ends at waist

Bisque lower arms are cast to well above elbows

Bisque lower arms, robustly modelled

Rosy-pink tint on finger-nails

Pasteboard bell forms the lower half of the doll

Metal frame within bell houses and protects the clockwork mechanism

Printed cotton dress is designed to conceal the doll's working parts

Brass winding key

Rivets attach the pasteboard bell to the base

Wooden base

1870s' AUTOMATED LADY *The clock-work mechanism inside this doll is wound with a brass key and is activated by an on–off lever next to the key. The wheel can be set so the doll rotates or moves forwards, simultaneously raising and lowering its arms and calling "Mama".*

HT: 38cm (15in)

Rotating wheel

Label of London doll-maker and seller, Charles Marsh (see page 35)

On–off lever

Winding key

Base Detail (LEFT) The three small wheels that protrude through the holes cut in the Automated Lady's wooden base have three separate functions: one stabilizes the doll; one is the drive wheel; and one sets its direction.

Stabilizer wheel

Drive wheel

Mohair wig, styled with side parting

Inset large blue glass eyes

Heavy, feathered eyebrows

Closed mouth

Bisque socket head, incised at back below hairline "J. STEINER/ BTE S.G.D.G./PARIS/ F₁RE A 9"

Composition arms, jointed at shoulders and elbows

Label reads "LE PETIT PARISIEN/ BÉBÉ J.STEINER/ MARQUE DÉPOSÉE/ MÉDAILLE D'OR/ PARIS/1889"

Typical feature: fingers are all roughly the same length

Composition upper legs and torso, jointed at hips

Composition lower legs, jointed at knees

Space between big and smaller toes

Post-1890 Bébé Steiner

(ABOVE) Steiner bébés are usually characterized by their pretty faces, with closed mouths and heavily painted eyebrows. Their bisque socket heads usually bear one of the Steiner marks incised on the nape of the neck. Ht: 38cm (15in)

Steiner Kicking Doll

(BELOW) An unusual feature of the dressed doll pictured at bottom is revealed in this detail: a bisque head with flange neck, which fits over the metal bar that turns the head from side to side. The doll's inset deep blue glass eyes and open, toothed mouth are typical of Steiner automata.

Unjointed composition arms

Kid and composition torso

Torso houses the clockwork mechanism

Head turns from side to side as doll moves

Beneath dress, key and lever activate the clockwork mechanism

Composition lower legs

Splay-toed feet are designed for kicking, rather than walking

Blonde mohair wig, with flat top and curls

Doll Marks

Mechanical dolls may be marked only on the clockwork mechanism.

The paper label on post-1889 dolls details the name, patent registration, and award.

Arrested Movement (LEFT & BELOW) The Kicker – seen here "in action" – found a popular market in the United States and Europe between 1870 and 1890. The clockwork mechanism that controls its head, arms, and legs also enables the doll to utter a plaintive cry. Ht: 46cm (18in)

The S.F.B.J. and Others

· 1899 to 1950s ·

DURING THE FINAL DECADES of the nineteenth century, more and more German dolls were imported into France, presenting a lively threat to the already competitive home market. Ten companies responded to this disquieting development by forming, in 1899, the *Société Française de Fabrication de Bébés et Jouets* (S.F.B.J.) – a union composed largely of French doll producers, including both Jumeau and Bru. Some German companies were also admitted, notably its largest single investor, Fleischmann & Bloedel.

In 1905, the S.F.B.J. registered its trademark: a circle divided into quarters, each segment containing one of the *Société's* four initials. Other marks on S.F.B.J. dolls use the same initials, with mould and size numbers.

S.F.B.J. dolls made after 1905 often have this printed paper label stuck to their bodies. The details on the label are usually repeated in the incised head marks.

Sleeping brown glass eyes; single-colour eyes are an S.F.B.J. feature

Bottom eyelashes are painted

Shoulder-length mohair wig, styled with a left-side parting

Pierced ears

Bisque socket head

Silk hat with upturned brim; doll costumes usually included matching headwear

Top eyelashes are made of animal hair

Open mouth, with a row of moulded top teeth, is characteristic of S.F.B.J. dolls

Composition arms, jointed at elbows

Dress is made from a lightweight fabric known as "washing silk"

Ball joints at wrists allow hands to rotate

Composition hands; separately moulded fingers and thumbs

Composition legs

At back of torso, paper label is stuck to the left side

Composition body, jointed at hips and shoulders

Book bound in tooled leather is a tiny replica of a 1903 German diary

Wickerwork valise, with bound cane handles

Ball joints at knees give lower legs backwards and sideways movement

Roughly modelled feet: toes are barely distinguished

C.1905 S.F.B.J. GIRL *Although many of the firms that joined the Société were renowned for the excellence of their products, dolls manufactured under the S.F.B.J. blanket were usually of a cheaper quality. This early model, a typical example of dolls made soon after the trademark registration, reveals no clue as to which member of the Société produced it.*

HT: 35cm (14in)

Machine-crocheted cotton socks

Simple, mercerized cotton ties

Cloth shoes, with cardboard-reinforced soles

Bisque socket head, marked on back and neck

Inset blue-grey glass eyes, with dark pupils

Brown mohair wig

C. 1910 S.F.B.J. DOLLY FACE GIRL (RIGHT) *The bisque socket head of this doll is incised on the back below the hairline "S.F.B.J./PARIS/60", and on the neck "2". The double figures indicate that the head was made from mould number 60 — a dolly face style that was a bestseller for the Société. The size, 2, corresponds to the height of the doll. Ht: 50cm (20in)*

Black velvet dress

Composition arms, jointed at wrists, shoulders, and elbows

A. LANTERNIER GIRL (BELOW) *Founded in 1855, the A. Lanternier & Cie. porcelain factory in Limoges, France made bisque dolls and heads from 1915 to 1924. The incised mark on this head bears the doll's name, Chérie. Other names on Lanternier heads are Favorite, La Georgienne, Toto, and Caprice. Ht: 68cm (27in)*

Replacement human hair wig

Inset blue glass eyes

Bisque socket head, marked on back

Dress conceals composition body, jointed at shoulders, elbows, wrists, hips, and knees

Dress conceals composition legs, jointed at hips and knees

Swiss cotton pinafore

Ankle-strap leather shoes, with ribbon bows

J. VERLINGUE BISQUE SWIVEL HEAD (RIGHT) *Some companies did manage to survive outside the S.F.B.J. The small Parisian business of J. Verlingue traded between 1915 and the 1920s. This head of one of its lady dolls is teamed with a gusseted kid body. Ht: 38cm (15in)*

Pierced ears

Highly tinted bisque swivel head and shoulder plate

Incised on the back of the head, below the hairline, the mark reads "PETITE FRANÇAISE/J V/FRANCE/1/ LIANE". The company's anchor trademark can be seen between the J and V.

Chestnut brown mohair wig

Sleeping brown glass eyes; top lashes are made of animal hair

Open mouth, with well-defined, moulded top teeth

Composition arms, jointed at shoulders, elbows, and wrists

MIGNON (RIGHT) *The tradename, Mignon, was used for dolls made by Felix Arena of Paris. It is coupled on this bisque socket head — made in Germany for Felix Arena — with the company's mark: a symbol resembling a biplane or box kite. The mark was registered in 1918 and was used for the following two years. Ht: 65cm (26in)*

Hands are moulded to show separate fingers and thumbs

Doll's cotton print frock is not original, but is in period style

Dress hides composition legs and torso, jointed at knees and hips

Fancily patterned, knitted wool socks

Leather-cloth boots, with leather soles, originally belonged to a small child

Leather shoes, with leather thong ties

German Marks of Distinction

· 1860s to 1920s ·

THURINGIA BECAME ESTABLISHED as Germany's most important porcelain-producing region from the start of the nineteenth century. Many firms, whose main product was porcelain tableware, manufactured bisque doll heads and sometimes also limbs on behalf of German and French doll-makers that did not have their own porcelain factories, but assembled bought-in doll parts and sold the finished dolls under their own tradename.

One such manufacturer was Simon & Halbig, established in 1869. Its production plant and facilities at Gräfenhain (near Ohrdruf in Thuringia) were within a stone's throw of the Alt, Beck & Gottschalck factory. Both firms produced many types and styles of high-quality bisque doll heads, among them were those moulded and painted to show highly decorative hairstyles (see pages 44–51).

Jutta doll bodies were manufactured by Cuno & Otto Dressel. The firm's winged helmet mark is stamped in red ink on the doll's right shoulder.

Ears are pierced on the lobes

Curled blonde mohair wig, with left-side parting

Moulded and painted eyebrows

Bisque socket head, marked on back below hairline

Sleeping violet-blue glass eyes, with top lashes of animal hair

Open mouth, with well-defined, moulded top teeth

Composition arms, jointed at elbows, shoulders, and wrists

Base of finger-nails is outlined with red paint

Joints at wrists allow hands to rotate

Composition torso, moulded as a child's body

Ball joints at hips give legs forwards, backwards, and sideways movement

Jointed knees; legs can bend backwards, but not forwards

Composition legs

Expressively modelled hands have separate fingers and thumbs

Red paint defines toes and toe-nails

Doll wears lace-trimmed Swiss cotton dress over two cotton petticoats and baggy knickers

SIMON & HALBIG HEAD

The bisque socket head, marked with the mould number, 1349, identifies this c.1910 doll. The number appears on the dolly face heads that were produced by Simon & Halbig for Cuno & Otto Dressel's Jutta dolls – a line made between 1906 and 1928.

HT: 55cm (22in)

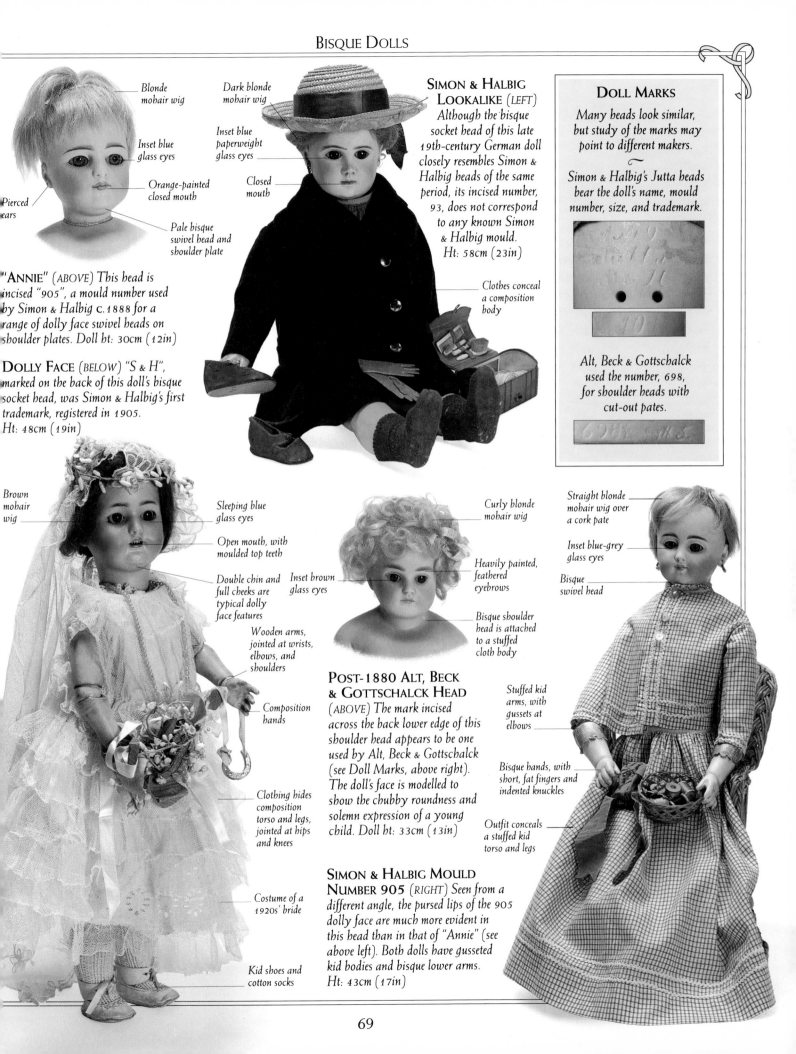

Blonde mohair wig

Inset blue glass eyes

Orange-painted closed mouth

Pierced ears

Pale bisque swivel head and shoulder plate

"ANNIE" (ABOVE) This head is incised "905", a mould number used by Simon & Halbig c.1888 for a range of dolly face swivel heads on shoulder plates. Doll ht: 30cm (12in)

DOLLY FACE (BELOW) "S & H", marked on the back of this doll's bisque socket head, was Simon & Halbig's first trademark, registered in 1905. Ht: 48cm (19in)

Dark blonde mohair wig

Inset blue paperweight glass eyes

Closed mouth

SIMON & HALBIG LOOKALIKE (LEFT) Although the bisque socket head of this late 19th-century German doll closely resembles Simon & Halbig heads of the same period, its incised number, 93, does not correspond to any known Simon & Halbig mould. Ht: 58cm (23in)

Clothes conceal a composition body

DOLL MARKS

Many heads look similar, but study of the marks may point to different makers.

Simon & Halbig's Jutta heads bear the doll's name, mould number, size, and trademark.

Alt, Beck & Gottschalck used the number, 698, for shoulder heads with cut-out pates.

Brown mohair wig

Sleeping blue glass eyes

Open mouth, with moulded top teeth

Double chin and full cheeks are typical dolly face features

Wooden arms, jointed at wrists, elbows, and shoulders

Composition hands

Clothing hides composition torso and legs, jointed at hips and knees

Costume of a 1920s' bride

Kid shoes and cotton socks

Curly blonde mohair wig

Inset brown glass eyes

Heavily painted, feathered eyebrows

Bisque shoulder head is attached to a stuffed cloth body

POST-1880 ALT, BECK & GOTTSCHALCK HEAD (ABOVE) The mark incised across the back lower edge of this shoulder head appears to be one used by Alt, Beck & Gottschalck (see Doll Marks, above right). The doll's face is modelled to show the chubby roundness and solemn expression of a young child. Doll ht: 33cm (13in)

SIMON & HALBIG MOULD NUMBER 905 (RIGHT) Seen from a different angle, the pursed lips of the 905 dolly face are much more evident in this head than in that of "Annie" (see above left). Both dolls have gusseted kid bodies and bisque lower arms. Ht: 43cm (17in)

Straight blonde mohair wig over a cork pate

Inset blue-grey glass eyes

Bisque swivel head

Stuffed kid arms, with gussets at elbows

Bisque hands, with short, fat fingers and indented knuckles

Outfit conceals a stuffed kid torso and legs

German Character Dolls

· 1880s to 1900s ·

WHILE MAKERS IN FRANCE continued to create dolls of an almost idealized "femininity" and beauty, German companies of the late nineteenth century turned their attention towards a novel idea: dolls with facial features modelled on those of real people. Although several manufacturers produced their own versions of these character dolls, as they were called, Kämmer & Reinhardt – founded in 1886 at Waltershausen in Thuringia by doll designer, Ernst Kämmer, and Franz Reinhardt, a salesman – was the first company to register "Character Dolls" as a tradename, in 1909.

Kämmer & Reinhardt made only doll bodies, but also produced complete dolls using bisque heads made to its specifications by one of the German porcelain factories. The heads for its Character Dolls were made by Simon & Halbig (see pages 68–69), and are said to have been modelled on the grandchildren of the company's two founding partners.

Bisque socket head, coloured pink to represent a Caucasian baby

Moulded, painted blonde hair

Pale, delicately painted eyebrow

Intaglio eyes, painted pale blue with black pupil.

Moulded and painted dark brown hair

Intaglio eyes, painted brown

Heavily painted dark eyebrows

Baby mouth, with bowed top lip and droopy lower lip

Robe conceals a bent-limb, flesh-pink composition body, jointed at shoulders and hips

Mouth is moulded into an open smile

Bisque socket head, coloured brown to represent an African baby

Deeply creased double chin

Second and third fingers are moulded together; separate thumbs

Bent-limb composition body, jointed at shoulders and hips, painted brown to match colouring of the head

HT: 38cm (15in)

THE BABY *The first of the Character Dolls to be registered, the Baby head bears the mould number, 100, together with the marks of both Kämmer & Reinhardt and Simon & Halbig. The same mould was used to produce both white and brown heads, despite the dissimilar facial characteristics of the Caucasian and African races that the two colours were intended to represent.*

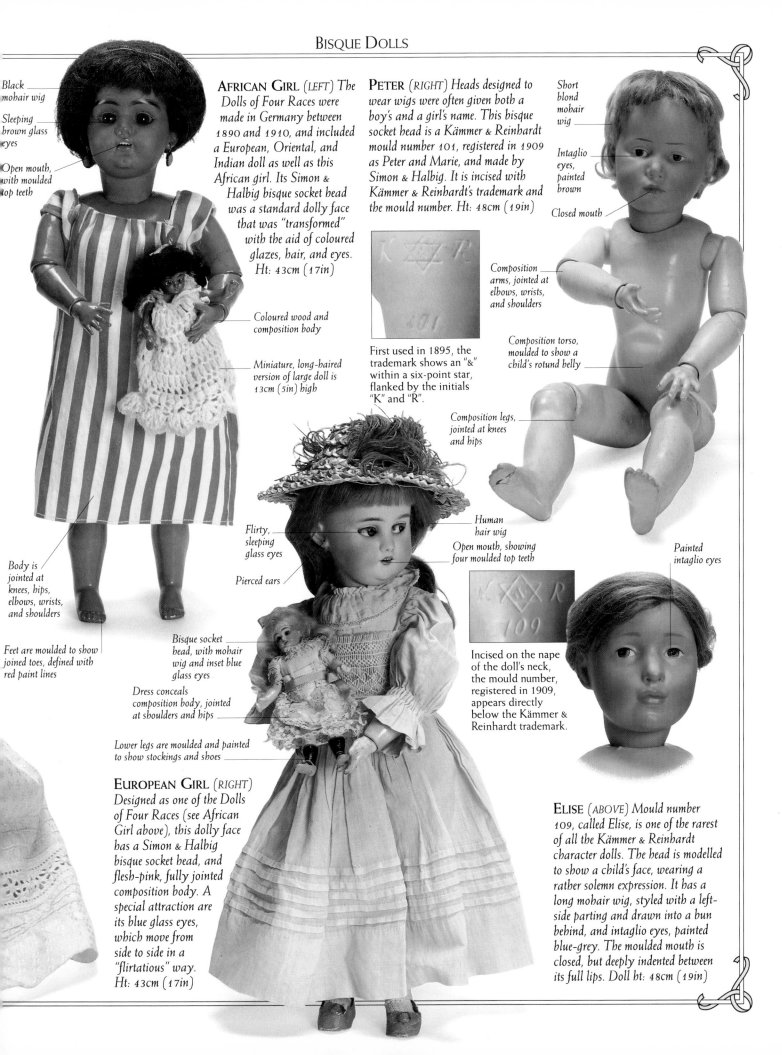

Black mohair wig

Sleeping brown glass eyes

Open mouth, with moulded top teeth

AFRICAN GIRL (LEFT) The Dolls of Four Races were made in Germany between 1890 and 1910, and included a European, Oriental, and Indian doll as well as this African girl. Its Simon & Halbig bisque socket head was a standard dolly face that was "transformed" with the aid of coloured glazes, hair, and eyes. Ht: 43cm (17in)

Coloured wood and composition body

Miniature, long-haired version of large doll is 13cm (5in) high

Body is jointed at knees, hips, elbows, wrists, and shoulders

Feet are moulded to show joined toes, defined with red paint lines

PETER (RIGHT) Heads designed to wear wigs were often given both a boy's and a girl's name. This bisque socket head is a Kämmer & Reinhardt mould number 101, registered in 1909 as Peter and Marie, and made by Simon & Halbig. It is incised with Kämmer & Reinhardt's trademark and the mould number. Ht: 48cm (19in)

First used in 1895, the trademark shows an "&" within a six-point star, flanked by the initials "K" and "R".

Short blond mohair wig

Intaglio eyes, painted brown

Closed mouth

Composition arms, jointed at elbows, wrists, and shoulders

Composition torso, moulded to show a child's rotund belly

Composition legs, jointed at knees and hips

Flirty, sleeping glass eyes

Pierced ears

Bisque socket head, with mohair wig and inset blue glass eyes

Dress conceals composition body, jointed at shoulders and hips

Lower legs are moulded and painted to show stockings and shoes

Human hair wig

Open mouth, showing four moulded top teeth

EUROPEAN GIRL (RIGHT) Designed as one of the Dolls of Four Races (see African Girl above), this dolly face has a Simon & Halbig bisque socket head, and flesh-pink, fully jointed composition body. A special attraction are its blue glass eyes, which move from side to side in a "flirtatious" way. Ht: 43cm (17in)

Painted intaglio eyes

Incised on the nape of the doll's neck, the mould number, registered in 1909, appears directly below the Kämmer & Reinhardt trademark.

ELISE (ABOVE) Mould number 109, called Elise, is one of the rarest of all the Kämmer & Reinhardt character dolls. The head is modelled to show a child's face, wearing a rather solemn expression. It has a long mohair wig, styled with a left-side parting and drawn into a bun behind, and intaglio eyes, painted blue-grey. The moulded mouth is closed, but deeply indented between its full lips. Doll ht: 48cm (19in)

~ German Doll-makers ~

· 1890s to 1930s ·

BY THE END OF THE 1800s, many German factories were involved in the increasingly lucrative doll industry. Some produced only heads, others only bodies; some made the whole doll, and others bought in the parts and simply assembled them. A number of these companies started small and expanded gradually. This growth enabled them to produce, assemble, and distribute dolls worldwide.

~ One such company was Cuno & Otto Dressel of Sonneberg, in Thuringia. Its already established history of trading in dolls and toys had led, by this time, to a flourishing business producing composition doll parts, including heads. Bisque heads were made for the company by leading manufacturers of porcelain, such as Simon & Halbig (see pages 68–69) and Armand Marseille (see pages 76–79).

Shoulder head is turned flatteringly to the side

Large, sleeping glass eyes

Blonde mohair wig

Open mouth shows four teeth

Kid upper arms sewn to upper torso

Fashionable dress made of finely pleated silk crepe

Solid torso made of kid

Lower arms are bisque

Hinged kid thighs allow doll to sit down

Silk damask muff

Lower legs made of cotton material

Gusseted knees

Separate triangle of cotton forms toes, giving feet some shape

Elaborate lace trimming on hem, bodice, and sleeves of dress

BISQUE GIRL, "IRENE" *The fine bisque shoulder head of this late 19th-century doll was made by Armand Marseille for Cuno & Otto Dressel. The shoulder plate is marked at the back, "COD 93-1 1/2 DEP". Although the doll's body is designed to look natural, it actually bears very little resemblance to the human form.*

HT: 48cm (19in)

Knitted, knee-length stockings

Silk shoes, with leather soles

Moulded and painted hair

Blue intaglio eyes

Open/closed mouth

Composition body with bent limbs

Bisque socket head

Doll is jointed only at hips and shoulders

The head mark probably dates from 1926.

BABY DOLL (ABOVE) The doll's face and mark resemble those of a Gebrüder Heubach character, but its head was made by Wiefel and Co. Operating from 1912 to the 1930s, this porcelain factory was taken over by Gustav Heubach and Robert Carl in 1926. Ht: 23cm (9in)

Blonde mohair wig

Sleeping eyes are light blue glass

Open mouth has five teeth

Sleeves conceal cloth upper arms and torso

Bisque lower arms

Beneath dress, doll has composition legs, jointed at knees

Silk and lace parasol

J.D. KESTNER DOLLY FACE GIRL (RIGHT) *Every company produced its own version of the Dolly Face doll, as a universally popular line alongside other less appealing designs. All these dolls, which could be dressed as girls or boys, have the rounded, slightly double-chinned face of a young child, an open mouth showing teeth, and inset or sleeping eyes. This example has unusual eyes that are brown with a black pupil. Ht: 47cm (18½in)*

Dress conceals composition body, jointed at wrists, shoulders, elbows, hips, and knees

C. & O. DRESSEL LADY WITH ARMAND MARSEILLE HEAD (LEFT) *These dolls were first made in 1893. The number 93 (see mark below) was registered by Armand Marseille with C.O.D. in 1892, and probably stands for 1893. A.M. shoulder heads are usually also marked "AM/Made in Germany". Ht: 37cm (14½in)*

Silk shoes stamped on leather soles "MADE IN GERMANY"

The mark, incised on the side of the shoulder plate, clearly identifies this particular model.

Bisque socket head with mohair wig

Sleeping eyes are operated by a lead weight

Stylish costume, made c.1920 from racing silks

Silk and lace parasol

GEBRÜDER HEUBACH DOLLY FACE GIRL (LEFT) *This c.1900 doll shows an example of a Dolly Face by another famous maker. In its bisque head and composition body, it looks quite similar to the Kestner version, but this model has sleeping blue glass eyes, and a tongue has been added to create a more realistic effect. Ht: 50cm (20in)*

Composition hands jointed at wrists

"Lady Betty Modish"

· 1902 to 1911 ·

THE GERMAN COMPANY of J.D. Kestner was founded in 1805, and operated throughout the nineteenth century into the 1930s from its premises in Waltershausen, Thuringia. Its first all-wooden dolls were followed by dolls with composition heads on cloth bodies. By the late 1890s, the company was manufacturing bisque doll heads from its factory in Ohrdruf. Cooperative trading agreements were common at this time, and many Kestner heads were sold to doll-making firms that did not produce heads of their own. Others were attached to Kestner composition bodies. Completed dolls were exported as far as the United States. Here, fortune smiled on one special doll and in 1902, "Lady Betty Modish" entered the whirl of fashionable Boston society.

"Gold" metal hair-band, set with pearls and horsehair cockade

Blonde human hair wig

Inset brown glass eyes, with finely painted lashes

Open mouth shows four top teeth

Pearl necklace matches the hair ornament

Composition hands, with separate fingers and thumbs

Shoulders are decorated with satin fabric rosebuds and curled ribbons

Evening gown, made of cream satin, with white net overskirt and low-cut bodice

Satin ribbons and appliquéd flowers, hand-stitched to overskirt

Long blonde mohair wig

Bisque dolly face socket head

Composition torso, with defined waist and curvy hips

Wooden balls at elbows allow arms to move

Composition upper legs, jointed at hips

Rounded knees and thighs

Wooden discs add strength to jointed parts

Inside body, elastic stringing holds the parts together

Composition arms, jointed at elbows and shoulders

Composition hands, jointed at wrists

Tops of legs are shaped so that legs can move freely

Wooden balls at knees allow upper and lower legs to move to and fro

Flat feet; red paint detail on moulded toes

HT: 46cm (18in)

MODEST MISS The dressed doll at right cuts a fashionable figure, with its lady doll bisque socket head made from mould number 162 and evening gown, designed and stitched by two Boston ladies. As the gown cannot be taken off, a similar Kestner doll shows the composition body that "Lady Betty Modish" is sadly unable to reveal.

Satin blouse, with centre
panel of guipure lace

Purple velvet
jacket; sleeves are
lined for warmth

Cuffs and collar
are trimmed with
rabbit fur

VISITING OUTFIT (LEFT) *Lavish costumes
for all occasions were created for "Lady Betty
Modish", despite the doll's attachment to its
evening gown. This sumptuous, richly
coloured ensemble is for winter wear.*

DOLL MARKS
*J.D. Kestner first registered
mould numbers for its
bisque shoulder and socket
heads in 1897.*

*Incised marks often include
"Made in Germany".*

*Kestner composition bodies
have a red ink stamp mark
on the torso or buttocks.*

Purple velvet-
covered cocked
hat, with ostrich
feather trim

Inset stiffened
lace crown

Purple velvet skirt,
made in six panels
for extra fullness

Pleated cerise
silk dust-ruffle

RIDING HABIT (BELOW) *In the early 20th
century, hunting was a very popular sport, but
no lady would have considered sitting astride a
horse. This costume is designed for riding side
saddle, with a specially cut skirt that permits
the merest glimpse of a leather-booted leg.*

52 tiny playing
cards: a complete pack

Cream silk stock, secured
with a "gold" pin

BOUDOIR ACCESSORIES (LEFT
& BELOW) *The miniature personal
items that "Lady Betty Modish"
takes into her "private
apartments" are as classy as
any piece of the doll's elegant
wardrobe. Still in pristine
condition, they are a unique
part of this original collection.*

Brown wool
jacket, with
nipped-in
waist

Knitted woollen
riding hose

Loop at top,
to pull socks
up legs

Nail buffer, with
ivory back and
chamois pad

Ivory nailbrush,
with hair bristles

Manicure
scissors

Metal
nailfile

Leather stationery
wallet, with writing
paper and envelopes

Long-sleeved,
striped silk
blouse

Wool skirt fastens
at side with four
fabric-covered
buttons

Cotton spats,
worn over
boots

Pearl button
fastening

Buckled straps go
under the feet to keep
the spats in place

Knitting in
progress: a
lacy bedjacket

Metal bag frame,
bound with
crochet cotton

Black and
tan leather
riding boots,
with metal
buckles

Silk damask
knitting bag

Armand Marseille Dolls

· 1890s to 1930s ·

BORN IN THE RUSSIAN CITY of St. Petersburg in 1856, Armand Marseille later emigrated with his family to Thuringia in Germany. The region supported a well-established toy- and doll-making industry, which soon captured the young man's interest. In 1885, he bought the porcelain factory of Liebermann & Wegescher in Köppelsdorf, and began to manufacture bisque doll heads here five years later. The business went from strength to strength, and Armand Marseille became one of the largest German manufacturers of bisque doll heads.

Most of the heads made from 1890 to 1920 are the socket type, well cast and finished. The open-mouth, smiling dolly face head of mould number 390 was the most popular. Later heads show a quite marked deterioration in the quality of their workmanship.

Short brown mohair wig, styled in a "pudding-basin" haircut

Inset dark blue-grey glass eyes

Wig is secured to the head with glue

Bisque socket head, incised "Armand Marseille/Germany/ 996/A.6.M."

Inside torso, arms are strung with elastic from left to right shoulder

Bent arms, made of composition

Hip joints allow doll to sit down

Inside torso, legs are strung to head with elastic

Square feet are flat, with no instep

Mouth is moulded to show a separate tongue and two top teeth

Enamelled golliwog, pinned to wool dickey

White silk facings and a collar edged with crocheted cotton

Full sleeves, gathered into narrow cuffs

Composition torso, modelled to show a child's rounded belly and chest

Hands have separate thumbs and fingers

Hip-length belt, a popular fashion of the 1920s

Straight, unjointed composition legs, with chubby knees

Indistinctly defined toes

Long, fine wool coat, with front button fastening

Wool trousers match the coat

White kid shoes, tied with purple-red satin ribbon

White cotton socks

LATE 1920s' BOY *The mould number, 996, incised on the nape of this doll's neck, appears in the records of Armand Marseille as a baby socket head, with inset or sleeping glass eyes, a moulded open/closed mouth, and a wig. Unlike most baby dolls, which feature moulded, unjointed bent limbs, this example has straight legs that allow it to stand without support on its flat feet.*

HT: 48cm (19in)

Mohair wig

Bisque socket head, incised "1894/AM 4/ oX DI"

"Germany/ 996/A.3.M." is incised on head

Closed, pursed-lip mouth

Bisque socket head

TYROLEAN BOY
(ABOVE) This late 1930s' socket head is typical of those produced by Armand Marseille after its boom years. Although the colouring of the head and facial features is quite well done, the finish is rather harsh and considerably less refined than that of earlier heads. Doll ht: 43cm (17in)

DOLLY FACE GIRL (LEFT) In the 1930s, this type of doll, with a pretty face and robust, partly jointed composition body, was considered to be an ideal and inexpensive playdoll for young children. Ht: 40cm (16in)

Outfit covers a composition and wood body, jointed at the knees, hips, elbows, and shoulders

Clothes hide composition torso, jointed at hips and shoulders, with straight legs and bent arms

Mohair wig

Mohair wig

Moulded eyebrows

Sleeping blue glass eyes

Inset blue glass eyes

Open mouth has four moulded top teeth

Open mouth shows four teeth

EARLY 1900s' BOY CRICKETER (ABOVE)
Wholesale dolls were often exported and sold unclothed. This dolly face boy's classic cricketing attire – wool shirt and flannels, with a striped blazer and cap – was made by a mother, based on her son's own sporting togs. A tin-box cricket bat completes the outfit. Ht: 35cm (14in)

FLORODORA (RIGHT) The tradename, Florodora, was registered in 1901 for mould number 1374, a bisque socket head. Produced until 1921, many heads were exported to the United States for George Borgfeldt's My Playmate line of dolls. Ht: 40cm (16in)

c.1900 RED CROSS NURSING SISTER (RIGHT)
The familiar dolly face socket head of Armand Marseille mould number 390 is teamed in this doll with an unmarked composition body. Many bodies are so similar in style that it is almost impossible to identify their individual makers if they have no marks. Ht: 40cm (16in)

Dress conceals fully jointed composition body

The shoe soles are stamped with two German script letters.

My Dream Baby

· 1920s to 1930s ·

UNTIL THE START of the nineteenth century, the word "baby" was used for all dolls, including those representing older children or adults. The very few dolls that were designed to portray babies had neither the facial features nor the body type of their human counterparts, but were simply made shorter than "older" dolls. By 1850, some manufacturers in France and Germany had registered *Bébé* and Baby as tradenames, but the dolls so named still resembled young children rather than babies.

In 1909, Kämmer & Reinhardt registered its first character doll baby head (see pages 70–71), along with a special design of bent-limb composition body, and baby dolls began to look like babies. Armand Marseille's mid-1920s' version was issued in Germany as My Dream Baby. Heads were sold to other doll producers, including the Averill Manufacturing Co. of New York, which used them for its Lullaby Baby doll line.

Spray-painted, muted colour suggests downy hair covering

Softly painted eyebrows

Sleeping blue-grey glass eyes, without lashes

Small, tightly closed mouth

Deep, low forehead

Small eyes are set wide apart

Squat, button nose, with flat bridge

Bisque socket head, marked on back "Germany/341/ 4.K/A.M."

Chubby hands, with separate thumbs and partly joined fingers

Lace trim at sleeve and neck edges

Composition arms, with bent elbows

Inside torso, arms are jointed at shoulders with elastic stringing

Red paint lines define joined parts of fingers

V-shaped red paint lines between thumbs and first fingers

Composition torso, modelled as a rounded baby body

Inside torso, legs are jointed at hips with elastic stringing

Composition legs, moulded to show dimpled bent knees

Cream silk baby robe

Deep creases between legs and feet

Slightly upturned, stubby feet

MOULD NUMBER 341 *Armand Marseille produced more than one style of My Dream Baby. This doll shows the better-quality type. It has a bisque socket head with closed mouth and a bent-limb composition body, designed so that the doll can sit with splayed legs, but not stand.*

HT: 40cm (16in)

Bisque socket head, marked on back "A. M./ Germany/ 51/3.K"

Painted hair, with small curls moulded on forehead

Puffy, swollen eyesockets, typical of a newborn baby

Open mouth has two moulded bottom teeth

Painted hair, no moulded detail

Fine brush-strokes indicate eyelashes

Sleeping pale blue-grey glass eyes

Composition body with bent limbs

CLOSED-MOUTH SOCKET HEAD (ABOVE) Although every head was cast from mould number 341 or 351, the hand-painting of the features makes each one look slightly different. This example, marked "A. M./Germany/341/0.K", has the characteristic My Dream Baby face, but with top and bottom lashes painted around the eyes. Doll ht: 30cm (12in)

DOLL MARKS

Mould number 341 identifies a bisque socket head with closed mouth.

Mould number 351 identifies a bisque socket head with open mouth. "K" for Kurbelkopf indicates a socket head.

MOULD NUMBER 351 (ABOVE)
Another version of the My Dream Baby bisque socket head, this example shows an open mouth with moulded bottom teeth, a design that seems at odds with the concept of a newborn infant. Ht: 30cm (12in)

BLACK BABY (RIGHT) Three other colours of head were issued as well as the white ones that represented babies of the Caucasian race. Described in the words that were used in the 1920s, they are: brown, for mulatto; cream, for Oriental; and black, for Negro, shown here. Ht: 60cm (24in)

Moulded and painted black hair

Inset very dark brown glass eyes

White bisque socket head, coloured brown

Wooden baby rattle, hand-carved in India

Dress conceals slightly bent legs of coloured composition, jointed at the hips

Closed-mouth white bisque socket head, coloured cream

Original ikat-patterned silk kimono

Inset black glass eyes, with painted lashes

Darker crossline accentuates fullness of lips

Hands, shaped as fists, have separate thumbs

Costume hides a composition body, coloured cream

Curved arms, jointed at shoulders, made of coloured composition

Broad feet, with poorly defined moulded toes

ORIENTAL BABY (ABOVE) Like the black baby, the Oriental head was cast from one of the standard moulds used for "white" dolls, with no attempt made at modelling ethnic features. The finger- and toe-lines, painted orange instead of red, are a special feature. Ht: 23cm (9in)

Bisque Baby Dolls
· 1900s to 1990s ·

THE POPULARITY OF BISQUE-HEADED baby dolls peaked during the 1920s, with the introduction of named models such as George Borgfeldt's Bye-Lo Baby in the United States and Armand Marseille's My Dream Baby in Germany. Many were the product of German manufacturers, whose skilled modelling of character heads satisfied the increasing demand for dolls with realistic features. Designed as newborn infants or older babies, the dolls have heads showing their makers' styles, attached to a common body type. A typical 1920s' baby doll has a bisque socket head – most often with moulded and painted hair – and a plump composition body. Its unjointed, curved limbs are strung with elastic at the shoulders, so that the arms can move, and at the hips, allowing the doll to sit.

Hair is indicated with feathered brushstrokes

Painted eyebrows

Large ears, moulded as one with the head

Human hair lashes, glued into inside top edges of eye sockets

Chin, mouth, and nose are modelled to show deep creases

Open mouth; tongue is moulded with bottom lip

Jointed shoulders allow arms to move to and fro

Chubby, curved arms; no elbow joints

Hands have separate thumbs; second and third fingers are moulded together

Creases at waist suggest fleshy folds

Composition torso, with rotund belly and rounded chest

Jointed hips allow doll to sit with wide-apart legs

Chubby, curved legs; no knee joints

Feet are modelled to show flexed toes, a typical baby movement

Head is modelled to show the features of a newborn baby

Inset blue glass eyes

Moulded top teeth

Traditional christening robe, made of white cotton lawn

Front of robe is edged all around with a border of broderie anglaise

Robe hides period baby undergarments: white cotton vest and nappy; cream wool long crossover bodice; and white, lace-trimmed cotton petticoat

MODEL BABY *The finely cast and detailed bisque socket head of this early 20th-century doll is incised "151", a mould number that was registered by several companies, including Hertel, Schwab & Co., to which the head is attributed. The composition body is also of high quality, and is a superb example of the bent-limb style that was specially designed for baby dolls.*

HT: 60cm (24in)

Painted eyelashes

Inset blue glass eyes

Small closed mouth

NEWBORN INFANT (LEFT) This character baby was made by Willy Weyh of Sonneberg in Germany in 1925. It has a bisque flange neck head with a stuffed cloth torso, arms, and legs, and moulded composition hands, cast to the wrist joints. Ht: 30cm (12in)

The size of the head, 2, appears below the name of the maker as part of the mark.

Brown human hair wig

Metal eyelids, with hair lashes

Sleeping blue glass eyes

Bisque socket head

The mark incised below the hairline on the back of the head shows the maker's initials and the mould number.

Second and third fingers are joined together, except at tips

Composition bent limbs

Clothes hide composition body, jointed at hips and shoulders

Curves of eye sockets are defined with brown paint lines

Painted light blue eyes

Closed mouth, modelled with very full lips

Hand-painted mark below left ear "LER 92/Tilly/160"

Double chin, a baby doll feature

Hair is lightly painted in parallel lines

Fine brown paint lines define upper rims of eye sockets

Moulded and painted eyes

At back of head, maker's mark reads "FB/0"

Open/closed mouth

ADVANCED BABY (ABOVE) Forsaking realism, some makers used wigs to soften the bald heads of their baby dolls, particularly those that were made to portray older children. This c.1916 example is the work of J.D. Kestner. Ht: 46cm (18in)

C.1911 CHARACTER BABY (LEFT) Inspired by Kämmer & Reinhardt's first character doll, Baby (see page 70), this model has a bisque socket head made by the German company, Fritz Bierschenk. Its bent-limb body is designed as that of a lusty young baby. Ht: 28cm (11in)

1992 BABY GIRL, TILLY (ABOVE) A traditionally styled doll that brings bisque up to date, Tilly was hand-crafted by English doll artists, Lynne and Michael Roche. The doll has a bisque flange neck head, with spray-painted hair. Its bent lower arms and legs are also bisque, while the upper limbs and rounded torso are made of firmly stuffed cloth. Ht: 20cm (8in)

Curved bisque legs, cast to above knee joints

Dress conceals a composition body, jointed at hips and shoulders

Lesser-known German Makers

· 1900s to 1930s ·

AS THE HUB OF THE GERMAN porcelain industry, Thuringia supported numerous small doll-makers as well as the factories that manufactured doll heads for large companies. The work of these lesser-known makers has often survived not because the dolls are of superior quality, but simply because they were made in great numbers. Considered as toys to be played with and thrown away when broken, the huge quantities that were produced to meet public demand also helped to sustain the business of smaller makers. These two pages show the work of less celebrated German makers. Each doll has a bisque head incised with the marks of a known and recognized manufacturer. Finding identifiable marks is a stroke of luck, as many makers did not mark their products.

Titian mohair or human hair wig

Painted top and bottom eyelashes

Sleeping blue glass eyes

Ears are pierced for earrings

Sleeping eyes, with metal lids, in half-closed position

Open mouth, showing four top teeth

Simon & Halbig bisque socket head, marked on back "79/10/Germany/ HANDWERCK"

Composition arms, jointed at elbows, shoulders, and wrists

Composition torso, moulded to show a child's pronounced belly and small chest

Separate thumbs and spread fingers

Arms are painted flesh pink

Cotton lawn dress, trimmed with satin ribbon, lace, and broderie anglaise

Composition upper legs, shaped at tops of thighs so doll can sit easily

Red paint lines define finger- nail ridges

Wooden balls give upper and lower legs easy movement

Composition lower legs, with curved calves

Chubby, creased ankles

Painted red toe and toe-nail detail

HEINRICH HANDWERCK

Founded in 1855 as a toy-making company, Heinrich Handwerck later switched to composition doll bodies, which were attached to Handwerck-designed Simon & Halbig bisque heads. This finely modelled c.1900 dolly face girl typifies one of the most popular styles of the period.

HT: 48cm (19in)

Toning, patterned cotton socks

Pigskin shoes, with metal buckles

The mark, incised on the back of the head, also includes "Germany /4" below the designer-maker's name. Max Handwerck operated in Waltershausen from 1900 until the 1930s.

Composition body, jointed at shoulders, elbows, wrists, hips, and knees

The Hermann Steiner mark shows an "H" entwined with "St.", and size number below.

Blonde mohair wig

Inset brown glass eyes

Open mouth, with four top teeth

Bisque socket head

Hands jointed at wrists

MAX HANDWERCK, GIRL

(*ABOVE*) The composition doll bodies made by this company were teamed with one of two types of bisque head, many of which were produced in the porcelain factory of William Goebel. Socket heads, like this one, came with sleeping glass eyes and mohair wigs. Shoulder heads were usually finished with moulded and painted hair and painted eyes. Doll ht: 68cm (27in)

HERMANN STEINER, DOLLY FACE

(*RIGHT*) In 1920, bisque doll heads joined the stuffed plush animals that had been Hermann Steiner's stock-in-trade since the establishment of the company in Neustadt in 1911. This example, made in the 1920s, has a composition torso and fully jointed wooden limbs. Steiner still produces toys but not dolls. Ht: 43cm (17in)

Blonde mohair wig, on a bisque socket head

Sleeping blue glass eyes, with hair lashes

C.1925 GIRL (*RIGHT*)

Arthur Schoenau and Carl Hoffmeister had already proved their ability as doll-makers when they joined forces in 1901 to form the Schoenau & Hoffmeister Porzellanfabrik Burggrub. The company produced its bisque doll heads – of which this is a good example – in its own porcelain factory. Ht: 70cm (28in)

Dress hides a fully jointed composition torso and limbs

Germany
S PB H
914
12½

The incised mark shows the initials of the factory name above the size and mould numbers.

Boots hide wooden legs, with very long thighs, jointed at knees and hips

Reddish brown coarse mohair wig

Sleeping googly blue glass eyes

Bisque socket head

Bisque arms, jointed at shoulders

J. WALTHER & SOHN, C.1920 GOOGLY-EYED DOLL

(*RIGHT*) The charming bisque character head of this doll was made in the Oeslau, Coburg porcelain factory of Johann Walther. It is incised on the back with the crown symbol of the firm, together with "W & S" entwined. Ht: 18cm (7in)

Dress hides composition legs and torso; lower legs have moulded and painted shoes and stockings

Ethnic and English Dolls

· 1860s to 1920s ·

THE STORY OF DOLLS and their makers has linked numerous countries not only through mutually beneficial trade and enterprise, but also as a result of historical events. Some of the most interesting and unusual of dolls have been made during periods of conflict, or as designers tried to create new and exciting models that would spark the imagination of the buying public and – in so doing – loosen its purse-strings. For many collectors, dolls of this kind have a very special charm that balances their sometimes idiosyncratic appearance. ∾ All the dolls described on these two pages illustrate how English and German manufacturers reacted to changes in their familiar worlds during the second half of the nineteenth century and the first two decades of the twentieth century – changes that led on one hand to broadened horizons and on the other to newly entrenched and insular attitudes.

Slanted, curved eyebrows: the only "realistic" facial feature

Closed mouth

Silk-covered card-board hat has a braided silk trim

Pierced ears: a common feature of late 19th-century German doll heads

Tinted bisque socket head

Elbow-length sleeves are lined with pink silk

Incised under hair, "220": the mould number for an Oriental head, registered in 1888

Mohair wig, braided into a long pigtail

Hands have separate thumbs and joined fingers

Composition arms, jointed at shoulders

Back of jacket shows its original olive green colour

Front of silk jacket has faded from its original olive green colour to dun brown

Woven silk damask underskirt

Clothes hide composition legs, jointed at knees and hips and strung to a composition torso

Split-sided tunic coat, made of dark blue silk

Pink wool is braided in with the pigtail and secures its end

Linen hose, with woven patterning

Pink silk also lines the body of the coat

Small feet evoke the Chinese custom of foot-binding

MANDARIN'S SON *Ethnic dolls became popular in the late 19th century, when new possibilities for world travel brought an awareness of other cultures to the masses. Companies that added such dolls to their product range used standard moulds not modified to show realistically ethnic features. This doll's bisque socket head, made in Germany by Bähr & Pröschild, hardly resembles the Chinese boy that it is meant to portray.*

HT: 30cm (12in)

Composition lower legs, moulded and painted to show Chinese-style slippers and socks

Black astrakhan wig

Inset very dark brown glass eyes

Standard bisque dolly face socket head, with applied colour

Open mouth, painted orange, with three moulded top teeth

Slightly curved composition arms

Beneath jerkin, arms are jointed at shoulders

Coral pink satin jerkin, embroidered with gold braid

Hands are coarsely modelled, with joined fingers and separate thumbs

Clothes conceal the tinted composition torso

Feet are crudely modelled, with ill-defined toes

Cotton muslin kilt: a type of one-piece pants

Tinted composition straight legs, jointed at hips

1860s' DOLL IN INDIAN STATE COSTUME (RIGHT) A glazed china head with an elaborately moulded hair style has been used for this unusual doll, which represents a male court official in Rajpur, India at the turn of the century. Originally designed to show the features of a girl, the face has been painted with a fine set of side-burn whiskers and a curled moustache. Ht: 55cm (22in)

Inset blue glass eyes

Pierced ears, hung with ornate earrings

Sleeves hide bisque arms, jointed at the shoulders

Very finely modelled hands

Clothes conceal bisque legs, jointed at hips to a stuffed cloth torso

Magnificent costume, made of linen, silk, and muslin

Slender fingers and thumbs

Gold anklets

Tiny feet, moulded and painted to show heeled, gaiter-type boots

RUNNING FOOTMAN (ABOVE)
The bisque socket head of this doll bears a raised mark similar to some of those used by Walther & Co., a company that produced doll heads in its own porcelain factory from 1908. The doll itself is thought to represent an Eygptian servant. Its head and composition body are tinted to show the tones of a dark-skinned man. Ht: 28cm (11in)

Legs swivel at hips, but shape of torso hinders sitting position

Stuffed cloth upper arms

Stoneware lower arms

Moulded and painted hair

Elongated, firmly stuffed torso

Stuffed cloth upper legs

Painted intaglio eyes

Open/closed mouth, with moulded tongue and top teeth

Stoneware lower legs

ENGLISH BABY (RIGHT) During World War I, supplies of imported German dolls were withdrawn from sale in Great Britain, yet buyers still wanted bisque-headed dolls. This doll illustrates a typical example of the stoneware heads that were produced by some English porcelain factories to fill the gap in the market. Ht: 50cm (20in)

The mark incised on the back of the head includes "H" and "L", for Hewitt & Leadbeater.

WILLOW POTTERY, BABY HEAD (LEFT) English pottery company, Hewitt & Leadbeater, manufactured Willow Pottery stoneware doll heads from 1914 to 1920. This shoulder head shows one of its many styles. Doll ht: 35cm (14in)

Mass-produced Bisque Dolls

· 1900s to 1940s ·

IN THE LATE NINETEENTH and early twentieth centuries, France and Germany cornered the market for bisque dolls. The glazed china and untinted bisque heads with elaborately moulded hairstyles, prim-faced lady dolls in gorgeous attire, and character dolls of this period are some of the finest-ever examples of doll-making. But after 1900, and particularly between World Wars I and II, new possibilities for world trade opened up, and encouraged the mass production of inexpensive dolls, as forward-looking manufacturers capitalized on an increasingly lucrative export market.

Such dolls are often of the "cheap and cheerful" variety. Many were produced to be sold at fairs and in amusement arcades, or as holiday souvenirs; some were made as ornamental pieces, aimed more towards adult than child buyers, and can hardly be thought of as playdolls; others originated as fictional characters.

The designer's surname appears as a signature, impressed into the base of the feet.

Long wisps of hair, painted from knob on crown to forehead

Top of head is moulded and painted to show a knob of hair

Large eyes, painted in the typically side-glancing position

Single moulded and painted knob of hair on either side of head

Moulded tiny button nose

Hair is painted in wispy brushstrokes at nape of neck

Mouth is a single moulded and painted line set in a broad smile

Shoulder joints have metal pins that allow arms to move

Tiny moulded wings, painted blue, a special Kewpie feature

Printed paper label shows the Kewpie tradename, registered by George Borgfeldt in 1913, and the doll's country of origin

All-bisque arms

"Starfish" hands, a typical Kewpie feature

Hands are moulded to show separate thumbs and spread, slightly "webbed", fingers

All-bisque body, moulded as one with the head

Diminutive rump; paintwork accentuates each tiny buttock

Moulded bellybutton, tinted with rosy pink highlights

Tinges of darker colour define "hipline" at base of torso

Moulded legs are joined together

Depressions between ankles and thighs give shape to backs of legs

Legs are modelled to show a young child's chubby thighs

Splotches of colour suggest knees

Short, stubby feet

ALL-BISQUE KEWPIE *Based on illustrations by Rose O'Neill in* Ladies' Home Journal *and elsewhere, the original Kewpies were modelled by Joseph Kallus and produced by George Borgfeldt, a company in New York where Mr Kallus worked as a designer. This doll is one of the earliest models, which were made in the porcelain factory of German doll manufacturer, J.D. Kestner.*

Narrow grooves give definition to the moulded, joined toes

HT: 18cm (7in)

Moulded and painted hair

Coarsely modelled facial features

Bisque shoulder head

Dumpy bisque lower arms

Well-modelled hair

Stuffed cloth upper arms

Bisque lower legs

Stuffed cloth upper legs and torso

Jester's hat is moulded as part of the head

Arms are pinned to shoulders with bent-ended wires

Plump cheeks, painted to show a florid complexion

Paint highlights costume details

Lower arms are moulded as gauntlets

Hips are strung with elastic

Lower legs are moulded to show wide trouser hems

Bisque lower legs, painted to show shoes

Stiffened canvas hat, with braid trim and wool flowers

Mohair wig

Painted facial features

Ceramic arms, jointed at shoulders

Ceramic legs, jointed at hips

Lower legs are painted to show boots

JAPANESE DOLLS (ABOVE)

When Germany suspended the production of bisque dolls during World War I, the United States turned to Japan for supplies. This pair shows the poor quality of Japanese dolls made for export. Ht: Boy 18cm (7in); girl 15cm (6in)

RECLINING LADIES (RIGHT)

High-quality bisque figurines were popular ornaments between 1900 and 1930, their willowy, nude – or semi-nude – bodies gracing many a boudoir dressing table or mantelpiece. These two beauties, made in Germany c.1920, are unusually adorned with mohair wigs. Ht: 13cm (5in)

1920s' CARNIVAL KEEPSAKE

(ABOVE) Made in Germany, this all-bisque figure has a one-piece head and torso, moulded and painted to show a jester's costume. Crude joints at the shoulders and hips allow the limbs to swing when the doll is jiggled. Ht: 6cm (2½in)

1930s' HOLIDAY

SOUVENIR (RIGHT) Though wearing the regional costume of Alsace in France, this doll is probably of German origin. Its head and torso, cast as a single unit, and unjointed limbs are all made of a low-grade ceramic material. Ht: 10cm (4in)

Gracefully angled head

Strawberry blonde mohair wig; moulded hair is more typical

Body is fixed into an alluring, "come-hither" position

Eyes and brows are delicately painted

Body is modelled to show a slim, curvy torso and slender limbs

Recumbent figures are the most often-seen type

Moulded and painted hair

Well-modelled eyes, nose, and open/closed mouth

Wired joints at shoulders

Legs are jointed to one-piece torso and head with elastic stringing

1930s' GERMAN BISQUE

BABIES (ABOVE) Inexpensively made in large numbers, small bisque dolls like these found a ready market among children as dolls' house figures. Many came fully clothed in pastel-coloured, crocheted garments. Ht: Largest 7.5cm (3in); smallest 4cm (1½in)

Feet are moulded and painted to show slippers

Rag Dolls

Doll manufacturers in England and the United States introduced the first commercially made rag dolls in the 1850s. Soft, safe, and warm to cuddle, a rag doll was often a child's first toy. These were generally less sophisticated than dolls made from other materials, such as bisque or wood, but had great charm, nonetheless. Unfortunately, rag dolls are not very hard-wearing; as a result, fewer survive than any other type of doll.

THERE IS OCCASIONALLY some confusion regarding the definitions of rag and cloth dolls. "Rag" is the general term used for dolls that are made of any fabric; this could be cotton, silk, velvet, felt, or any other suitable material. "Cloth", however, is a more specific term, used only to describe dolls made of linen or cotton, including calico (a coarse, plain, usually unbleached cotton) and muslin (a fine, plainweave cotton fabric). Traditionally, rag dolls are stuffed with cloth, sawdust, straw, or kapok, which is a type of cotton wool. Since the 1950s, foam, foam chips, or old nylon stockings and tights have also been used.

Rag Doll Origins

For centuries, rag dolls had been made by mothers in the home simply as toys for their children to play with. The quality and design of these dolls had a tendency to vary greatly, depending on the skill and imagination of the maker, and the availability of the materials. However, any type of fabric could be used, and many a doll was made from an old rag, or woollen remnants that could be found in the home.

Factory-made Rag Dolls

From the 1850s onwards, rag dolls began to be produced commercially by English and American doll-makers. Designs were printed in colour on flat sheets of fabric, and were subsequently cut out, stitched, and stuffed. Sometimes only a flat representation of the front and back of the doll were shown; occasionally additional features and gussets were sewn on to make the body appear more life-like and to give it a three-dimensional quality.

∽ Alternatively, the dolls' features could be painted rather than printed. This was a particularly common practice in

GRANDMA COLE (LEFT)
This doll, representing a grandmother, is one of the members of the Cole Family (see page 93), created c.1901. It is thought that the doll may be a portrait of the doll-maker, Roxanna Elizabeth McGee Cole of Conway, Arkansas, United States.
Ht: 55cm (22in)

"SOLID COMFORT"
(RIGHT) *The famous American doll-maker, Izannah F. Walker, produced this doll in 1873. It is made entirely from cloth. The facial features, hair curls, and black boots were delicately painted on by hand in oil colours. It is clothed in a printed, lace-trimmed cotton dress over plain cotton undergarments.*
Ht: 43cm (18in)

FACE MASKS *(ABOVE) These 1920s' masks, made of cotton stretched over a moulded buckram base, were attached to prepared cloth heads and stockinet bodies. Ht: 16cm (6in) and 14cm (5½in)*

MAGAZINE ILLUSTRATION *(RIGHT) Published in* The Graphic *in 1879, "Rich girl, poor girl, both fond of dolls" illustrates how young girls, regardless of their social status, are fascinated by dolls.*

the United States. The doll would be made up, and the facial features and hair were then painted on by hand in oil colours. The features were also sometimes stitched, or could be painted and then stitched. Human hair or mohair was occasionally sewn onto the head or made into wigs that were glued or stitched in place for a more realistic effect.

Rag Dolls in the Twentieth Century

By the twentieth century, manufacturing methods had greatly improved, and it was possible to emulate the more sophisticated, jointed dolls made of materials such as bisque and composition. Many companies, such as Steiff (see pages 96–97) and Lenci (see pages 100–101) began to use felt for the heads, as opposed to cloth, for a more life-like result. When treated with stiffening, felt can be pressed over a mould to give a doll raised features. It is stiff enough to hold glass eyes or a wig and is easily painted. Sometimes doll bodies, as well as heads, were made of felt.

∽ Doll-makers also began to use a knitted silk or cotton fabric called stockinet. Owing to the soft, stretchy quality of the material, it is generally used for bodies rather than heads. However, if stretched over a moulded, hollow, buckram (stiffened cloth) base, it is sufficiently rigid and can be painted. Between the 1920s and 1930s, manufacturers produced a range of dolls with long, lean, stockinet bodies, styled on the fashionable body shape of the time. These soft bodies were attached to rigid, painted face masks (see above).

∽ Velvet is also occasionally used in doll-making, but rarely for heads. However, the English doll manufacturer, Norah Wellings (see pages 102–103), produced a considerable number of heads made of velvet. These were used particularly in the production

of her ethnic dolls. Velveteen, a short, thick-pile cotton fabric, was sometimes used as a substitute for velvet in the manufacture of cheaper quality dolls.

∽ Today, rag dolls are still popular. They are made of modern, washable materials and, if the health and safety guidelines are followed, are easily maintained. A few of the old manufacturers still survive, and continue to make rag dolls in the traditional ways of their predecessors.

RAGGEDY ANN *(RIGHT) Raggedy Ann began life as a cartoon illustration created by Johnny Gruelle, an American artist. In 1915, he registered "Raggedy Ann" as a trademark, and made and sold hand-crafted Raggedy Ann dolls. A candy heart with the words "I love you" was put in the chest of each doll. This model was made in China by Playskool, Inc., a subsidiary of Hasbro, Inc., in 1987. Ht: 30cm (12in)*

American Home Industry

· 1890s to 1930s ·

LIKE THE WOODEN DOLLS of the nineteenth century (see pages 14–15), American cloth dolls of this period have a charm that belies their rather solid appearance. Many designs started as playthings, made by mothers for their children. As the dolls became popular and treasured items among family and friends, the maker was urged to increase output, and the dolls went into small studio or factory production. These two pages show examples of work by such makers.

Emma E. Adams of Oswego, New York began making dolls in the 1890s. In 1893, at the Chicago World's Fair, the Columbian Exposition Commission awarded one of her dolls a "Diploma of Honorable Mention" and named it Columbian Doll: "Columbia" is the female personification of the United States. Among the very first American patriotic dolls, the Columbians were produced until 1910.

1893 Columbian Exposition ribbon, from Miss Columbia's scrapbook journal.

Curly blonde hair, painted in oil colours

Flat, painted features

Oil colour continues from head down to top of chest

Lower arms are stiffened with small wooden stick inside

Banner ribbon in traditional patriotic colours, with commemorative enamelled pin

Lower arms are painted in flesh-toned oil colours

Stuffed muslin body, shaped to define waist

Seams at tops of thighs and knees allow limited movement

Cotton dress and undergarments are all handmade

Original buttoned shoes and socks

CHILDREN'S CHARITY ENVOY *Miss Columbia is perhaps the most famous of the Columbian dolls. Made in 1899, and given by Miss Adams to wealthy Bostonian, Elizabeth Richards Horton for her International Doll Collection, it toured the world raising money for charities, especially those benefitting children.*

HT: 48cm (19in)

Bisque sailor doll, German c.1900

wooden, Queen xandra & ward VII

GIFTS AND SOUVENIRS (LEFT)
During its three-year journey, the Miss Columbia doll received a great many tokens, given for good luck, or as cheery remembrances of people seen and places visited.

HOSPITAL DOLLS (RIGHT) Martha
Jenks Chase, a doctor's wife in Pawtucket, Rhode Island, developed the Hospital Dolls in 1910. Life-size and realistic, these baby and adult figures were used widely in hospital training, hence their name. The stockinet head is stretched over a mask, moulded to show facial details. Stitched seams provide jointing for the body. The entire doll is oil painted. Ht: 60cm (24in)

Wooden water-bottle

Fish pincushion, from Japan

Mohave Indian clay pipe

Thumb is applied separately from fingers and hand

Stitched mark of St. Thomas's Hospital in London

Cloth doll, from the Philippines

Woolly hair is made of lint

MISS COLUMBIA'S CONSORT (LEFT)
This Uncle Sam doll, made in 1901 by Mrs. Covey of Los Angeles, California, travelled with the Miss Columbia doll as its male counterpart and "companion", representing the United States. Its cloth body is unjointed, and its head and hands are oil painted. Ht: 50cm (20in)

ALABAMA INDESTRUCTIBLES
(RIGHT) Designed by Ella Louise Gauntt Smith of Roanoke, Alabama, these handmade dolls were factory-produced for the Ella Smith Doll Co. from 1900 to 1925. The ears are a distinctive feature. Ht: 37cm (14½in)

Round cloth pate at top of head

Applied ears

Painted blonde hair on forehead and around edges of face

Human hair wig

Oil paint covers the entire body

Stiffened, moulded cloth head

Flange neck allows head to turn

Body is jointed at shoulders and hips

Thumb is separate from fingers, but cut from same piece of cloth

Coat conceals solidly stuffed torso and limbs

Feet and legs are painted to resemble boots

Silk trousers, jacket, and star-spangled vest

KAMKINS DOLL
(RIGHT) Louise R. Kampes designed these dolls, which were made in her Atlantic City, New Jersey studios between 1919 and 1928. The head of this example is marked at the back, under the hairline "Kampes/Atlantic City". Ht: 46cm (18in)

Leather shoes

Clothes were made by out-workers to Mrs. Kampes's design

Painted and Sewn Dolls

· 1880s to 1900s ·

TOWARDS THE END OF THE NINETEENTH century, many companies were manufacturing rag dolls in quantity, although they still made the dolls individually. The facial features were often sewn by hand: eyes, ears, noses, and mouths were stitched onto good quality fabrics such as fine cotton, silk, and stockinet. A skilled needlewoman could make a fairly realistic face from a flat, rather moon-like surface. Alternatively, the dolls' facial features were hand painted in oil colours; sometimes they used a combination of painting and sewing.

By the turn of the century, rag dolls were more sophisticated. As is the case with Philadelphia Baby, shown here, the heads were often made of stockinet that had been stretched over a firm papier mâché base and moulded into shape. With its rigid head, this type of doll had painted, rather than sewn, facial features.

Brown painted hair worn away in places to reveal stockinet

Moulded, well-defined features

Soft, rosy pink skin tones are painted onto face

Large, painted brown eyes with black pupils

Well-defined mouth, painted pink

Separate ears are stuffed and shaped

Sleeveless dress with embroidered anchor at neck

Shoulder head is painted in flesh-toned oil colours

Floppy arms are stitched to torso at shoulder seams

Lower arms, painted in flesh-toned oil colours

Sailor-style smock, with blue and white-striped trim and red bow

Cloth body, shaped to define waist

Five life-like fingers stitched on each hand

Stitched seams at knees allow movement

Lower legs, painted in flesh-toned oil colours

HT: 55cm (22in)

PHILADELPHIA BABY *This is one of a range of Philadelphia Baby dolls produced c. 1900 for J.B. Sheppard & Co., a department store in Philadelphia, Pennsylvania, United States. The dolls varied in size from 46cm (18in) to 55cm (22in). The shoulder head and facial features are painted in oil colours, as are the lower arms and lower legs. It has a soft cloth body.*

Five toes stitched on each foot; no shoes

Solid head, made of strong calico, filled with hardwood

Stitching throws eyebrows and nose into relief

COBO DOLL *(LEFT) Rag doll-makers Alice Le Hureys and Judy Guilles manufactured this model in Cobo, an area in Guernsey, in the Channel Islands, c.1900. Its facial features are crudely painted and stitched.*
Ht: 37.5cm (15in)

SANTA CLAUS *(RIGHT) From the 1880s to c.1917, a type of doll known as Worsted dolls began to be produced commercially. This example dates from c.1890, and was probably made by Emil Wittzack of Gotha in Thuringia, Germany.*
Ht: 35cm (14in)

Black bead eyes

Needle-stitched stockinet head

Lower arms, painted in flesh-coloured tones

Hand-knitted, red-and blue-striped outfit

Brown cotton gift sack carried on Santa's back

Red and green woollen tassels, and metal bells

Small bisque doll, carried in the crook of each arm

THE COLE FAMILY *(BELOW) Roxanna Elizabeth McGee Cole started making dolls in the United States in 1868. She died in 1907, but her daughter-in-law, Molly Hunt Cole, took over the running of the business. This family of five was created c.1901, and is unique. All the dolls are made of fine muslin, which is hand painted and delicately stitched.*

Flannel boots, stitched to grey trousers at knees

Lower legs, painted in flesh-coloured tones

GRANDMA COLE Ht: 55cm (22in)

THE MAID Ht: 45cm (17½in)

BABY Ht: 38cm (15in)

JOSIE JUNE Ht: 45cm (17½in)

MAY Ht: 45cm (17½in)

Maid's uniform: apron; mobcap; checked dress; and lace-up shoes

Long robe conceals flannel petticoat, nappy, and small white slippers; wicker rattle attached to baby's wrist

White, lacy dress and broad-brimmed bonnet; hair drawn in pencil and painted in watercolours; holds small bisque doll

Skirt and jacket, and blouse with lace fichu; accessories include reading glasses and knitting needles and wool; human hair is sewn on

Smock worn over gingham dress; cotton undergarments; holds small bisque doll

Printed Cloth Dolls

· 1900s to 1980s ·

AS DEMAND FOR COMMERCIALLY made rag dolls increased, factories began to produce printed cloth dolls, sometimes known as cut-out cloth dolls. The front and back of the doll were printed onto cotton sheets and were generally sold in sheet form to be cut out, sewn together, and stuffed with kapok, straw, or even sawdust, by the buyer. They represented a variety of characters – some were well known, such as a celebrity or storybook character; others represented types, such as a pretty girl or soldier.

~ Although the first printed cloth dolls were made in the last half of the nineteenth century, most of the dolls that survive were manufactured after 1900. The chromo-lithographic process caused the fabric to deteriorate, as did rough handling and washing; in some cases, the stuffing was eaten away by animals or insects.

Doll's name is printed on cap

Idealized features: "rosebud" mouth and large eyes

Outfit represents the Liberty Bell in Philadelphia

Patriotic stars and stripes on cap and tee-shirt

Hanging loop attached at shoulder seams

Liberty Bell's crack reproduced on doll

Company name printed at base of bell

Printed cloth label shows limited-edition number (891)

All-in-one cloth body stuffed with kapok

MISS LIBERTY BELLE *Produced in 1976, this doll commemorates the Bicentennial of American Independence on the front, and the Sesquicentennial on the back. It is named after the Liberty Bell in Philadelphia, Pennsylvania, United States. Printed by the* Toy Works (Hodge Podge) *in Massachusetts, United States, it is a limited-edition doll.*

HT: 36.5cm (14½in)

Distinctive queue, or pony-tail

Printed cloth body, ready-stuffed with kapok

"Tails" give an extra dimension to the doll

Cereal packet features Sunny Jim character

RED RIDING HOOD
(RIGHT) This cut-out doll pattern was printed in the United States c.1970. For economic reasons, cut-out doll patterns were usually printed continuously onto a large piece of cloth, which was then sold by the yard (or metre). These shapes were printed on a 46cm- (18in-) wide cotton strip. Ht: 42cm (16½in)

Red cape is a separate cut-out shape

Design shows how doll should look when made up

Front and back of doll to be stuffed and sewn up

Red kerchief

SUNNY JIM (LEFT) In 1905, A.C.
Fincken, the manufacturer of Force Wheat Flakes, a breakfast cereal launched in 1901 in the United States, issued a printed cloth doll to promote their product. Sunny Jim, a caricature of an early 1800s' gentleman, could be obtained by sending coupons and a small sum of money to the manufacturer. Both Force Wheat Flakes and the doll are still available today. This model dates from c.1970. Ht: 41cm (16in)

STRUWWELPETER (RIGHT) The well-
known German storybook character, Struwwelpeter ("Shock-headed Peter"), was the creation of Dr. Heinrich Hoffmann. Since the publication of Hoffmann's cautionary tales in 1845, Struwwelpeter, the disobedient boy who refused to cut his hair or nails, has been portrayed in doll form many times. This printed cloth model was made in the Far East. Ht: 33cm (13in)

Yellow and beige wool sewn onto head

Facial features printed onto cloth

Fronts and backs of all four dolls printed on single sheet

PRINTED DOLLS
(LEFT) Printed onto a cotton sheet, each of the dolls are named: Cora, Agnes, Sylvia, and May. They were designed by Samuel Finburgh and first printed in 1916. In the 1970s the designs were reprinted by Hulbert Fabrics A.U.L. for the H.M.S.O. (Her Majesty's Stationery Office), which supplied the Bethnal Green Museum of Childhood in London. Ht: 39cm (15½in)

Clothes based on the storybook illustration

2.5cm- (1in-) long nails are made of vinyl and glued onto cloth hands

Printed label indicates doll is copyright of Heinrich-Hoffmann-Museum GmbH

Steiff Dolls

· 1900s to the present day ·

THE STEIFF COMPANY, established by Margarete Steiff in 1877, is still in business today. Although probably best known for its teddy bears, it also produced a wide range of dolls and other soft toys. These two pages show a selection of Steiff rag dolls made in the early 1900s. Steiff dolls of this period were usually made of felt, and the range of characters they portrayed was diverse. Many were caricatures of types, such as policemen, circus entertainers, or sailors, with exaggerated and often comical features. Some represented storybook characters.

Distinguishing features of Steiff dolls include a centre or diagonal seam on the face, and the company's "Button-in-Ear" trademark (see Doll Marks, opposite). If the button is missing from the doll, there are usually tell-tale signs where it was once punched through the felt.

Shiny, black boot-button eyes sewn into face

Smile indicated with red paint

Limp grey mohair sewn to head

Socket head, made of moulded felt

Unpainted cloth body, jointed at shoulders

Posture of old woman: drooping bustline, sagging stomach, and rounded shoulders

Jointed hips allow some movement

Thumb is separate from fingers, but cut from the same piece of cloth

Large hands appear rather swollen

Knees are fixed in a bent position

Large feet; no toes

HT: 48cm (19in)

OLD WOMAN *First marketed in 1913, this doll was re-issued in the late 1980s. It is an unusually life-like portrayal of an elderly woman with a sagging posture. The legs are the most startling feature: bent and gnarled, they even show traces of varicose veins.*

Wide mouth
is stitched and
painted red

Curly white mohair
plush hair extends
around the back
of the head

Shirt decorated
with red bow tie
at neck and small
black buttons

Blue felt suit,
trimmed with
ribbed brass
buttons

Large, round felt
patches represent
spectacles

Back of Steiff
button is visible
in left ear

Black boot-button
eyes sewn onto felt
spectacles

HEAD DETAIL (ABOVE) *Available
between 1905 and 1914, this all-felt
doll bears a Steiff metal button in its
ear (see Doll Marks, right). These
buttons were usually attached to
the doll's left ear, and could face
either forwards or backwards.*

Hands in clenched fist
position, fingers
indicated by stitching

DOLL MARKS

*"Button-in-Ear" was registered
as a trademark in May 1905.*

*Dolls made after 1905 bear
a metal button marked
"STEIFF" in raised lettering
(see below).*

*In 1908–1909 a cloth label,
printed with the product
number, was attached to the
metal button.*

*From 1926 a chest label
was added to Steiff dolls.*

GROSSPAPA (LEFT) *With his
white hair and knobbly knees,
Grosspapa (or Grandpapa) clearly
represents an elderly man. His
upright posture and clenched fists
indicate that he is a proud and
robust character. Ht: 37cm (14½in)*

Felt legs are also
intended to be
trousers

Long, pointed
shoes, worn with
felt spats, are made
of brown leather

Blond mohair
plush hair, sewn
onto head and
clipped short

Nostrils are painted
red for realistic effect

Lips and flesh tones
are painted soft red

Green felt braces,
embroidered with
yellow chain stitch

Fingers indicated
by beige mercerized
cotton thread

Shaped fingers
and thumbs

Characteristic Steiff
seam down centre of face

Seams on either side
of the eyes give doll
interesting expression

"Button-in-Ear"
faces backwards

Lips made of a
separate piece of felt,
sewn in and painted

Felt breeches, trimmed
with chain stitch, are
tied at knee

"GEORGE" (LEFT) *Steiff's
tradename for this model was
actually Hans, but the doll shown
here was renamed "George" by its
owner. It is an all-felt construction,
and is similar to Anthony (right),
but is twice the size. Ht: 60cm (24in)*

ANTHONY (LEFT) *Made
by Steiff in 1909, Anthony
was distributed by Borgfeldt
in the United States. It was
available in five sizes, from
28cm (11in) to 60cm (24in);
some models contained a voice
box in the torso. The traditional
Tyrolean costume is completely
original, and made of
good-quality materials.
Ht: 28cm (11in)*

English Manufacturers

· 1920s to 1950s ·

BETWEEN 1920 AND 1940, RAG DOLLS enjoyed a new wave of popularity. Working at the same time as Lenci in Italy and Käthe Kruse in Germany (see pages 100–101), English companies produced many new models of rag dolls in quantity for the home and international markets. These represented a wide range of character types. Often they were made as souvenirs, portraying a famous figure, such as a new king.

One of the most successful English companies to make rag dolls was Chad Valley Co. Ltd. Originally a printing firm called Johnson Brothers, it was established c.1850 in Birmingham. The firm was renamed Chad Valley in 1897, and diversified to manufacture games, jigsaw puzzles, and soft toys. The first dolls were produced c.1920.

Reddish brown mohair is sewn on to form side-parting

Facial features moulded from stiffened felt, and painted

Socket head is made of firmly stuffed felt

Kapok-stuffed calico body, jointed at shoulders and hips

Velvet arms, covered by the cotton uniform

Separate, but not applied, thumb

Hands are stitched to indicate fingers

Shiny, black American-cloth shoes

Cotton dress is part of the doll's structure and cannot be removed

American-cloth trim on cuffs and collar

Hygienic Toys label attached to right wrist

The label, tied to the right wrist indicates that the doll is safe for children.

CHAD VALLEY HYGIENIC TOYS MADE IN ENGLAND THE SEAL OF PURITY

Cotton stockings conceal velvet legs

CHAD VALLEY CO. LTD., NURSE *A fine example of a Chad Valley doll, this model was first issued c.1930. The Hygienic Toys/Seal of Purity label indicates that this model is made of safe, good-quality materials. It distinguishes the doll from many Eastern European imports made during this period, which contained sawdust, moss, or animal hair.*

HT: 48.5cm (19½in)

DEAN'S RAG BOOK CO. LTD., LUPINO LANE (LEFT) The wire frame base, covered with padding, is completely flexible and allows the limbs of this 1939 doll to be bent into different positions. Lupino Lane was the star of the musical, Me and My Girl. Ht: 31.5cm (12½in)

This printed label is attached to the sole of the doll's right foot.

Label indicates actor's name and song from the musical

Woollen checked suit is part of body structure

Doll's limbs are completely flexible

CHAD VALLEY CO. LTD., SEVEN DWARFS (BELOW) In 1937, Walt Disney released his animated cartoon, Snow White and the Seven Dwarfs. In 1938, Chad Valley produced the characters from the cartoon in doll form. The faces are individually moulded from felt and painted, giving each dwarf a unique facial expression and personality. Ht: 16.5cm (6½in)
© The Walt Disney Company

HAPPY

MERRYTHOUGHT LTD., HAPPY AND SLEEPY (ABOVE & RIGHT) Merrythought was founded in 1930, and is still in business to this day. In the mid-1950s, the firm made a set of Walt Disney's Snow White and the Seven Dwarfs. Ht: 24.5cm (10in)
© The Walt Disney Company

SLEEPY

Fingers indicated with stitching; separate, but not applied, thumb

J.K. FARNELL & CO. LTD., H.M. THE KING (RIGHT) J.K. Farnell was established as a toy-maker c. 1870 in Acton, London, and began producing dolls in 1915. This doll, manufactured in 1937, commemorated the coronation of George VI, after the abdication of his brother, Edward VIII. Ht: 38cm (15in)

The label is fixed under the doll's right pocket flap.

"Sleepy" features painted onto moulded felt face

Black teased-wool bearskin, with 5cm- (2in-) high, woollen plume

Facial features moulded from stiffened felt, and painted

Costume is replica of Royal Highlanders' uniform

Metal sword painted black with gold tip

White plush sporran with black braid tassels

A label, attached to the sole of the foot, bears the name of the manufacturer

A woven label, concealed by the jacket, is sewn to the body of each dwarf shown below.

BASHFUL

SNEEZY   SLEEPY   DOPEY   GRUMPY   DOC   HAPPY

Trousers are part of the legs   Removable felt jackets   Pink cotton bodies and backs of heads   Label reads "THIS IS HAPPY"

European Manufacturers

· 1920s to 1950s ·

BY THE 1920S, several European manufacturers were producing very high-quality rag dolls. Sometimes known as "art dolls", these were often designed and painted by talented artists, and modelled by highly skilled craftsmen. German doll-maker, Käthe Kruse, and the Italian firm, Lenci, were two of the leading manufacturers of rag dolls. Both of these companies are still in business to this day.

Käthe Kruse, wife of sculptor, Max Kruse, was a talented painter, who began making dolls c.1911. Convinced that bisque dolls were not suitable toys for children, she believed that dolls should be realistic, unbreakable, and easy to play with. Lenci was founded in Turin in 1918 by Elena Scavini. It is thought that she named the firm after her pet-name, Lenci.

Side-glancing, painted brown eyes, with black pupils

Nostrils are painted in red

Typical Lenci mouth is closed and painted in red

Reddish blond mohair is sewn onto head

Boyish features are moulded and painted

Separate, shaped ears

Socket head made of stiffened felt

Two fingers are joined on hand; typical Lenci feature

Smock was made at same time as doll

Joints at shoulders and hips allow some movement

Torso, like the head, is made of stiffened and moulded felt

"Piglet" is a 1950s' copy of the toy made for author A.A. Milne's son, the original Christopher Robin

HT: 47.5cm (19in)

LENCI, BOY *Made in the 1920s, this is a fine example of a Lenci doll. Although it bears a remarkable resemblance to E.H. Shepard's illustrations of Christopher Robin, the hero of A.A. Milne's famous Pooh Bear stories, there is no evidence to suggest that Lenci modelled the doll on this character. It is extremely life-like, and has a charming, slightly wary expression.*

100

Black plush hair, sewn on

Moulded bulbous eyes; right eye is partly closed

Shaped fingers and thumbs; stitching indicates gloves

LENCI, BELLBOY (LEFT) This bellboy character, made by Lenci c.1920, was available as a black or white doll. The number identifies this doll as a fairly early Lenci model: the model numbers began with 100 and rose to over 2000 by 1930. The small button attached to the bellboy's cuff is the first style of Lenci button produced. Ht: 28cm (11in)

Raised, moulded button attached to left cuff reads "Lenci"

Red felt suit

Black oilcloth shoes, with white felt spats

Highlights painted in white onto iris

LENCI, GIRL (LEFT) This c.1922 doll has typical Lenci features: brown painted eyes looking to the side, a small, rosebud mouth, and a rather sullen expression. Lenci designs are very distinctive; however, the untagged dolls are often quite difficult to identify, as many other manufacturers tended to imitate many of the company's designs. Ht: 32cm (12½in)

All-in-one cotton and lace undergarment

Original cream felt dress, trimmed with dark turquoise felt

Fingers are indicated by stitches; separate thumb, but cut from same piece of fabric

This metal button, attached to the doll's undergarment, is the second style of Lenci button produced.

Characteristic three seam lines at back of head

Human hair wig; hairs are sewn onto a thin silk skullcap, three at a time

Moulded and painted face intended to resemble that of a child as closely as possible

C-shaped ears applied to head separately

KÄTHE KRUSE, BABY (RIGHT) It is said that Käthe Kruse made her first doll from a potato and a towel filled with sand. By 1911, she was producing high-quality rag dolls in quantity. The construction of this 1920s' baby doll is complicated; it has been assembled from numerous panels of cloth, which have been sewn together. Ht: 41cm (16in)

Dress conceals cloth body and limbs, stuffed with a soft but hard-wearing filling

MAGDA BOALT, SWEDISH DOLL (RIGHT) Sometimes known as the Swedish Käthe Kruse, Magda Boalt is probably Scandinavia's best-known doll-maker. A one-time hairdresser, she began by making small wigs for dolls, using remnants of human hair. In 1944, she made her first doll. This model was manufactured c.1950. Ht: 48cm (19in)

Wrist originally bore a label with doll's name

Body has two seams at front and back; five-panel leg construction

Black leather shoes, with metal buckles

Foot is lined with card and stamped with product number

Norah Wellings

· 1919 to 1960 ·

NORAH WELLINGS BEGAN HER CAREER in 1919 with the Chad Valley Co. Ltd. (see pages 98–99). In 1926, she opened her own factory, Victoria Toy Works, in Shropshire, England, where she designed and made dolls until 1960. During this time, she also designed dolls for Chad Valley. For this reason, many dolls produced by these two firms are quite similar. However, those manufactured at the Norah Wellings factory can be identified by a woven label sewn to the body (see Doll Marks, opposite).

Norah Wellings dolls are generally made of felt, velvet, and velveteen, and represent children and adults. She produced many ethnic dolls, as well as numerous storybook characters. Probably the finest Norah Wellings dolls were made in the 1930s.

Heart-shaped face, moulded fro[m] stiffened felt

Side-glancing blue eyes, painted in oil colours

Two red painted dots accentuate the nostrils

Reddish brown mohair is sewn to head

Swivel head is turned to side

Orange, peasant-style felt dress with laced bodice

Shoulder joints allow some movement

Original wooden-bead bracelets, attached to both wrists, cannot be removed

Only two fingers sewn together, an unusual feature

Jointed at hips to allow movement

Legs are shaped to define calves and ankles

Toes indicated by stitching; label sewn to base of left foot

Orange felt shoes, with metal buttons

ORANGE GIRL *This large, 1930s' felt doll has a swivel head, the body is stuffed and jointed at the shoulders and hips, and the facial features are moulded and painted. The hands are of special interest, as only two of the fingers are joined together. Usually, the fingers of Norah Wellings dolls are indicated by stitching, with a separate thumb.*

HT: 44cm (17½in)

102

SAILORS (LEFT) These c.1928 dolls were sold on board passenger liners as souvenirs. They were made in two styles: "grinning" sailors (top), with felt feet and large, protruding, pointed ears; and "smiling" sailors (bottom), with velvet feet and flat ears. Ht: 21cm (8½in)

Hat, stamped with name of ship

Woven label, sewn to sole of left foot

HARRY THE HAWK (BELOW) During World War II, Norah Wellings made dolls representing characters from the Army, Royal Navy, and Royal Air Force. This mascot doll, Harry the Hawk, raised funds for men serving in the Royal Air Force (R.A.F.) during the war. Ht: 18cm (7in)

Felt parachute, in patriotic colours

DOLL MARKS
Sewn-on cloth labels were firmly stitched to Norah Wellings dolls.

The labels are black, blue, or beige, depending on the colour of the doll.

MADE IN ENGLAND BY NORAH WELLINGS

Labels are usually sewn to the foot, but can appear on the wrist or doll's back.

MADE IN ENGLAND BY NORAH WELLINGS

Brown felt intended to represent leather gauntlets

Outfit is based on authentic R.A.F. flying combat overalls

Felt flowers worn in hair

ORIENTAL GIRL (LEFT) This 1930s' all-felt doll is not merely a standard model dressed in oriental clothing. The face has been carefully designed to portray particular racial characteristics; the colouring is as true to life as possible. A Norah Wellings label is sewn to the foot. Ht: 31cm (12½in)

Fingers are indicated by stitching; separate thumb

Label indicates R.A.F. benefits from sales of the doll

"HARRY THE HAWK" ROYAL AIR FORCE COMFORTS FUND

Felt, Japanese-style kimono

Coloured-velvet uniforms are part of dolls' bodies

GUARDSMEN (RIGHT) Like the sailors shown above, two styles of guardsmen dolls were available: those that grin, and those that smile. Both wear the same uniform, and were made in a range of sizes, some as large as 91cm (36in). These models were made in the 1930s. Ht: Largest 84.5cm (33½in); smallest 25cm (10in)

Woven label sewn to sole of right foot

Celluloid Dolls

By the last quarter of the nineteenth century, celluloid began to compete with the traditional materials used in doll-making such as bisque, wood, paper, and cloth. It was a versatile substance, made from pyroxylin (cellulose nitrates) and camphor. Economical and easy to produce, celluloid was used extensively for the manufacture of dolls, as well as many household items, until the mid-1950s, when it was superseded by other plastics.

CELLULOID WAS DEVELOPED and first used for dolls by the Hyatt Brothers of New Jersey, United States, in the late 1860s. The firm registered the name Celluloid in 1869, and worked under the new tradename of the Celluloid Novelty Company. Although the product was patented, the term is often used to describe all types of pyroxylin mixtures, regardless of the manufacturer.

∽ Celluloid was not only manufactured for the doll-making industry. A number of companies in Europe and the United States made celluloid as a substitute for many natural materials, such as tortoiseshell, bone, ivory, coral, and even marble. It was made into a variety of items, from spectacle frames and hairclips to billiard balls, teething rings, children's bathtime toys, dice, and rulers.

∽ Celluloid dolls were manufactured by placing the substance in its solid state into a two-piece metal mould. Steam or hot air was then blown into the mould under pressure; this would soften the celluloid, and cause it to conform to the shape, and bond the two halves of the moulded celluloid. When cool, the mould was removed and the doll was decorated.

Mass-produced Celluloid Dolls

When celluloid was first used for dolls at the end of the nineteenth century, it was a relatively expensive material. By the first quarter of the twentieth century, it had become extremely cheap to produce. Factories

CLAUDINET AND CLAUDINE
(*LEFT*) *Advertised in a French catalogue in 1937, this pair of dolls is fashionably and expensively dressed; both sets of clothing show smocking on the yokes. They were available individually or as a pair. Ht: Claudinet 64cm (25½in); Claudine 57cm (23in)*

MINIATURE KEWPIE
(*RIGHT*) *This all-celluloid Kewpie doll was probably made in the United States or Germany in the 1930s. The tufts of hair and facial features are moulded and painted, and it bears blue wings, characteristic of many Kewpie models, on its back. The doll is marked "Design 43980 Patent". Ht: 5cm (2in)*

BOAT RACE FAVOUR (LEFT)
In 1939, spectators of the famous University Boat Race could buy a small novelty doll, or "favour", dressed in the colour of their team's crew: Oxford was dark blue, Cambridge was light blue. This small celluloid doll, probably made in Japan, is an Oxford favour. It wears a pom-pom and carries a pair of oars. The safety pin was used to attach the doll to the supporter's clothing. Ht: 7.5cm (3in)

manufacturers, exactly as the porcelain factories made and sold heads of bisque. The heads were sent to companies within Germany, and to England and the United States, where they were attached to stuffed or composition bodies. Manufacturers who assembled dolls from component parts made by the Rheinische Gummi- und Celluloid-Fabrik included Kämmer & Reinhardt, C. & O. Dressel, and J.D. Kestner.

The End of the Celluloid Era

In many ways, celluloid was an ideal material for doll-making. It was light, and easy to mould and decorate; but its extreme inflammability naturally caused great concern worldwide. A less serious problem was that it faded in bright light, which meant that the features became bleached with time. It also crushed if the doll was squeezed tightly, or trodden on. If poor quality celluloid was used, as was often the case in the 1930s and 1940s, it was thin, and disintegrated quickly. With the invention of plastics in the mid-1950s, celluloid was replaced by materials such as vinyl, which were thought to be safer and more reliable.

in Germany, France, the United States, and Japan were producing celluloid dolls in the thousands. Famous manufacturers of celluloid dolls include: the Rheinische Gummi- und Celluloid-Fabrik and J.D. Kestner in Germany; Petitcollin in France; the Wilson Doll Company in England; and the Averill Manufacturing Company, E.I. Horsman, Parsons–Jackson, and the Celluloid Novelty Company in the United States.

Most of the celluloid dolls produced in Europe were manufactured in Germany. Probably the best known factory was the Rheinische Gummi- und Celluloid-Fabrik, founded in 1873. Products made by this company can usually be recognized by the famous turtle-in-a-diamond trademark (see pages 106–107). In addition to producing celluloid dolls, this company also made celluloid heads for other

TYROLEAN PAIR (RIGHT)
The turtle trademark on the dolls' backs and the wrist tags indicate that this pair was made for Käthe Kruse by the Rheinische Gummi- und Celluloid-Fabrik in the early 1950s. The boy has sleeping eyes with lashes; the girl has moulded, painted eyes. Ht: Boy 40cm (16in); girl 39cm (15½in)

JAPANESE BOXER (LEFT) *Like most Japanese celluloid dolls mass-produced in the 1930s, this figure is small, brittle, and cheaply made. Japanese celluloids made at this time were often amusing trinkets or novelty items produced for the West, rather than for the Japanese market. Ht: 10cm (4in)*

German Manufacturers

· 1870s to 1960s ·

ESTABLISHED IN BAVARIA in 1873 by Friedrich Bensinger, the Rheinische Gummi- und Celluloid-Fabrik was the major producer of celluloid in Germany. Today, the company produces vinyl dolls from its original factory in Mannheim–Neckarau; since the early 1950s, it has operated under the name Schildkröt-Spielwaren GmbH. *Schildkröte* is the German word for "turtle", and the company's main trademark was that of a walking turtle encased in a diamond, which was moulded on the doll necks and bodies. In some cases the diamond is omitted, or the turtle is enclosed in a circle, square, oval, triangle, or hexagon. Other manufacturers of celluloid also used the trademark of a turtle to represent durability; however, the raised turtle-in-a-diamond was exclusive to the Rheinische Gummi- und Celluloid-Fabrik.

The turtle mark and model number and signature of Käthe Kruse appear on the back of the doll.

Inset blue glass eyes

Moulded nose; nostrils painted in red

Moulded and painted brown hair

Eyebrows are painted in brown

Dress has small orange-red bow at neck of cape collar

Head and torso moulded as one; head cannot turn

Celluloid body, jointed at shoulders

Straight arms are shaped to define elbows

Blue cotton dress conceals white one-piece undergarment

Moulded fingers, with separate thumbs

Jointed hips allow some movement

Straight legs are shaped to define knees

Feet point inwards; moulded toes

Wrist tag, with turtle-in-a-diamond trademark

Cream machine-knitted socks

Red leather shoes, with metal buckles

KÄTHE KRUSE, BLUE-DRESS GIRL *In the mid-1950s, Käthe Kruse worked with the Rheinische Gummi- und Celluloid-Fabrik to produce all-celluloid dolls, and dolls made of Tortulon – a new plastic that resembled hard vinyl. This model is made entirely of celluloid, yet manages to retain the facial characteristics of a Käthe Kruse rag doll (see pages 100–101).*

HT: 35cm (14in)

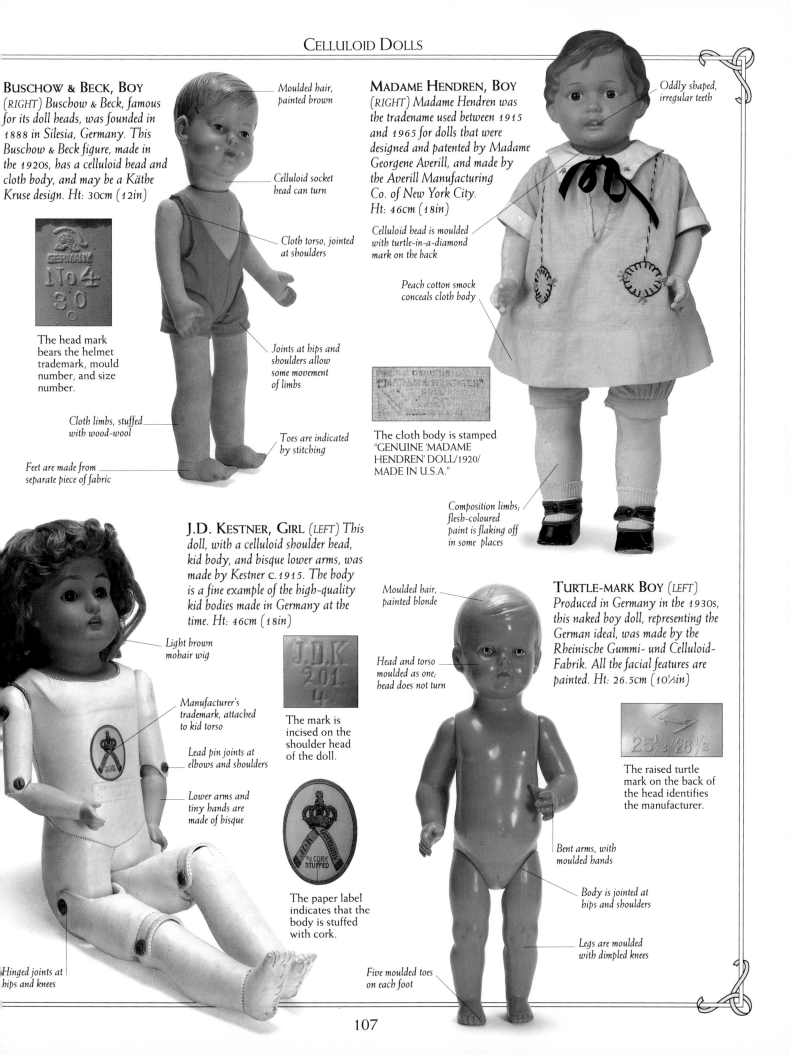

BUSCHOW & BECK, BOY

(RIGHT) Buschow & Beck, famous for its doll heads, was founded in 1888 in Silesia, Germany. This Buschow & Beck figure, made in the 1920s, has a celluloid head and cloth body, and may be a Käthe Kruse design. Ht: 30cm (12in)

The head mark bears the helmet trademark, mould number, and size number.

Moulded hair, painted brown

Celluloid socket head can turn

Cloth torso, jointed at shoulders

Joints at hips and shoulders allow some movement of limbs

Cloth limbs, stuffed with wood-wool

Toes are indicated by stitching

Feet are made from separate piece of fabric

MADAME HENDREN, BOY

(RIGHT) Madame Hendren was the tradename used between 1915 and 1965 for dolls that were designed and patented by Madame Georgene Averill, and made by the Averill Manufacturing Co. of New York City. Ht: 46cm (18in)

Oddly shaped, irregular teeth

Celluloid head is moulded with turtle-in-a-diamond mark on the back

Peach cotton smock conceals cloth body

The cloth body is stamped "GENUINE 'MADAME HENDREN' DOLL/1920/ MADE IN U.S.A."

Composition limbs; flesh-coloured paint is flaking off in some places

J.D. KESTNER, GIRL (LEFT) This

doll, with a celluloid shoulder head, kid body, and bisque lower arms, was made by Kestner c.1915. The body is a fine example of the high-quality kid bodies made in Germany at the time. Ht: 46cm (18in)

Light brown mohair wig

Manufacturer's trademark, attached to kid torso

Lead pin joints at elbows and shoulders

Lower arms and tiny hands are made of bisque

The mark is incised on the shoulder head of the doll.

The paper label indicates that the body is stuffed with cork.

Hinged joints at hips and knees

TURTLE-MARK BOY (LEFT)

Produced in Germany in the 1930s, this naked boy doll, representing the German ideal, was made by the Rheinische Gummi- und Celluloid-Fabrik. All the facial features are painted. Ht: 26.5cm (10½in)

Moulded hair, painted blonde

Head and torso moulded as one; head does not turn

The raised turtle mark on the back of the head identifies the manufacturer.

Bent arms, with moulded hands

Body is jointed at hips and shoulders

Legs are moulded with dimpled knees

Five moulded toes on each foot

Mass-produced Dolls

· 1900s to 1980s ·

FROM THE 1900S TO MID-1950S, millions of celluloid dolls were produced. Some were good quality, such as those manufactured by the Rheinische Gummi- und Celluloid-Fabrik, but many were quite poorly made. Throughout the 1920s and 1930s, celluloid novelty dolls were very popular. Cheap and cheerful, these little trinkets were usually mass-produced in Japan, and given away as fairground prizes, or sold at the seaside for a small sum.

By the mid-1950s, doll manufacturers in Germany, the United States, France, and England had stopped using celluloid for dolls, owing to its inflammability. Instead, they preferred to work with new and safer plastics, such as vinyl. In some Eastern European countries, such as Poland, celluloid dolls continued to be produced until the late 1980s.

The "K" trademark identifies the doll manufacturer, Kaliskie Zaklady.

Upper eyelashes made of black nylon bristle; lower lashes painted in brown

Dark brown nylon wig, in fashionable style of the day

Hair tied at back of neck with green nylon ribbon

Checked-cotton mini-dress in style of 1960s–1970s

Socket head allows head to turn

Plump upper arms; jointed at shoulders

Moulded fingers are slightly webbed; separate thumb

Rounded stomach of a toddler

Bent lower arms with moulded hands

Straight legs are sturdy and thick-set

Centre seams visible on legs

Small feet with indistinct, moulded toes

POLISH DOLL, BEATA *This all-celluloid toddler doll was produced by the Polish manufacturer, Kaliskie Zaklady, in the 1960s or 1970s — over a decade after the West had ceased making celluloid dolls. The doll is otherwise composed of modern materials: the sleeping eyes are made of plastic, and the wig is nylon.*

HT: 27cm (10½in)

Fashionable, slip-on PVC shoes

The raised mark on the back of the doll shows Petitcollin's trademark of an eagle's head.

Moulded and painted mouth, eyes, and nose

Crudely painted facial features

Bright pink pom-pom hair

Betty-Boop look-alike

Black doll with movable limbs

Fine organdie apron with gold-ribbon and white-lace trim

Lead weight in base, makes doll bounce back up

Full, checked-cotton skirt with gold-ribbon trim

NOVELTY DOLLS (ABOVE) *These novelty dolls were made in Japan in the 1920s and 1930s. The figure on the right is a tumbling doll. If it is pushed over, it will bounce back up again. Ht: Largest 6cm (2½in); smallest 4.5cm (2in)*

FRENCH COSTUME DOLL (LEFT) *Dressed in French provincial costume, this doll was made in the 1920s by the Petitcollin company of Paris, founded in 1914. The costume is highly ornate, but the doll itself is made of thin, rather brittle celluloid. Ht: 22cm (8½in)*

Moulded "earphone" hairstyle; hair painted blonde

Inset blue glass eyes; painted brows

Moulded and painted ribbed stockings and shoes

Moulded hair; faint signs of paint remain

"Foreign" usually indicates that a doll was made in Japan.

Two black dots indicate eyes; no lashes

Dress made c. 1960; the fabric is possibly older

Moulded, closed mouth is crudely painted

Well-formed hands, with separate fingers and thumbs

Mould cast lines have not been cleaned

JAPANESE PAIR (RIGHT) *Mass-produced in Japan in the 1920s and 1930s, these small figures are cheap-quality, all-celluloid dolls. The facial features are moulded and crudely painted, and much of the dolls' colour has now faded. Ht: Largest 12.5cm (5in); smallest 4.5cm (2in)*

GERMAN DOLL (RIGHT) *With its blue eyes, blonde hair, and tidy appearance, this doll reflects the 1930s' Germanic ideal. The turtle-in-a-diamond trademark indicates that it was made by the Rheinische Gummi- und Celluloid-Fabrik. Ht: 38.5cm (15½in)*

Modern Dolls

Although some American composition dolls made in the early twentieth century were thought almost revolutionary at the time, the real "modern" era in the history of dolls begins in the 1940s – the decade that saw the start of the plastics boom and the move to production on a massive scale. Yet not all modern dolls are plastic, nor are they all mass-produced. The past 50 years have seen an extraordinarily wide range of different models being made.

WORLD WAR II HAD A MAJOR impact on the doll industry in Europe. Suddenly, most production ceased where an industry had been built up over centuries. When peace did at last return, it brought with it revolutionary new plastics – developed to help the war effort and now available for all manner of applications. ∽ Light, strong, and easily moulded into an infinite variety of forms, the new plastic materials demanded new equipment and new technologies for production. Although initial investment costs were very high, manufacturers found that they could produce millions of dolls that were all identical, or create a range of dolls based on the same basic model, making only minor modifications to give each doll its characteristic features.

Plastic dolls of the late 1940s are vastly different from those of today. They were made of hard plastic and, although they looked like the composition dolls they largely replaced, they were lighter, tougher, and more durable. The arrival of the polyethylene compounds followed, introduced in the mid-1950s. Commonly referred to as vinyl, it is a much more flexible material, available in both hard and soft forms.

The Difference with Vinyl

The introduction of vinyl brought a key difference to doll hair: whereas composition and hard plastic dolls had wigs, or moulded and painted hair, the use of soft vinyl allowed hair to be "rooted" into the head. Facial features, hands, and feet tend to be less well moulded, and defined in vinyl dolls than in those made of composition or hard plastic. Most dolls today use a combination of vinyls: soft for the head and limbs, and hard for the body.

RAYNAL DOLL *(RIGHT)*
An enormous success in the 1950s, Raynal dolls were manufactured in Montreuil-sous-Bois, near Paris. They were made of rhodoid, a type of celluloid, with synthetic hair. Some had sleeping eyes. Ht: 57cm (22½in).

SHOPPING FOR CLOTHES
(LEFT) An assistant at Harrods store in London in the 1950s helps a young customer to choose clothing for her doll. This personal approach to selling is in marked contrast to the aggressive marketing techniques of later 20th-century decades.

WAAC-ETTE

WAVE-ETTE

of doll-makers Lynne and Michael Roche (see pages 81 and 128), dolls are still created by the traditional methods. Only a few of each model are produced, and wood or other natural materials take the place of modern synthetics. These dolls are usually classified as art dolls – to be displayed rather than played with by children as toys.

A Popular Appeal

The popularity of modern dolls tends to be much more transient than that of their predecessors. New models come and go continually as the power of advertising and the influence of the media, in particular television and films, encourage ephemeral fads and fashions that change almost overnight.

～ While the charm of many traditional models guarantees their continuing appeal, novelty dolls are very much in demand, from character dolls drawn from cartoons and comic books, like the Batman and Robin models shown below, to baby dolls with ever more realistic features (see pages 122–123). But the great commercial successes of the age are the "dressing" dolls, especially those that are available not only with changes of clothing, but also with every conceivable accessory. Mattel's Barbie (see pages 116–117), which truly embodies the "more-is-better" values of today's society, is produced at a rate of 55,000 a day; 600 million have been sold since the doll's launch in 1959.

Strong competition and financial difficulties have forced the closure of many of the small individual companies that survived the war years; today most doll manufacturers belong to giant corporations. Over the last 20 years even these have been forced to merge or close down entirely. Usually, the most marketable products have been sold on, either as a profit-making concern, or in name only: the Sindy doll, for example, was once an English product made by Pedigree, but is now owned by the American company, Hasbro (see pages 120–121).

Small-scale Producers

Doll-making, in contrast to large corporate enterprise, still survives as a cottage industry to this day. Across the world, in studios and workshops, such as those

ROBIN

BATMAN

SUPERMAN

Vogue Dolls, Inc.

· 1940s to 1960s ·

JENNIE GRAVES was already established as a designer and producer of fine dolls' clothing when she founded Vogue Dolls, Inc. in 1948. Since the 1930s, she had purchased American- and German-made, undressed dolls, clothed them with her own creations, and sold them through stores nationwide; but in 1948, she introduced Ginny, a doll of her own design. Other dolls were added – each with its own personalized accessories, and outfits based on contemporary fashions – to create the Ginny Doll Family. The range included Ginnette (Ginny's baby sister), Jill (her older sister), and Jeff, who could be either Jill's boyfriend or the two sisters' brother. Every doll that was created represented the company's family tradition of producing quality dolls "that are made to be loved".

Light brown corduroy hat, trimmed with blue satin

Brown sleeping eyes, with painted brows and lower lashes

Closed mouth, painted red

Elephant-shaped blue buttons cover the hook and eye fastenings

Light brown corduroy jacket and skirt, lined with blue satin

Black and gold "Vogue" label stuck on skirt

Skating costume covers a blue satin, all-in-one undergarment

White socks just visible inside skates

Paper-like, white cloth skates have metal blades

Auburn mohair wig

Upper eyelashes are made of animal hair

Composition head and body, jointed only at neck, shoulders, and hips

Hands are moulded into an expressive up-and-outwards attitude

Legs are quite straight below the knee, but have shapely thighs

Feet are flat and stubby, with no instep

THE SKATER *This 1947 doll wears Vogue clothes designed by Jennie Graves, but pre-dates the original Ginny. It has the same all-composition construction as the first Ginnies, which were somewhat shorter, standing only 20cm (8in) tall. The Skater is one of a group that represents various sporting activities: there is also a skier, a golfer, and a tennis player.*

HT: 35cm (14in)

Synthetic wig, made of Dynel

Red-painted finger- and toe-nails

Seamed, thigh-high stockings

Clear plastic open-toe, heeled shoes, decorated with sparkles

Head turns from side to side when doll is "walked"

Moulded and painted hair

Body is jointed only at shoulders and hips

White flannel dress jacket

Cummerbund around waist matches bow tie

Jill's corsage, trimmed with a pink bow, matches her dress

Trousers embellished with satin tuxedo stripe

Black and silver Lurex thread socks

Black plastic shoes, fastened with ribbon

JILL AND JEFF (LEFT) In his smart evening clothes, Jeff is all set to escort his friend — or sister — Jill to the school end-of-term prom. The dolls are models that were both copyrighted in 1957. They are made of hard vinyl, and have blue sleeping eyes, with moulded lashes and painted eyebrows. Ht: Jill 24.5cm (9¾in); Jeff 25cm (10in)

Body made of beige nylon plush fabric

Felt ears

Glass eyes

Printed tartan overcoat, labelled "GINNY'S PUP"

Untinted, moulded curls on forehead and around face

Wig made of black Dynel

Golden brown sleeping eyes, with moulded lashes

Separate thumb fits into the doll's mouth

GINNY'S PUP (ABOVE) This miniature toy terrier is one of the many accessories made especially for Ginny. Ht: 9cm (3½in)

GINNETTE (RIGHT) Made in the 1960s of tinted soft vinyl, Ginnette has the typical dumpy limbs of a baby doll, and a nursing mouth designed to take a feeding bottle or the doll's thumb. Ht: 20cm (8in)

MISS 2000

All-composition Ginny doll model, jointed at shoulders and hips

MISS 2000 (LEFT) The "Half-Century Group" was designed between 1948 and 1950. It featured the futuristically clad Miss 2000 and the Misses 1900, 1910, 1920, 1930, 1940, and 1950. A complete set is a real find. Ht: 20cm (8in)

Reverse of wrist tag

Ginny Doll Family
FASHION LEADERS IN DOLL SOCIETY

Front of wrist tag reads "Hi! I'm Ginnette/Created by VOGUE DOLLS Incorporated, Malden, Mass."

Dimpled bent limbs

American Manufacturers

· *1900s to the present day* ·

A NUMBER OF DOLL MANUFACTURERS were established in the United States throughout the first quarter of the twentieth century, and some of them survive today in some form or another. Most of these manufacturers gained international reputations for their production or design of composition dolls – expertise that they later skilfully adapted to suit the new and exciting potential of plastic.

The Ideal Novelty & Toy Company of Brooklyn, New York City, got off to a flying start when founders Morris Michtom and A. Cohn launched their "unbreakable" composition dolls. During the 1930s, Ideal issued a number based on famous film personalities: its Shirley Temple range, in particular, was extremely successful. After World War II, Ideal turned its skills to creating dolls made of all kinds of plastic; many were bestsellers.

Genuine woven straw hat

Gold-coloured plastic "Shirley Temple" brooch

Curly nylon "Shirley Temple" wig

Sleeping plastic eyes, with nylon upper lashes

Reverse socket head

Facial features are modelled on those of Shirley Temple

Smiling open mouth, with teeth

Shoulder joints allow arms to rotate

Printed cotton shirt has corduroy collar and white plastic buttons

Slightly bent arms

Middle fingers of right hand are moulded together

Doll is dressed as fictional character, Rebecca of Sunnybrook Farm

Straight legs, with shapely thighs

Joints at hips allow movement of legs

Blue cotton knee-length trousers

Separate fingers on left hand

Body is all-vinyl construction

Flat feet allow the doll to stand unaided

Moulded toes, with toe-nail detail

Corduroy cuffs on roll-ups of trousers

Knitted knee-length cotton socks

SHIRLEY TEMPLE *The Ideal Novelty & Toy Company first issued Shirley Temple dolls in the 1930s, when little Shirley was the number one box-office attraction in the United States. This 1960s' hard vinyl version is modelled on the heroine of the film Rebecca of Sunnybrook Farm, in which Shirley Temple starred in 1938.*

Black plastic slip-on shoes

HT: 30cm (12in)

Original packaging, with clear film front and Ideal logo

Rooted nylon hair, styled into ringlets

1982 SHIRLEY TEMPLE (ABOVE) Ideal marketed this updated Shirley Temple in its Classic Doll range. The head is made of soft vinyl, with a hard vinyl body that looks much the same as the 1960s' model. The clothing is cotton, with cloth lace-up shoes. Ht: 22cm (8½in)

© IDEAL 1982 HONG KONG

The copyright mark indicates that the doll was made in Hong Kong for Ideal in 1982.

1930S' SHIRLEY TEMPLE (RIGHT) One of the original Shirley Temple models, this doll was designed by Bernard Lipfert. Side-glancing eyes and a head of golden "Shirley Temple" curls give it an irresistible appeal. From 1934 to 1938, more than six million dolls of this popular young actress were sold. Ht: 64cm (25½in)

Flirty, sleeping eyes move from side to side and open and close

Composition reverse socket head

Bent composition arms

Cotton shoes conceal straight composition legs

CAMPBELL KID (BELOW) Just one of a range used to advertise Campbell's soups, this composition doll was licensed for production to E.I. Horsman in 1911. Horsman went on to produce a number of character dolls made of plastic. Ht: 30cm (12in)

Painted facial features

Composition arms are jointed at shoulders

Chest label advertises Campbell's soups

Campbell's KID A HORSMAN DOLL

ANNE SHIRLEY (BELOW) Effanbee (the trademark of Fleischaker & Baum, in New York) drew on L.M. Montgomery's novel, Anne of Green Gables, to create its all-composition Anne Shirley in 1936. The high quality of Effanbee's composition dolls was maintained with later plastic models. Ht: 38cm (15in)

Human hair wig, a replacement dating from the early 1960s

Sleeping eyes

Composition arms are jointed at shoulders

Moulded hair, with baby curls

Composition flange neck head

Bent composition limbs

Overalls conceal composition legs, jointed at hips

Doll wears lacy-knit coat over long knitted dress and bootees

Flat feet are painted to resemble shoes and socks

1924 GRUMPY (LEFT) This cloth and composition doll from Effanbee was first issued in 1914. Grumpy dolls proved very popular, and many companies included one in their range. Ht: 36.5cm (14½in)

Smock conceals all-composition construction

Cotton smock with heart motif

The Changing Face of Barbie
· 1959 to the present day ·

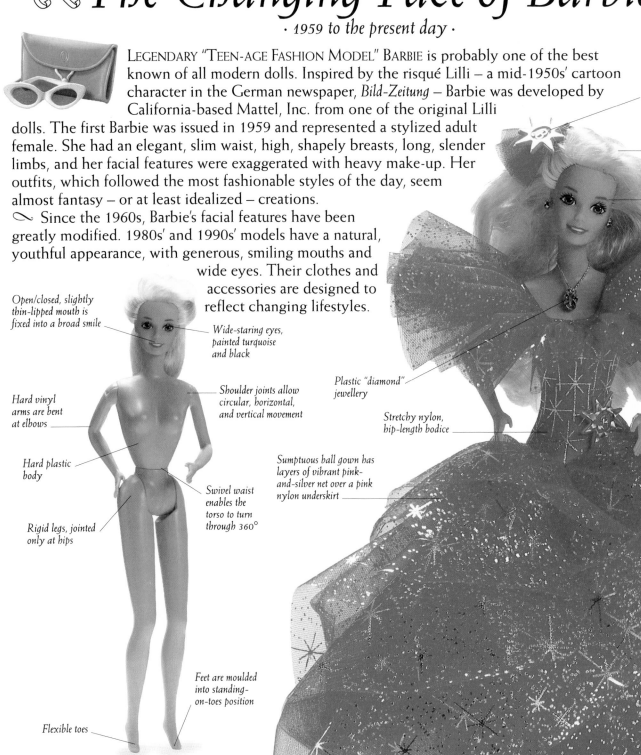

LEGENDARY "TEEN-AGE FASHION MODEL" BARBIE is probably one of the best known of all modern dolls. Inspired by the risqué Lilli – a mid-1950s' cartoon character in the German newspaper, *Bild-Zeitung* – Barbie was developed by California-based Mattel, Inc. from one of the original Lilli dolls. The first Barbie was issued in 1959 and represented a stylized adult female. She had an elegant, slim waist, high, shapely breasts, long, slender limbs, and her facial features were exaggerated with heavy make-up. Her outfits, which followed the most fashionable styles of the day, seem almost fantasy – or at least idealized – creations.

Since the 1960s, Barbie's facial features have been greatly modified. 1980s' and 1990s' models have a natural, youthful appearance, with generous, smiling mouths and wide eyes. Their clothes and accessories are designed to reflect changing lifestyles.

Simulated mother-of-pearl hair decoration

Nylon (saran) hair is rooted into the head

Reverse socket head, made of soft vinyl

Open/closed, slightly thin-lipped mouth is fixed into a broad smile

Wide-staring eyes, painted turquoise and black

Plastic "diamond" jewellery

Hard vinyl arms are bent at elbows

Shoulder joints allow circular, horizontal, and vertical movement

Stretchy nylon, hip-length bodice

Hard plastic body

Swivel waist enables the torso to turn through 360°

Sumptuous ball gown has layers of vibrant pink-and-silver net over a pink nylon underskirt

Rigid legs, jointed only at hips

Feet are moulded into standing-on-toes position

Flexible toes

"HAPPY HOLIDAYS" BARBIE
A standard model, made in China, this Special Edition 1990 Barbie comes with a signed photograph. She has numerous outfits and can also wear those of similar-sized dolls.

HT: 30cm (12in)

Arched
eyebrows

Flirtatious, side-
glancing eyes, with
moulded eyelashes

Pert mouth

Painted eyes look
straight ahead

Pouting red
lips, drawn
into a slight
smile

DOLL MARKS

The Mattel, Inc. mark and copyright date are impressed into the back of the head.

©MATTEL, INC. 1966
CHINA

The body mark appears at the back of the torso on the waist or right buttock.

The Barbie logo is distinctive and has changed little over the years.

Barbie

1950s' LILLI (ABOVE) The original Lilli dolls were vampish, reflecting the exploits of the cartoon character. This German model is made of hard vinyl, and has a reverse socket head. Ht: 30cm (12in)

1962 "BUBBLE-CUT BARBIE" (ABOVE) With her short hairdo – new for 1962 – "Bubble-cut Barbie" has all the sophistication, but none of the toughness, of the Lilli dolls. Ht: 30cm (12in)

1991 FULL-OF-LIFE BARBIE (ABOVE) Registered in 1990, this model glows with youth and vitality. The doll has a lean body and wears bright, easy-care clothes from the "Ski Fun" set. Ht: 30cm (12in)

BARBIE'S FERRARI (RIGHT) This doll-sized car, made in Italy in 1990 for Mattel, is a scale-model version of a Pininfarina 328 GTS. Inside, a 1990 Barbie wears an outfit from the "Springtime Fashions" set.

"Chrome" wheel-
hubs, with Ferrari
horse logo

Authentic styling details include rear-view
wing mirrors and snap-in seat belts

Soft polyethylene
head, with rooted
nylon hair

Outfit is a
perfect replica
of the official
American
Airlines
uniform

"AMERICAN AIRLINES STEWARDESS" (RIGHT) Clothes transform the basic Barbie into myriad roles. This set was made c.1963, and is modelled here by one of the earliest dolls. Ht: 30cm (12in)

Miniature regulation
flight bag has zip
fastener that works

Regulation
black
shoulder
bag

Catalogue
contains
outfits for
Barbie,
boyfriend Ken,
and best-
friend, Midge

Original
1950s'
Mattel,
Inc. logo

Emergency
phone numbers

School books with
carrying strap

BABY-SITTER KIT (LEFT) The "Barbie baby-sits!" set, just one of Barbie's many accessories, was introduced in 1962, and came complete with a pair of reading glasses, a telephone for essential calls, and pretzels to munch.

Sandals replace
original classic
heeled pumps

English Manufacturers

· 1950s to 1980s ·

ENGLISH DOLL-MAKING thrived in the middle years of the twentieth century. A number of firms that had begun production in the 1920s and 1930s coped admirably with the new developments in manufacturing techniques and materials, created their own distinctive style and designs, and were often very successful. By the mid-1980s, however, financial difficulties had driven many companies out of business altogether. Others had become absorbed by larger international corporations, which moved the manufacture of their dolls to other countries, especially those in east Asia, where labour was cheaper and production costs were lower. The dolls illustrated on these pages were made by some of the most prestigious firms of the 1950s to the 1980s.

Printed card in metal ring, attached by a string to the doll's wrist.

Long rooted nylon hair can be brushed into a fringe

Doll wears a good-quality, cotton gingham dress over white cotton knickers

Socket head can turn

Stylized facial features

Painted brown eyes, with painted black upper lashes and a tinge of blue eyeshadow above

Hard vinyl body is jointed at shoulders

Torso is made in two parts but does not turn

Wrist tag is the doll's only marking

Joints at hips allow movement of legs

Moulded hands, with joined fingers and separate thumbs

Straight legs, with rounded calves

Flat feet, with no instep, enable the doll to stand unaided

Leather shoes, with snap-fastening ankle straps

TRENDON, SASHA DOLL *Sasha Morgenthaler of Zurich, Switzerland, designed the Sasha range of hard vinyl dolls, first produced by Trendon Ltd. of Stockport, Cheshire, in 1965. Girls, boys, and babies were available in three colourings: the flesh tone changed, according to whether the doll had blonde, brunette, or black hair. This example is Sasha Brunette No. 103, issued in 1970.*

HT: 40cm (16in)

Prototype heads are made of plaster, painted in watercolours

Final chosen version of the Daisy head

DAISY PROTOTYPES (ABOVE)
Mary Quant designed a number of different types of face for Daisy until she was satisfied that the features of the doll represented those of a typical English "model girl".

PEDIGREE, KELLY (RIGHT) Kelly, a fully poseable fashion doll, was designed by Bruce Beresford and produced by Pedigree Soft Toys Ltd. exclusively for a chain of retail stores in the United Kingdom. Kelly was briefly available at the end of 1979. Ht: 28cm (11in)

Various hair colours are available

Daisy, with the original English-language packaging for a fashion outfit

Side-glancing eyes suggest a youthful girl, full of fun

Rooted nylon hair

Painted facial features

Reverse socket head is made of soft vinyl

MARY QUANT'S DAISY (LEFT) The dress designer, Mary Quant, together with Flair Toys, introduced Daisy in 1973 and it was produced for ten years. Although Mary Quant designed all of the clothing, much of it was manufactured in Hong Kong, along with the doll itself. Ht: 23cm (9in)

Socket head can turn

Chestnut brown rooted saran hair

Mary Quant's trademark gives the doll its name

Sleeping blue plastic eyes, with nylon lashes

Painted closed mouth

Dress conceals soft vinyl body

Cotton dress designed by Hazel Smith

ROSEBUD (RIGHT) Eric and Hazel Smith of Northampton registered the name, Rosebud, as a trademark for a range of dolls in 1947. This model, manufactured in 1963, has a pretty dolly face. Ht: 47cm (18½in)

Straight legs are jointed at hips

Moulded and painted hair

Inset eyes, without lashes

Body is jointed at shoulders

Bent limbs

Joints at hips allow legs to move

White vinyl shoes, with button fastening

All-plastic, injection-moulded body

RODDY DOLL (LEFT)
Using a combination of their names, doll-makers D.G. Todd and J. Robinson created a range of dolls called Roddy in the late 1930s. This typical injection-moulded baby doll was manufactured c.1955. Ht: 30cm (12in)

Buttoned armchair is made of vinyl

Sindy and Patch

· 1960s to the present day ·

A FASHION DOLL with a youthful image, Sindy was designed by Dennis Arkinstall and first issued by the Pedigree Doll Company of Canterbury, Kent, England, in 1962. Marketed as "the doll you love to dress", Sindy was available with a wide range of different outfits and accessories that reflected the changing styles of the time. The doll soon had family and friends, including Patch, the younger sister, and Paul, the boyfriend (see page 127).

Sindy was remodelled in 1971 and given a more shapely, elegant form to keep up with fashion trends. Then in 1987, when Pedigree ceased trading, Hasbro of the United States bought the doll. Sindy has since been completely redesigned and now has an active, sporting image to suit current fashions.

Long rooted nylon hair can be combed and even styled with rollers

Retroussé nose

Closed mouth is painted red

Plastic "diamanté" choker fits closely around neck

Reverse socket head is made of soft vinyl

Painted side-glancing eyes, with painted lashes

Hard plastic body is jointed at shoulders

Within the limbs, a special inner framework permits the elbows, knees, and ankles to be posed

Lurex evening gloves stretch to above elbow height

Hands have long, thin, separately moulded fingers

Long, shapely, soft vinyl legs are jointed at hips

Swivel waist allows the torso to turn a full 360°

Stylish lurex evening dress, with ruched and gathered sides

Elegant matching evening bag, with "gold" chain

Mould lines are visible down centre of legs

Feet are shaped to fit into high-heeled shoes

Green plastic slip-on high heels

1971 SINDY *The "second-generation" Sindy boasted a completely new body, created by Ian Daniels. It has a special framework inside the vinyl "skin", which allows the elbows, knees, and ankles to move freely yet also stay in one position. At that time, Sindy's wardrobe offered many different accessories and outfits, including this glamorous evening dress.*

HT: 27cm (10½in)

- Rooted curled blonde hair of coarse nylon
- Soft vinyl head
- Painted features
- Clothes conceal hard vinyl body and soft vinyl limbs
- Beneath sweater, lower torso carries raised mark "MADE IN HONG KONG"

- Platinum blonde nylon hair
- Soft vinyl reverse socket head, with painted facial features
- Within the limbs, internal joints allow the elbows and knees to bend
- Costume conceals hard vinyl body, jointed at hips and shoulders

1962 SINDY (LEFT)
Dressed in clothes typical of the early 1960s, this was the first Sindy model of the range. The body has a more girlish form than that of the doll that followed, and the feet are flat. Ht: 30cm (12in)

1990S' "TOP MODEL" SINDY (LEFT)
Reissued by Hasbro, modern-day Sindy has a sporty look and a wide, confident smile. This example has encased joints at the elbows and knees. Ht: 28cm (11in)

DOLL MARKS
The logo on the packaging reflects changing styles.

~

The first Sindy signature was in a simple script, suggesting a youthful hand.

The 1990s' signature is more stylish, and often in two colours instead of one.

"FUN BIKE" SINDY (BELOW)
Reflecting a new-found passion for cycling among children and fitness fanatics of all ages, in 1990 Hasbro produced a Sindy model with "pedal power action" and, of course, her very own mountain bike. Ht: 27cm (10½in)

- The insignia of the letter "S" enclosed in a heart shape makes Sindy accessories instantly recognizable

"TOBOGGAN TIME" PATCH
(BELOW) Issued as Sindy's younger sister in 1966, Patch is shorter than Sindy and, because of her youth, has a less well developed body and a flatter chest than that of her sister. Ht: 23cm (9in)

- Cyclist's helmet, echoing current concerns about safety
- Soft vinyl head
- Clothes conceal hard vinyl body, jointed at shoulders and hips
- Open joints at knees allow legs to bend and stretch

- Sindy from the late 1960s

- Rooted short nylon hair
- Painted features, with freckles

- Bike is in working order: wheels, pedals, and legs move together

SINDY'S WARDROBE (ABOVE)
Among the many accessories for Sindy are a wardrobe, a house, and a car. Dolls with complete sets of clothing and accessories have been popular for many years.

- Dazzling "fluorescent" colours, fashionable in the early 1990s

- Bicycle is 30cm (12in) long

- Hard plastic toboggan

- Clothes conceal soft vinyl limbs and hard vinyl torso

∼ Baby and Toddler Dolls ∼

· 1940s to the present day ·

ENCOURAGED BY ADVANCES in equipment and technology in the 1930s, manufacturers of baby dolls began to produce models that were ever more realistic. Those that "performed" in some way – feeding, wetting, or crying – proved to be long-term favourites. In recent years, designers have even created dolls that look as if they have nappy rash, and those that will "eat" solid food. With the aid of batteries, some dolls will laugh, crawl, and even repeat words that are spoken to them. ∼ Many models portray newborn babies, and are often available complete with hospital identity tags and navel bindings, as well as birth certificates. Some dolls are anatomically correct, made either as boys or as girls. But these have proved controversial, being considered by some people to carry realism too far.

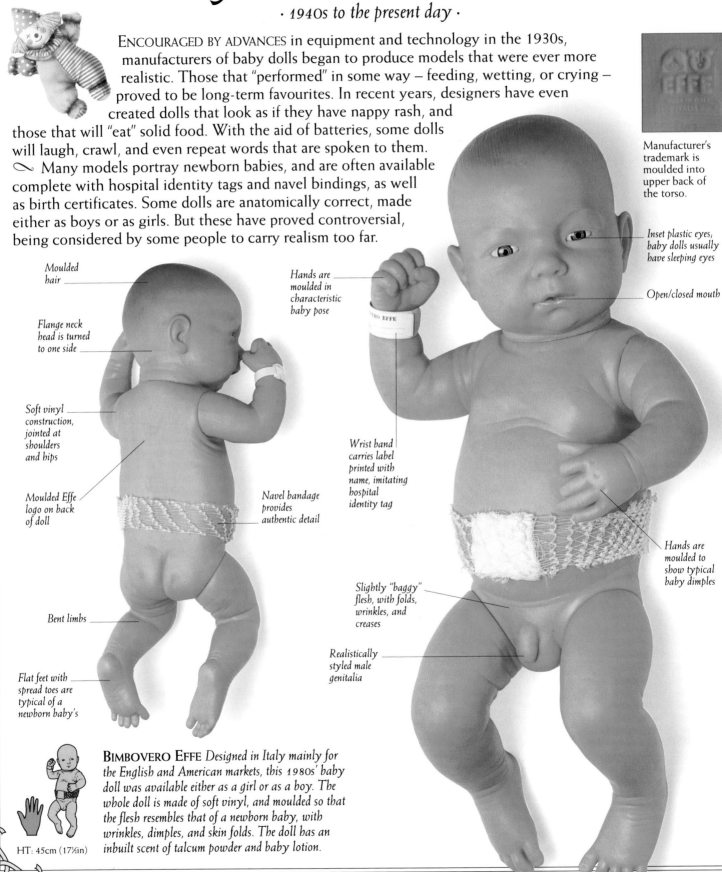

Manufacturer's trademark is moulded into upper back of the torso.

Moulded hair

Flange neck head is turned to one side

Soft vinyl construction, jointed at shoulders and hips

Moulded Effe logo on back of doll

Bent limbs

Flat feet with spread toes are typical of a newborn baby's

Hands are moulded in characteristic baby pose

Navel bandage provides authentic detail

Wrist band carries label printed with name, imitating hospital identity tag

Slightly "baggy" flesh, with folds, wrinkles, and creases

Realistically styled male genitalia

Inset plastic eyes; baby dolls usually have sleeping eyes

Open/closed mouth

Hands are moulded to show typical baby dimples

BIMBOVERO EFFE *Designed in Italy mainly for the English and American markets, this 1980s' baby doll was available either as a girl or as a boy. The whole doll is made of soft vinyl, and moulded so that the flesh resembles that of a newborn baby, with wrinkles, dimples, and skin folds. The doll has an inbuilt scent of talcum powder and baby lotion.*

HT: 45cm (17½in)

Cardboard cradle forms part of the doll's packaging

Open mouth, with toothless gums

Rooted blonde nylon hair

Cheeky expression changes when doll's torso is squeezed

Dress covers abdomen, containing voice box

Name of doll is printed on the side of the cradle

FIRST LOVE (ABOVE)

A newborn baby girl doll, First Love, was marketed in the 1980s by the English Pedigree Doll Company, although it was actually manufactured by Berjusa of Spain. The doll is made of soft vinyl and smells of baby lotion. Ht: 35cm (15in)

Dress conceals all-composition body, jointed at shoulders and hips

Spotted cotton dress and bonnet, over white petticoat and flannelette nappy

Side-glancing painted blue eyes, with painted lashes

MOVING MOUTH BABY

(LEFT & ABOVE) Squeezing the abdomen of this baby doll makes its mouth open and close, and elicits a squeak. Manufactured in Hong Kong and copyrighted by Mattel in the United States in 1966, the doll is made of vinyl, and jointed at the shoulders and hips. Ht: 18cm (7in)

Pink shoes, with lace trim, match the dress and pants

Bent limbs

Decorative red ribbons are sewn onto dress and bonnet

SUNSHINE BABY (LEFT)

Produced by Vogue Dolls in the 1940s, Sunshine Baby is a true classic of its era. Ht: 20cm (8in)

Vogue Dolls® is a registered trademark of Dakin, Inc. All Vogue Dolls designs © 1993 Dakin, Inc., Woodland Hills, California, USA, reproduced here courtesy of Dakin.

"POTTY TIME" QUINTS

(BELOW) The "Drink and Wet" set is just one in the Quints range copyrighted in 1991 by Tyco Industries, Inc. of New Jersey, in the United States, and made in China. These tiny toddler dolls each have a pair of pants and a feeding bottle, and come with a bench containing five heart-shaped potties. Ht: 6cm (2½in)

Blonde hair is tied up in a pony-tail with ribbon

Reverse socket head

Soft vinyl construction, jointed at shoulders and hips

Curly rooted saran hair

Open mouth for bottle

Colour-coordinated pants match the potty seats

Each of the five potty seats is identified with a colour and number

Hole at bottom of torso for liquid to come out

Plastic feeding bottles can be filled with water or milk

Royal Doulton and Nisbet

· 1980 to 1985 ·

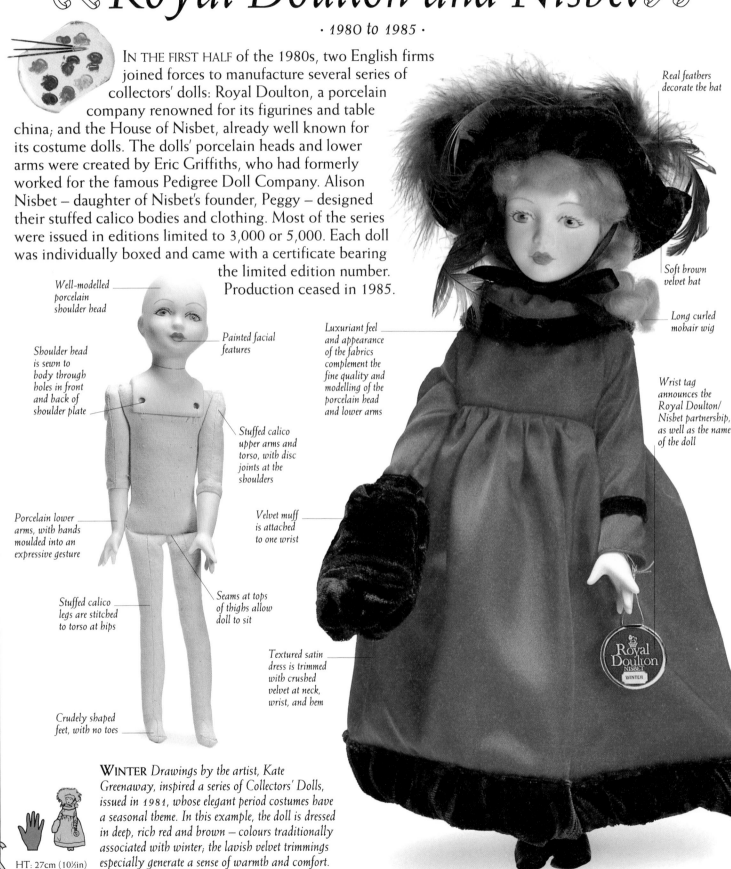

IN THE FIRST HALF of the 1980s, two English firms joined forces to manufacture several series of collectors' dolls: Royal Doulton, a porcelain company renowned for its figurines and table china; and the House of Nisbet, already well known for its costume dolls. The dolls' porcelain heads and lower arms were created by Eric Griffiths, who had formerly worked for the famous Pedigree Doll Company. Alison Nisbet – daughter of Nisbet's founder, Peggy – designed their stuffed calico bodies and clothing. Most of the series were issued in editions limited to 3,000 or 5,000. Each doll was individually boxed and came with a certificate bearing the limited edition number. Production ceased in 1985.

Real feathers decorate the hat

Soft brown velvet hat

Long curled mohair wig

Luxuriant feel and appearance of the fabrics complement the fine quality and modelling of the porcelain head and lower arms

Wrist tag announces the Royal Doulton/ Nisbet partnership, as well as the name of the doll

Well-modelled porcelain shoulder head

Painted facial features

Shoulder head is sewn to body through holes in front and back of shoulder plate

Stuffed calico upper arms and torso, with disc joints at the shoulders

Porcelain lower arms, with hands moulded into an expressive gesture

Velvet muff is attached to one wrist

Stuffed calico legs are stitched to torso at hips

Seams at tops of thighs allow doll to sit

Textured satin dress is trimmed with crushed velvet at neck, wrist, and hem

Crudely shaped feet, with no toes

WINTER Drawings by the artist, Kate Greenaway, inspired a series of Collectors' Dolls, issued in 1981, whose elegant period costumes have a seasonal theme. In this example, the doll is dressed in deep, rich red and brown – colours traditionally associated with winter; the lavish velvet trimmings especially generate a sense of warmth and comfort.

HT: 27cm (10½in)

Side of shoulder plate | Hole for pouring in bone china slip

THREE-PIECE HEAD MOULD

(LEFT) The plaster mould for the porcelain head is in three parts, held together by thick elastic bands. Bone china slip is poured into the hole at the top and, when it has hardened, the casts are removed. Called "blue heads" because of their colour at this stage, they need to be smoothed down before firing.

DOLL MARKS

Every doll bears the Royal Doulton copyright mark on the shoulder plate.

~

Special collections have their own individual copyright mark.

D.N.19
© ROYAL DOULTON
TABLEWARE LTD. 1981
KATE GREENAWAY
DOLL COLLECTION

Limited-edition dolls come with a certificate of authentication.

Royal Doulton
NISBET

FACE PAINTING (RIGHT) After the heads
are smoothed and fired, they are given either a pink or an ivory matt glaze, then the facial features are painted and fired several times to set each colour. The outline of the eyes and lashes come first, then the irises and pupils. Adding blush-pink colour to the lips and cheeks gives the finishing touch. Head ht: 6cm (2½in).

Collectors' series doll heads are all identical

Eye colour changes according to model of doll

Feather duster, made of real feathers

SATURDAY GIRL (LEFT)

"Saturday's child works hard for its living", from the children's birthday rhyme, provides the theme for one of the first dolls produced under the Royal Doulton/Nisbet name. Ht: 27cm (10½in)

Shoulder-length blonde mohair wig

Doll wears a maid's uniform

Stuffed calico hands, with the fingers indicated only by stitches; later models have porcelain hands

Cardboard label hanging from wrist identifies the doll and the series to which it belongs

Flange neck head

Painted hair and features

Full, pouting lips give the doll a distinguished mouth

Plastic socket joints at shoulders and hips allow the limbs to move freely

Porcelain lower arms

Porcelain lower legs to above knees

FIRSTBORN (ABOVE) The
baby doll of the Royal Doulton/ Nisbet series was issued in 1982. Its dumpy calico body is rather out of keeping with the well-cast porcelain head and lower limbs, but the doll's charm lies in its appearance when clothed. Ht: 30cm (12in)

Men and Boys

· 1960s to the present day ·

THE RATIO OF MALE TO FEMALE dolls has always tended to be small, reflecting the industry's belief that boys do not play with dolls. But more male models are now being produced, as it becomes clear that children of both sexes like to play with dolls of all kinds.

〜 The best-known male doll is Action Man, or G.I. Joe as it was named in the United States, first issued in 1964. Action Man was inescapably macho, and very much a military man. As anti-war feelings grew in the late 1960s, so Action Man's popularity waned, and the doll was re-presented in the form of a "global adventurer". Production ceased in the 1980s, but in 1993 Hasbro, the copyright-holder, re-launched the doll with new and updated accessories.

Raised, moulded mark on torso indicates manufacturer and licence-holder.

Waterproof suit made of unbleached calico

Moulded hair; later models have flock hair

Painted eyes and eyebrows

Moulded and painted scar on cheek

Soft vinyl socket head turns a full 360°

Diving belt has metal weights

Torso is fully formed, with well-moulded pectoral muscles

Identity tag bears Action Man logo

Waterproof calico mittens, elasticated at the wrist

Jointing at waist allows torso to swivel 360°

Well-modelled hands, showing knuckles and finger-nails, are specially designed to grip "equipment"

Hard vinyl body, with ball and socket joints at hips and waist

Hinged ball and socket joints at knees, elbows, shoulders, wrists, and ankles allow them to move freely

Shapely legs have distinctive calf muscles, with visible tendons

Plastic helmet finished to look like brass; air hose attaches to the back

Long, arched feet have well-shaped toes with toe-nails

Plastic sheath knife is strapped to the calf with elastic

Plastic boots, with metallic weighted clogs

1964 ACTION MAN *Described as "The movable fighting man!", the first Action Man has 20 moving parts and can be posed to run, kneel, sit, crawl, stand, or lie flat. When immersed in water, the deep-sea diver set shown here creates surprisingly realistic underwater effects.*

HT: 30cm (12in)

The "Official Action Soldier", dressed in U.S. Army regulation denims

ACTION MAN'S SCOUT CAR (BELOW) All manner of toy military vehicles have been produced for Action Man, and models have been updated in line with actual changes taking place in the armed forces.

Scout car based on World War II vintage

Moulded and painted hair

Felt cowboy hat

Metal toy gun on wrist ribbon

Wrist tag reads "Hi! I'm Jimmy"

Blue cotton dungarees conceal soft vinyl body, with dimpled limbs

JIMMY (ABOVE) Similar to Ginnette (see page 113), this doll was also made by Vogue Dolls, Inc. Ht: 20cm (8in) Vogue Dolls® is a registered trademark of Dakin, Inc. Vogue Dolls designs © 1993 Dakin, Inc., Woodland Hills, California, USA, reproduced here courtesy of Dakin.

MATTEL'S 1961 KEN (BELOW) The advertising slogan, "He's a doll", introduced Ken, Barbie's boyfriend (see page 116), in 1961. The first model had a semi-hard vinyl head and hard vinyl body. The doll's expression and slender physique suggest a clean-living, shy young man. Ht: 30cm (12in)

Luxuriant, rooted nylon hair

Shirt conceals bent arms, with modified ball joints at shoulders

Torso pivots slightly at the waist

Set includes hair gel, booklet with styling tips, and five hair accessories

Moulded and painted hair

Movable head

Painted green eyes

Blond flock "crew-cut" hair

Painted eyes, with moulded lids and lashes

Suit conceals straight, unjointed arms and legs

Small hands, with indented finger-nails

Simple packaging, printed in one language

Sophisticated packaging, printed in several languages

Doll's name is printed on tee-shirt

Hard vinyl limbs, tinted to give the doll a suntanned appearance

1991 "ULTRA HAIR" KEN (ABOVE) As with Barbie, Mattel has made major alterations to Ken, to keep pace with changing trends. This model has the well-muscled body of an athletic young man, and hair that can be coiffed with styling gel. Ht: 30cm (12in)

1991 "COOL SHADES" PAUL (RIGHT) A boyfriend for Sindy (see page 120), Paul was first issued by Pedigree in the 1960s, withdrawn in 1971, then reissued in 1987. This version is dressed for the beach and wears RayBan look-alike sunglasses. Ht: 30cm (12in)

❧ New Doll Ideas ❧

· 1960s to the present day ·

THE BOOM YEARS of the twentieth century saw a change of pace in the doll world. Although the traditional models were as popular as ever, novelty dolls came and went as styles changed. Some reflected the political atmosphere of the time, such as the movement against nuclear weapons, the anarchy of Punk rock – or the renewed emphasis on the importance of the family unit. The versatility of plastic, combined with the ingenuity of the manufacturers, allowed ever more complex designs.

〜 Not all modern dolls are plastic. Michael and Lynne Roche of Bath, England, are among a number of individual makers who have returned to using mainly natural materials for their dolls. Beth, one of their range, shows the best of English doll-making in the 1990s.

The maker's mark appears beneath the hairline on the back of the head.

Initials of Lynne Roche and date of manufacture appear below left ear.

Red-blonde mohair wig

Well-shaped bisque socket head

Painted mouth

Inset blue glass eyes

Yellow knitted cardigan has coloured wooden buttons

Traditionally shaped wooden body

Ball joints at the elbows, shoulders, and wrists

Bisque hands are large and expressive

Signature of Michael Roche, maker of the body, inscribed on the right buttock.

Ball joints at hips allow doll to sit

Ball joints at knees allow flexibility

Calves are smooth and well carved

Cat-shaped toy, made of printed cotton, fits snugly into back pocket of doll's dungarees

Blue denim dungarees are fastened at front with wooden buttons

Flat feet are carved to show toes

Red leather shoes, with button fastening

BISQUE AND WOODEN DOLL, BETH *Created by Michael and Lynne Roche in Bath, England, in 1992, Beth embodies the 1990s' revival of interest in traditional crafts and the use of natural materials. The doll has a finely modelled bisque head and hands, and a turned wooden body. Its clothing, made of wool and cotton, with leather for the shoes, is also of excellent quality.*

HT: 28cm (11in)

JUDITH "MOTHER & BABY" *(RIGHT) This innovative – if unrealistic – "pregnant" doll, issued in 1992, was designed by Villy Nielsen A/S in Denmark and manufactured by the Lucky Bell Plastics Company in Hong Kong. Ht: 28cm (11in)*

1985 PUNK ROCKER

(LEFT) A representative of the Punk scene that began in the mid-1970s, this hard vinyl doll is one of a pair issued by Marian Kenny Designs in England. Ht: 19cm (7½in)

FATHER
Ht: 30cm (12in)

Soft vinyl head, with moulded hair and painted features

Shirt conceals hard vinyl body, jointed at shoulders and hips

Clothes for boy twin coordinate with those for father

Soft vinyl head

Large, rounded tummy lifts off to allow baby to be removed, then spring-loaded flat tummy moves into place

Loose-fitting cotton and polyester clothing conceals hard vinyl body

Moulded sandals, with painted details

C.N.D. MARCHERS *(ABOVE)*
The rise of the peace movement in the 1950s and 1960s inspired the design of these two supporters of the British Campaign for Nuclear Disarmament. Manufactured in hard vinyl, the dolls are dressed in beatnik style and wear C.N.D. medallions. Ht: 19cm (7½in)

MOTHER
Ht: 30cm (12in)

Maternity clothes, as well as accessories for the baby, are available

BOY TWIN
Ht: 10cm (4in)

THE HEART FAMILY *(BELOW) Mattel, in the United States, created its own nuclear family in 1985, when it packaged two adult dolls together with twin baby dolls. In the six years the Hearts were in production, the range grew to include grandparents, baby cousins, and neighbourhood kids.*

Vinyl accessories include high-chair, baby bath, and pony rocker

Hard vinyl baby doll, with bent limbs

GIRL TWIN
Ht: 10cm (4in)

Mother's outfit matches that of little girl

National Dolls

National dolls take many forms, ranging from folk-art dolls crafted by indigenous peoples to record their culture, and patriotic dolls that celebrate popular heroes or historic events, to souvenir dolls in national costumes, which are not always made in the country they are intended to represent. In some cases the design or material used has changed over the years, but many national dolls are still made in accordance with centuries-old traditions.

THE NOTION OF NATIONAL DOLLS developed from the eighteenth century onwards, as many more Europeans ventured abroad. People collected dolls as mementoes of the countries they had visited. In some countries where no tradition of national dolls existed, Europeans introduced the concept, with the aim of recording the different ways of life and costumes in these places – often to commercial advantage.

Dolls in China and Japan

The best-known of the national dolls are the Japanese Festival Dolls. For more than 400 years, these figures have been used for very specific purposes. Boys are taught the virtues of manliness, loyalty, and chivalry; and girls are trained to understand the duties and virtues of being a good wife and mother. The children also learn of the nation's history and its culture through this process. These dolls are put on display only once a year, on the appropriate festival day – 3 March for girls, and 5 May for boys (see pages 132–133).

 At *Tango no sekku*, the Boys' Festival, the doll display is set out on a two- or three-tiered stand.

Dolls representing *Samurai* warriors and legendary characters are featured, as well as miniature models of swords, banners, hats, and horses. *Obina matsuri*, the Girls' Festival, is more complex. As a mother and daughter set out the dolls on a five- or seven-tiered stand, the mother explains the significance of each figure. Models of the Emperor and Empress, court officials, musicians, and servants are included among the dolls. Miniature household furnishings are also shown, and are placed on the lower tiers. Various personal objects representing the dowry of a bride from a noble or *Samurai* family, as well as offerings of rice cakes and *sake* are also displayed here.

 Over the years, the dolls have hardly changed at all. The makers endeavour to remain faithful to the traditional models with as much accuracy as they can, and do not develop or improve the design.

 Kokeshi are another quite different variety of traditional Japanese doll.

SOUTH AFRICAN MISSION DOLL (*LEFT*) *This stuffed felt doll, wearing an exquisitely beaded costume, was made in Durban, in a Red Cross Rehabilitation Centre, c.1960. Such dolls were sold in support of the centre. Ht: 33cm (13in)*

MEXICAN PAPIER MACHE DANCER (*RIGHT*) *A traditional design of brightly painted papier mâché was the inspiration for this Mexican doll, which was made in 1991. It is a folk-art doll, and is rather crude, but colourful. The doll's arms and legs are jointed with elastic. Ht: 33cm (13in)*

JAPANESE KOKESHI CRAFTSMAN *(LEFT) Each maker of the traditional turned wooden kokeshi may give his dolls a slightly different shape and paint them in his own particular design. Whole "families" of kokeshi are made, in a wide range of sizes.*

NEW ORLEANS SUGAR-CANE CUTTER *(RIGHT) This wax figure is one of a series of dolls portraying the traditional trades of New Orleans, United States. It was created by a member of the Vargas family, some time between 1915 and the 1930s. Ht: 18cm (7in)*

They have been made in the north-eastern region of Japan since the early seventeenth century. *Kokeshi* are fashioned from turned wood and given a decorative painted finish. These dolls are limbless, having only a head and a body. Originally designed as religious symbols, *kokeshi* became toys for children; nowadays they are sold mainly as souvenirs.

~ In China, children played not with dolls, but with small brightly coloured clay figures, often representing animals. Dolls in the Western style were introduced by Europeans to help to preserve a record of the way of life in China. Many dolls such as these were made at missions that had been set up towards the end of the nineteenth century to aid children in need. Found mainly in the southern provinces of Kiangsu, Fukien, and Chekiang, carved wooden dolls, such as those from the Door of Hope Missions (see pages 134–135), were dressed by the children and sold to raise funds for the missions themselves. Dolls were also sold as souvenirs in the markets and bazaars of China. These were made out of wire and clay, or painted plaster, and represented theatrical dancers and performers.

BRAZILIAN RAG COUPLE *(RIGHT) These are rather sophisticated Brazilian rag dolls, made in the 1930s, with embroidered bodies and facial features and anatomical detail. Their costumes are cleverly worked, the woman's having additional decoration in the form of coloured pieces of tin foil. In both cases, the finger-nails are shaped using small pieces of opaque celluloid. Ht: 46cm (18in)*

Dolls of Russia

The *Matryoshka*, or Nesting Dolls, have long been associated with Russia (see pages 136–137), although the idea for dolls that fit inside each other probably comes from China. Various styles of doll were traditionally made in Russia, as in other eastern European countries, to record the peoples, costumes, and culture of the different regions; now they are produced mainly as souvenirs for tourists. Customarily, wood was used to make these dolls, but in recent years, rag has often been used.

~ National dolls, especially the folk-art kind, are always popular with foreign visitors, but they have a value far greater than mere souvenirs. They provide paid employment for the makers, help to record the customs and traditions of the country, and preserve the craft of doll-making itself.

Japanese Dolls

· 1900s to 1960s ·

MANY JAPANESE DOLLS are designed not as playthings but as ornaments, often depicting some aspect of Japanese history or culture. The intriguing *sakura-ningyō* (cherry dolls) may be modelled on *kabuki* dancers, or they may portray some aspect of everyday life. It has long been a favourite pastime among young women to make and dress these figures. Today, cherry dolls are also produced commercially, mainly as souvenirs or for export, but they are still popular items for display in Japanese homes. ∾ The decorative category known as *hina-ningyō* (festival dolls), also serve a second purpose. Brought out only on the children's festival days each year, these dolls, which are handed down from generation to generation, are used to illustrate the traditions of the nation.

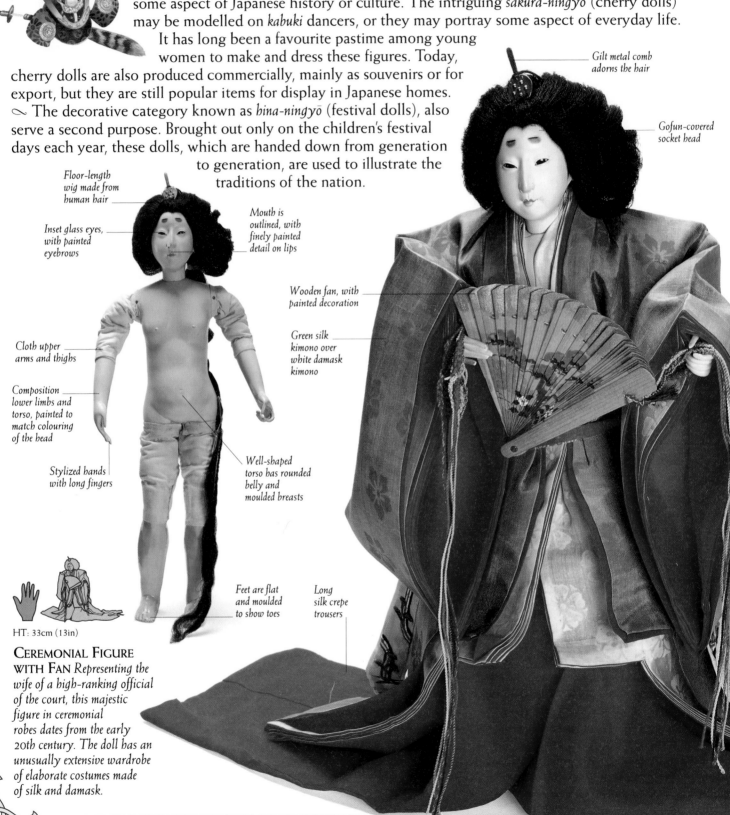

Gilt metal comb adorns the hair

Gofun-covered socket head

Floor-length wig made from human hair

Inset glass eyes, with painted eyebrows

Mouth is outlined, with finely painted detail on lips

Wooden fan, with painted decoration

Green silk kimono over white damask kimono

Cloth upper arms and thighs

Composition lower limbs and torso, painted to match colouring of the head

Stylized hands with long fingers

Well-shaped torso has rounded belly and moulded breasts

Feet are flat and moulded to show toes

Long silk crepe trousers

HT: 33cm (13in)

CEREMONIAL FIGURE WITH FAN *Representing the wife of a high-ranking official of the court, this majestic figure in ceremonial robes dates from the early 20th century. The doll has an unusually extensive wardrobe of elaborate costumes made of silk and damask.*

Plaster composition head and hands

MOUNTED WARRIOR
(LEFT) An important element of Tango-no-sekku, the Boys' Festival, this ornate figure is part of the set that conveys the code of the Samurai, Japan's aristocratic warrior class. Ht: 25cm (10in)

SHOKI, THE DEVIL CHASER
(RIGHT) By tradition, Japanese families displayed an image of the legendary character, Shoki, at the Boys' Festival in the belief that he would protect their sons from evil. This figure is a late 19th-century doll, designed to hold only one pose. Ht: 55cm (22in)

Horse is made of a padded wire armature covered with animal skin

Silk brocade costume, with gold-painted paper armour

Padded costume is part of construction of doll and cannot be removed

Elaborate robes made of padded silk brocade

Ornaments are carved from wood, then gilded

Carved and lacquered wooden stand

CEREMONIAL PAIR (BELOW)
The figure on the left of this boxed set is described in detail opposite. The other doll represents a man, ready to be dressed as a top-level official of the emperor's court.

Gofun-covered lower limbs and torso

Patterned silk kimono, with long sleeves

Stand is made of lacquered and painted wood

Gilded wooden feet

Man's face is natural colour; high-ranking lady's face is white

Bottom layer of 3-tiered black lacquered presentation box; other layers hold clothes and accessories (see page 149)

Feet wear toed socks

SILENT ENVOY (ABOVE) Yamato-ningyō, dolls representing children in traditional dress, were originally designed as gifts for royalty to present to honoured guests. Later, such dolls might be sent as "envoys of friendship" to other countries. Ht: 33cm (13in)

Hair is a silk wig

Face mask is made of painted, stiffened fabric

Male figure dressed in silk undergarment; ceremonial robes are included in the set

MAIDEN WITH HATS (RIGHT)
This sakura-ningyō, or cherry doll, portrays a kabuki character performing the "Dance of the Seven Hats", an interpretation of a Japanese folk tale. The doll is commercially made and dates from the 1950s. Ht: 35cm (14in)

Fixed-pose body is made of padded cloth over a wire armature

Hats are made of silk over buckram, trimmed with gold

Doll is mounted on a varnished wooden stand

Chinese Dolls

· 1900s to 1950s ·

FROM THE EARLY NINETEENTH CENTURY to about 1950, almost all dolls and toys in mainland China were made in missions set up to help destitute children – whether slaves, child widows, or prostitutes. Europeans were the driving force behind the missions and were concerned to retain the culture of the country while making attractive souvenirs that could be sold to raise funds for the centres' work.

Two important missions were based in Shanghai and Canton under the name Door of Hope. At the Shanghai centre, which was opened in 1901, the girls were taught needlework, a skill they could use to dress wooden dolls, for which they were paid. The Canton mission made similar dolls using composition.

Painted eyes and hair

Heads are carved from pear or box wood and polished smooth

Bright colours and decorative embroidery indicate child is of higher social class than plainly uniformed nurse

Back of head is carved into a bun shape

Baby is 14cm (5½in) tall

Pink silk "sling" ties the baby to the nurse's back

Child's legs are made of stuffed cloth

Traditional suit of tunic over three-quarter length trousers

Hands are carved from wood and then polished

Trousers conceal carved wooden legs

Front of costume has faded through exposure to sunlight

Fingers are fashioned together, but thumbs are separate

Clothing is made from scraps of fabric, donated by well-wishers

AMAH AND BABY *Made at one of the Door of Hope missions between 1928 and 1930, these two dolls depict an amah – a child's nurse – carrying a baby on her back. In keeping with the custom for the working class at the time, the nurse's feet are not bound, although those of the baby's mother would be, since she enjoys a higher social status.*

Shoes are black silk, with rolled tops and white soles

HT: 27cm (10½in)

MISSION DOLL FAMILY (BELOW)
This family of dolls from the 1930s is made of cotton, and has embroidered features. The dolls' fingers are formed from loops of cotton. Ht: Largest 7.5cm (3in); smallest 5cm (2in)

The name, "SHAOHSING INDUSTRIAL MISSION, SHAOHSING, CHEKIANG PROVINCE, CHINA", is printed at the top of the card

Moulded and painted facial features

Female doll holds composition and cloth baby

Composition head and limbs; body is made of padded cloth over wire armature

FARMER AND WIFE (BELOW)
These dolls, dressed in the dark blue associated with the post-war revolutionary period, are part of a set designed in the 1950s by Ada Lum. Their purpose was not only to provide a record of rural Chinese costumes, but also to give work to refugees who had fled to Hong Kong from mainland China in the wake of the revolution. Ht: 46cm (18in)

Woollen hair is braided into pigtail

Stuffed cotton head and body

Waistband has foil and paper decoration

Long silk dress, with three-quarter length kimono

Silk costume is richly embroidered

PEKING OPERA CHARACTERS
(ABOVE) Two figures from a set made c.1900, these rare display dolls represent dancers of the Peking Opera. The man's high status is denoted by the elaborate embroidery on his silk costume. Ht: Woman 28cm (11in); man 29cm (11½in)

MANDARIN WITH LONG FINGERS (RIGHT)
Known to have been bought in Hong Kong c.1930, this doll may be one of those from the Door of Hope Mission at Canton. Similar dolls were adapted for use as puppets by attaching bamboo rods to their wrists. Ht: 25cm (10in)

Ornamental head-dress is made of stiffened, painted paper

Head and limbs made of painted composition over wood

Embroidered eyebrows and eyes

Lips are painted

Dolls are dressed in matching, everyday outfits

Long fingers traditionally indicate doll represents the aristocracy

Silk brocade costume, heavily ornamented and embroidered

Female has embroidered shoes of a type worn only indoors

Seagrass shoes for outdoor wear

~ Russian Dolls ~

· 1800s to the present day ·

TOYS, INCLUDING DOLLS, have been made in Russia and its neighbouring republics for many centuries. In Russia, the tradition of making toys sprang from the monastery of Holy Trinity–St. Sergius (founded in 1337), where religious souvenirs were produced for pilgrims. The surrounding area, from Zagorsk (now called Sergiyev Posad) near Moscow to Bogorodskoye near Kirov, subsequently became the most important toy-producing region in the country.

~ The *Matryoshka* or Nesting Dolls are possibly the best known of all Russian dolls. Made of turned, hollowed wood and painted in bright, vibrant colours, they decrease in size so that each fits inside the next largest. The groups usually vary in number between six and ten, but much larger sequences of 15 or more nesting dolls have also been produced.

Painted features and hair show regional characteristics

Traditional costume of a lady's nursemaid

Small child at base of doll is carved from same piece of wood

Base shows original grain line

Figure is carved from a single piece of wood

Widest side of triangle forms a flat back

Decoration is continued around the back of the figure

TRIANGULAR FIGURE *Wooden dolls of this type have been popular in Russia since the early 1800s. Most were made during the winter by peasants living in forest regions, for sale in town markets in spring. This late 19th-century example comes from Bogorodskoye and is one of a set representing wealthy provincial ladies and their nurse-maids. It is carved from one solid piece of wood and hand painted.*

HT: 18cm (7in)

COSY RAG DOLL (BELOW)

From the 1930s to 1950s, many cloth dolls, in peasant or regional costume, were made as souvenirs. Variations on the theme abound: the padded-cloth skirt of this 1960s' doll covers a samovar or teapot. The head is made of composition, as are the lower arms, on a stuffed cloth torso. Ht: 35cm (14in)

DOLLS FROM FOUR REPUBLICS (RIGHT)

All 1960s' souvenirs, these figures represent four different republics. This kind of doll was usually made of moulded, compressed paper, sometimes mixed with pulped rag, and painted. Ht: 9cm (3½in)

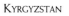

Solid, not hollow, construction

Tissue paper accessories

Varnish protects painted features and delicate skin tones

Thin paper hands and arms

UKRAINE

TAJIKISTAN

ARMENIA

KYRGYZSTAN

Braided hair of sheep's wool or beaten flax

Upper arms made of loosely stuffed cloth, sewn to body

Padded cloth cosy underneath skirt

DANCING COSSACK (LEFT)

This jolly character, c.1980, was inspired by one of Gogol's short stories. The head and lower arms are plastic, as are the lower legs, which are moulded to show boots. The body, upper arms, and upper legs are stuffed cloth. Special features are the star-shaped hands and open mouth. Ht: 19cm (7½in)

Curly wool hat

Moulded and painted moustache

Cotton blouse, with printed "embroidery"

Woven fabric sash

Nylon trousers "tucked" into moulded boots

Figure is fixed into dancing-on-heels position

1992 POLITICAL SEQUENCE

(LEFT) Nesting dolls have been made in Russia for centuries, yet the idea probably originated in China. They usually represent famous characters, peasants, or animals. The smallest doll is solid wood. Ht: Largest 11cm (4¼in); smallest 13mm (½in)

YELTSIN

Solid wood is turned on a lathe, halved around the centre, and hollowed out

GORBACHEV

BREZHNEV

KHRUSHCHEV

STALIN

LENIN

TSAR NICHOLAS II

Patriotic Character Dolls

· 1890s to 1918 ·

WHETHER MADE AS DIGNIFIED, true-to-life representations of their human counterparts, or as caricatures, patriotic dolls often mark a particular historical event, or celebrate a country's pride in its national identity. Heads of state and war heroes are usually serious portrait dolls. The c.1840 Pierotti Queen Victoria (see page 37), for example, was the family's personal tribute to the monarch on her marriage to Prince Albert of Saxe-Coburg-Gotha. On the other hand, politicians – an age-old target for gibes and ridicule – are commonly shown as caricatures.

In the United States, one of the best loved of all portrait dolls is the symbolic figure, Uncle Sam. Traditionally depicted as an older man with an austere yet smiling face, white hair, a goatee, and always wearing the Stars and Stripes on some part of its clothing, this mascot is the male personification of the United States. The name is used, even today, to bring a touch of familiarity to official government language.

Stars on hatband match those on waistcoat, and are adapted from the United States' flag

Metal button, showing a 48-star flag, may be a later addition to the doll's costume

Felted material of top hat was originally blue, one of the three colours of the Stars and Stripes flag of the United States

Clothing conceals composition or papier mâché body, jointed at shoulders, elbows, hips, and knees

Moulded and painted eyebrows

Inset blue-grey glass eyes

Hair and goatee are made of mohair, glued to the head and chin

Exaggerated features, typical of portraits of fictional characters

Back of the neck bears incised mark, "S1", indicating the socket head is made by Simon & Halbig

Wrinkles and skin folds are defined with red paint

Lower torso is slightly padded in front, to make a small paunch

Metal "pocket watch" hangs from the waistcoat on a striped ribbon fob

Head measures 7.5cm (3in) from crown to base of neck and 20cm (8in) around widest part of forehead

Single-breasted frock coat, made of blue felt, with metal buttons at front and back

GERMAN BISQUE UNCLE SAM *This version of the Uncle Sam character reflects one country's response to another's patriotic fervour. Using Simon & Halbig socket heads, the dolls were manufactured and marketed by Cuno & Otto Dressel of Sonneberg, Germany, in 1896. They were exported to the United States, prior to the explosive start of the Spanish–American War in 1898.*

Patriotic red- and white-striped trousers

Black cloth "patent leather" shoes, decorated with metal buckles

Machine-knitted, brown cotton socks

HT: 35cm (14in)

Composition socket head, with moulded and painted hair

Painted intaglio eyes

Detailed replica of full-size uniform

1ST EARL KITCHENER OF KHARTOUM (ABOVE) Disabled British soldiers and seamen of World War I immortalized Lord Kitchener, Secretary of State, as a cloth-bodied doll with composition head, hands, and boots. Ht: 48cm (19in)

Uniform conceals stuffed cloth body

ALBERT I, KING OF THE BELGIANS (LEFT) Representing King Albert I of Belgium as Chief of Staff of the Belgian Army, this portrait doll was made in England in 1915. It is part of the same series as the doll portraying Lord Kitchener (see left). Ht: 48cm (19in)

Composition socket head, with painted intaglio eyes

Composition hands end just above wrist joint

HYGIENIC TOYS MADE IN ENGLAND B

Chad Valley dolls often have a woven cloth label machine-stitched to the sole of the foot.

WORLD WAR I TOMMY SOLDIER (RIGHT) Portrait dolls depict not only famous characters, but also those whose identities are unknown. Modelled as a boyish-looking young man, this c.1916 doll wears the khaki uniform of a private, or tommy, in the British Army. The cloth strips, or "puttees" as they are known, were a typical feature of soldiers' uniforms during World War I. Ht: 38cm (15in)

Head is made from stiffened, moulded felt, with painted facial features and hair, and stitched ears

Felt clothing conceals unjointed cloth body, stuffed with kapok

STANLEY, 1ST EARL BALDWIN OF BEWDLEY (ABOVE) This rag doll, a caricature of a former British Conservative Prime Minister, is one of a series of political figures created by Chad Valley Co. Ltd. (see pages 98–99) in the 1930s. Ht: 30cm (12in)

PRESIDENT WILLIAM McKINLEY

ADMIRAL GEORGE DEWEY

ADMIRAL WILLIAM THOMAS SAMPSON

Broadcloth uniforms, with epaulettes, stripes, and insignia

Simon & Halbig bisque socket heads, with moulded, painted hair and facial features

Uniforms conceal fully jointed composition bodies

Feet are moulded and painted as boots

1898 SPANISH–AMERICAN WAR HEROES (RIGHT) Doll-makers worldwide celebrated the United States' victory in this 100-day war. According to museum records, these three portrait dolls were sent to the United States "compliments of Cuno & Otto Dressel, Sonneberg", at the request of the then U.S. Consul-General in Germany. Ht: 38cm (15in)

Unusual Dolls

In the world of dolls, there have always been a few that are strikingly out of the ordinary: they may have a unique feature of some kind, or have been made from an unusual material, or perhaps put to an intriguing use. One or two of the oddities described here are play dolls; but by far the most unusual are ornamental or display figures. Much sought-after in their time, they are justifiably collectors' items today.

THE FINAL YEARS of the nineteenth century were a time of great creativity and energy in the world at large. In all sectors of industry and society, people were eager to experiment with an unusual idea, or to try the latest invention. In the design and manufacture of dolls, too, there were many innovations at this time: for example, lead-weighted sleeping eyes replaced the earlier push-pull wired type, and sound mechanisms allowed a doll to "speak". But probably one of the strangest was the introduction of multiple heads and faces. On some dolls, one head can be exchanged for another that has a different hairstyle or different expression, and perhaps even a different flesh tone.

The most popular dolls of this type, however, have a single head moulded with two or three faces (see pages 142–143). The head is mounted on a spindle set into the torso, and the various faces are revealed by turning a handle on top of the head.

The Use of Metal

One development at this time was the use of metal. Mainly used for doll heads, metal was in some cases used for the whole figure. One of the major producers of metal heads was the German firm of Buschow & Beck. The heads were exported to England and the United States, where they were attached to stuffed cloth or composition bodies. The metal was usually coated tin, although painted brass and pewter were also used. The heads themselves were unbreakable, but the paintwork quickly discoloured and was easily chipped. Such dolls soon fell out of favour.

Pedlars on Display

Some of the most unusual dolls are found among those intended primarily for display or as decoration. In England in the nineteenth century, there existed a fashion for dressing any doll that was to hand as a pedlar. The character of the doll lay in its costume – a red hooded cloak, or a black or print dress, and white pinafore – and in the wicker tray or basket it carried containing a wide variety of household goods, knick-knacks, and

BOUDOIR DOLL *(LEFT) Reclining against damask cushions in its gorgeously exotic dress, this boudoir doll is an unusual model, as it comes with several outfits. Most have only one, stitched to the doll's body. Ht: 60cm (24in)*

TEAPOT HALF DOLL (LEFT) *This miniature half doll, holding a cascade of flowers in its slender arms, has been attached to a crocheted wool tea cosy. Made in Germany, it has moulded hair and painted features. Doll ht: 5cm (2in)*

METAL HEAD (RIGHT) *This shoulder head bears the mark "MINERVA", a tradename of the German firm Buschow & Beck. Relatively few metal-headed dolls were made. Head ht: 12cm (4¾in)*

haberdashery (see pages 144–145). The majority of Pedlar Dolls were dressed at home, but some were produced commercially, albeit on a small scale.

Half Dolls and Boudoir Dolls

Among the oddest phenomena are the Half Dolls produced during the 1920s and 1930s. These, too, were designed primarily as ornaments – but with a difference, since they were also used to disguise or decorate household objects. Consisting of a hollow head and torso, the half doll could be stitched or glued onto items such as tea cosies, hair and clothes brushes, dusting powder jars, even covers for the telephone. Virtually any material was used – wood, bisque, plastic – but most, by far, were made in porcelain, at factories in France, Germany, and Japan. Some half dolls are still made today, but the modern versions tend to be gaudy imitations of the originals.

◠ It was at approximately the same time that the Boudoir Doll emerged, an essential accessory for the woman of fashion in Europe, as well as in the United States. Their long, lean bodies were made of composition or padded cloth over a wire frame, and their faces were moulded

and covered with painted silk or stockinet. Resembling sultry-eyed "ladies", these beauties languished on beds, divans, sofas, and pianos. They soon became popular as mascots for taking along on car, train, or aeroplane journeys; young women would take them to dances, and even out visiting. Also called vamps, wobblies, or flappers in the United States, many boudoir dolls were dressed to represent the modern woman, in clothing that was considered the height of fashion in the 1920s: Charleston dresses, strings of beads, and cloche hats; mock fur coats; silken pyjama suits; luxuriously long close-fitting satin gowns.

◠ Weird and wonderful dolls are still being made today, in the tradition of the late nineteenth-century art dolls. E.J. Taylor, an American living in London, creates fascinating characters, modelling their strong expressive features in a special craft clay (see pages 146–147). Designed solely for display, these dolls are regarded by many people as works of art.

LADY WITH HAT (LEFT) *Of all the half dolls, those that portray fashionable women of the 18th century were especially popular. This graceful figure is made of bisque, and has delicately painted features and gold decoration on its dress bodice. Ht: 20cm (8in)*

POWDER PUFF LADY (RIGHT) *This bisque half doll, used as the cover for a box of dusting powder, has a crinoline-style costume made of strands of green wool, decorated with red. The elaborate wig is typical of such figures. Ht: 7cm (2¾in)*

Multiple Heads and Faces

· 1860s to 1980s ·

FROM THE 1860S ONWARDS, a number of patents were taken out for dolls with two or three different faces moulded on the same head. Fritz Bartenstein and Carl Bergner, both of Germany, were among the major manufacturers of these in the nineteenth century, and Herr Bergner's firm continued until the 1930s. Although a doll with a range of facial expressions does allow play to be more realistic, the doll itself can look quite hideous because of the head-cover that extends from the shoulder plate to hide the "reserve" faces. The principle of changing faces is still used today, for example in rag storybook dolls, which reveal the faces of different characters as the cloth pages are lifted.

Another similar, if less bizarre, novelty is the doll that has one body and a set of three or four different heads, which may represent a boy and a girl, each with a happy and a sad expression. Such a doll may also have interchangeable limbs, one set being made in a different flesh tone.

HT: 40cm (16in)

TWO-FACED DOLL *Probably made by Fritz Bartenstein in Germany in the 1880s, this doll has an egg-shaped head, moulded with two faces and two sets of ears. The detail in the screaming face is pleasingly authentic: apart from the open mouth, the flesh tone is darker than that of the smiling doll, the eyebrows are knitted together into a frown, and the nostrils are red.*

Mohair wig is attached to the head-cover

Composition swivel head coated in wax

Painted facial features; eyes are inset blown glass

Two-tiered cape, made of nun's veiling, edged with crocheted cotton lace, with satin ribbon tie

Head is turned by a metal and wooden peg

Fabric-covered carton cap, moulded as an extension of the composition shoulder plate

Cotton robe, with broderie anglaise bodice and flounces

Doll says "Mama" when voice-box within torso is activated by a cord at waist

Hands are painted composition; rest of limbs are made of wood and stuffed pink calico

THREE-FACED BISQUE DOLL

(RIGHT) A cumbersome head-cover makes this doll seem particularly unrealistic. A ring at the crown of the wig turns the faces, and a string at waist level operates a speaking mechanism. The doll, which has a composition and calico body and wooden limbs, was possibly made by Simon & Halbig for Carl Bergner in the 1890s. Ht: 30cm (12in)

Bisque socket head

Inset blue glass eyes

Mohair wig on carton head-cover conceals two faces

Happy face, with smiling mouth

Crying face, with furrowed brow and open mouth

Screaming face, with frown and teardrop

Sleeping face has no eyes, only permanently closed eyelids

Happy face, with "laughing" eyes

Moulded and painted facial features

Sleeping face has closed eyelids

Pixie suit covers stuffed cloth body

THREE-FACED PIXIE (LEFT)

A 1960s' ceramic baby doll, manufactured in the United States, this may have been based on a model made in celluloid in the 1930s. The doll has no head-cover: the hood of the clothing is designed to conceal the extra faces and the turning mechanism. Ht: 42cm (16½in)

THREE-IN-ONE (BELOW) This

multiheaded, multilimbed model was made in 1916 by the Doll Pottery Company, one of the few companies set up in England in World War I to produce ceramic doll parts. The set includes parts for a dark-skinned boy and a pale-skinned girl. Head ht: 9cm (3½in)

Moulded and painted hair and facial features

Ceramic hands and head

Stoneware shoulder head

Head is sewn or pinned to stuffed cloth torso through holes in the shoulder plate

Cloth upper limbs

Two faces portray wicked Stepmother (left) and sad Cinderella (far left); others show Fairy Godmother, Prince Charming, and Cinderella in a ball gown

STORYBOOK DOLL (LEFT)

This 1980s' stuffed cotton figure, which tells the traditional tale of Cinderella, is a multiheaded doll of a different kind. Each of the multiple skirts lifts up to reveal the face of a new character, with the text of the story printed on the skirt below. Ht: 23cm (9in)

The text features the character shown

CINDERELLA

WICKED STEPMOTHER

Stoneware lower limbs are fastened with cord or thread to fabric upper limbs around flange at top

Pedlar Dolls

· 1820s to 1990s ·

AS A "CONVERSATION PIECE" in fashionable drawing-rooms in nineteenth-century England, few objects could rival the fascinating Pedlar Doll. Given pride of place on a whatnot or the mantelpiece, and usually sitting beneath a glass dome to protect it from dust, the pedlar doll would be dressed in the traditional red-cloaked costume, carrying a tray or basket overflowing with miniature wares. Most popular between 1820 and 1860, pedlar dolls are enjoying a revival in the 1990s.

Although itinerant traders travelled all over Europe, pedlar dolls were a peculiarly English phenomenon. Even so, most were made in Germany and dressed in England. The heads are usually wood or composition, but kid, apples, and wax were also used. The bodies are often made of wood, composition, or stuffed or padded cloth.

The maker's mark is stamped in ink on the back of the torso.

Moulded and painted facial features

Costume is typical of 19th-century female pedlar

Bonnet is moulded with the head and hair

Cap frill is made of lace dipped in slip, then fired with the head

Bisque shoulder head attached to the body by strips of sticky-backed fabric

Stuffed calico upper arms and torso; disc joints at shoulders

Hands are large and gnarled, like those of an old woman

Bisque lower arms, cast to above wrists

Stuffed calico upper legs, stitched to torso at hips

Bisque lower legs, with moulded and painted stockings and shoes

Basket contents include bead necklaces, books, toys, and miniature dolls

MARTHA THOMPSON DOLL *Some pedlar dolls came with an empty basket, to be filled at home with a variety of tiny items, ranging from haberdashery to kitchenware. This pedlar was made in the United States by Martha Thompson in the late 1950s, and dressed and equipped by English doll collector, Faith Eaton, in 1992.*

HT: 30cm (12in)

Grey mohair wig, stuck on head

Spectacles made of copper wire

Simple painted facial features

Wooden head and torso, with peg-jointed limbs

Equipped with a wide range of knick-knacks and miniature household utensils

APPLE-HEAD PEDLAR (RIGHT)
A pickled apple forms the head of this unusual pedlar, which was made in England c.1830. The apple is carved and painted to recreate the wrinkled, weather-beaten features of an old street vendor. Ht: 15cm (6in)

Glass bead eyes set into pickled apple head

Open mouth showing teeth

PEG WOODEN PEDLAR (LEFT)
Made originally as a peg wooden, (see pages 18–19), this pedlar dates from about 1900. It was adapted in the 1960s by Hilda Fonteyn, a doll enthusiast living in northern England. Ht: 33cm (13in)

Colourful clothing hides a crudely made cloth body

Doll is mounted on a varnished wooden stand

Inset silk hair

Wax shoulder head, moulded with bosom and arms

Painted facial features

Original contents of basket can help to date the doll's manufacture

Painted hair and facial features

Carved wooden head and torso, with peg-jointed limbs

"HENRIETTA" (RIGHT) Most pedlar dolls represent old women, so this example of a young lady is particularly striking. The graceful wax-headed figure, with beautifully formed hands, was made c.1860 by English wax-modeller, Henrietta Wade. Ht: 25cm (10in)

NOTION NANNY
(RIGHT) Made in the United States during the 1960s, this doll is said to represent a typical pedlar of the Ozark range of mountains, which run across parts of Oklahoma, Arkansas, and Missouri. Notion Nanny is one of the American names for pedlar dolls. Ht: 27cm (10½in)

Woven basket holds doll-size metal utensils

Padded cloth legs and torso over wire armature

Wooden mount is normally covered by glass dome, which sits in the groove

Soles of feet are painted to resemble shoes

A Master Doll-maker

· 1970s to the present day ·

TRAINED AS A COSTUME DESIGNER at Parsons School of Design in New York, E.J. Taylor began making dolls in 1973. The first models he created were clowns based on characters from Italy's *commedia dell'arte* theatre. The next year he designed a group of half-man and half-animal figures. Then, in 1976, Mr. Taylor created a figure, which he called Lady in White, for Tiffany's jewellery store in New York, and this proved so successful that, two years later, Saks Fifth Avenue asked the artist to produce three more "garden ladies".

Mr. Taylor's dolls all have an extraordinary quality: their heads and hands are modelled from Sculpey, a clay material developed in the United States that can be fired to a ceramic-like hardness in domestic oven temperatures; the bodies are made of papier mâché moulded over a wire armature.

Half-closed eyes with heavy eyelids, accentuated with peach colouring

Well-shaped hands with long, elegant fingers, modelled in Sculpey

Straw bonnet is tinted to match the delicate tones of the painted facial features

Traditional Sussex trug contains dried roses

Facial features modelled from Sculpey clay have a life-like quality

Closed full-lipped mouth is drawn back and indented at the corners

High, spare cheekbones and slackened jaw showing "bone" structure beneath

Clothes conceal body made of papier mâché moulded over a wire armature

Damask silk costume made from a fringed shawl, trimmed with bead buttons

LADY IN WHITE *The first of a set of four "garden ladies", the Lady in White was designed and made in 1976, as a display piece for Tiffany's jewellery store in New York City. The figure represents an elderly, aristocratic-looking woman dressed in a costume reminiscent of those from the early decades of the 20th century.*

HT: 75cm (30in)

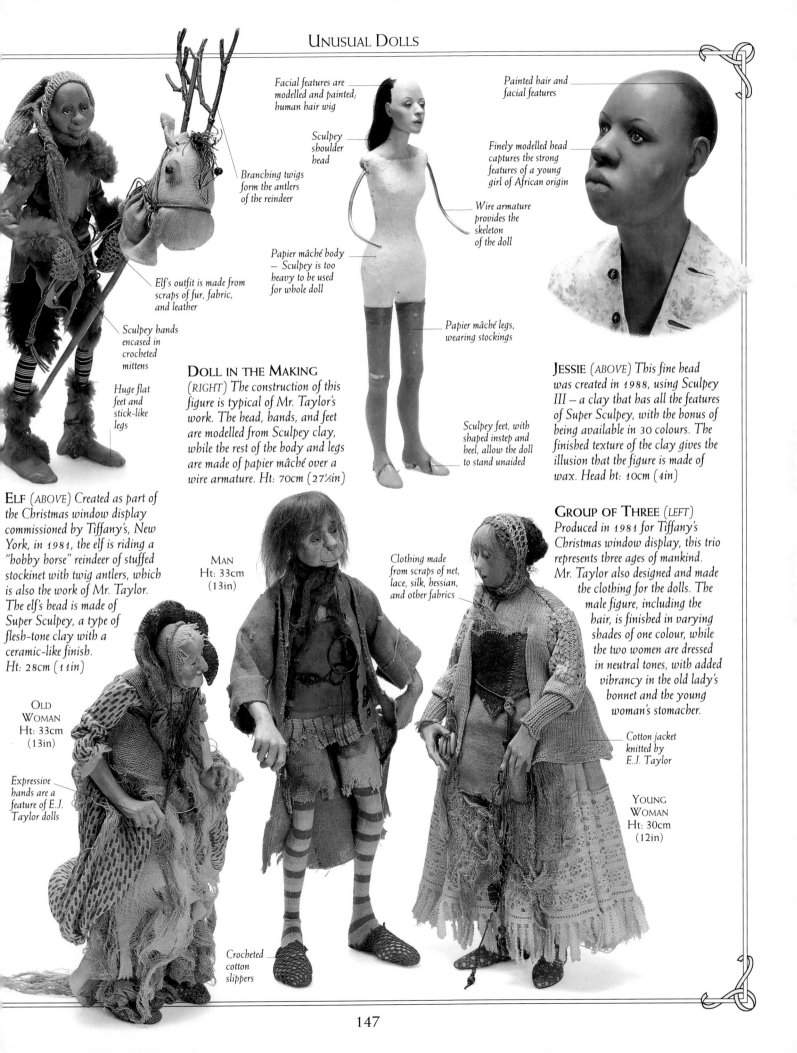

Facial features are modelled and painted; human hair wig

Sculpey shoulder head

Branching twigs form the antlers of the reindeer

Elf's outfit is made from scraps of fur, fabric, and leather

Sculpey hands encased in crocheted mittens

Huge flat feet and stick-like legs

Papier mâché body – Sculpey is too heavy to be used for whole doll

Wire armature provides the skeleton of the doll

Papier mâché legs, wearing stockings

Sculpey feet, with shaped instep and heel, allow the doll to stand unaided

Painted hair and facial features

Finely modelled head captures the strong features of a young girl of African origin

DOLL IN THE MAKING

(RIGHT) The construction of this figure is typical of Mr. Taylor's work. The head, hands, and feet are modelled from Sculpey clay, while the rest of the body and legs are made of papier mâché over a wire armature. Ht: 70cm (27½in)

JESSIE (ABOVE) This fine head was created in 1988, using Sculpey III – a clay that has all the features of Super Sculpey, with the bonus of being available in 30 colours. The finished texture of the clay gives the illusion that the figure is made of wax. Head ht: 10cm (4in)

ELF (ABOVE) Created as part of the Christmas window display commissioned by Tiffany's, New York, in 1981, the elf is riding a "hobby horse" reindeer of stuffed stockinet with twig antlers, which is also the work of Mr. Taylor. The elf's head is made of Super Sculpey, a type of flesh-tone clay with a ceramic-like finish. Ht: 28cm (11in)

MAN
Ht: 33cm
(13in)

Clothing made from scraps of net, lace, silk, hessian, and other fabrics

GROUP OF THREE (LEFT)

Produced in 1981 for Tiffany's Christmas window display, this trio represents three ages of mankind. Mr. Taylor also designed and made the clothing for the dolls. The male figure, including the hair, is finished in varying shades of one colour, while the two women are dressed in neutral tones, with added vibrancy in the old lady's bonnet and the young woman's stomacher.

Cotton jacket knitted by E.J. Taylor

OLD
WOMAN
Ht: 33cm
(13in)

Expressive hands are a feature of E.J. Taylor dolls

YOUNG
WOMAN
Ht: 30cm
(12in)

Crocheted cotton slippers

Useful Information

Most collections have modest beginnings: a doll from childhood, or perhaps one found in the attic, which belonged to your mother or grandmother, or one bought at random, simply because you liked the look of it. A mild curiosity about the history of one particular doll sparks an interest in the whole fascinating subject — an interest that may soon become an all-consuming passion, even taking over your home and your life.

THE MAJORITY OF BEGINNERS tend to acquire each and every doll they see; but gradually they become more selective, developing a liking for certain kinds of doll and choosing these in preference to all others. As you become more knowledgeable, through books, clubs, talks, and exhibitions, you may decide to specialize, perhaps choosing dolls of a particular material or ones created by an individual or a single company; or you may collect only portrait dolls or dolls with fancy moulded hair. Even collectors of modern dolls often limit the selection to just one type.

As soon as you have started your own collection, however modest, you should consider not only how to house it, but also how to look after it (see pages 150–153). It is as well to think carefully before adding to it to any great extent. Before long, you may find your entire home has become a display cabinet.

Where and What to Buy

If you are a beginner, it is advisable to buy your dolls from a reputable auction house, such as Christie's or Sotheby's, or a well-established doll-dealer. The big auction houses have salesrooms or affiliated branches in many parts of the world. If you are in any doubt about a dealer's reputation, be sure to consult another, more experienced collector, or check with your local doll club. Collecting modern dolls is much easier, of course, as you simply buy the doll directly from the maker, or if it is a mass-produced doll, from your local

COLLECTABLE WAX *(LEFT) A lovely wax doll such as this figure, made in the 1890s by Lucy Peck (see page 35), can be bought at a relatively low price because of the general belief that wax is unstable. Although wax is affected by changes in its surroundings, a sudden drop in temperature is the most damaging. Ht: 50cm (20in)*

ORIGINAL BOXED SET *(RIGHT) Acquiring a doll in its original state is a joy for any collector. The doll in this bisque set, made in the late 19th century by J.D. Kestner of Germany, is still tied to its box around the ankles, and at the waist underneath the pinafore. Ht: 46cm (18in)*

Ink stamp, usually found on the back of the torso

Moulded mark on celluloid head

Incised mark on bisque head

Paper label

Cloth label, stitched to clothes

IDENTIFYING MARKS (*ABOVE*)
From the 1890s, international law decreed that dolls (in common with all other products) must be marked or labelled with their country of origin. Marks and labels also help to date a doll and identify its maker, as well as the model. Head marks sometimes include a mould number. Corresponding size numbers may also appear on the head and body.

Card wrist tag, found only on 20th-century dolls

MISGUIDED IMPROVEMENT
(*RIGHT*) *This fine bisque swivel head doll, made c.1890 by the Parisian company, Bru Jne. & Cie, has been spoiled by replacing the original mohair wig with a modern nylon one, which is both too large and too heavy. Dolls that have suffered "improvements" like this may cost less to buy than others.*

the French bisque dolls of the 1860s to 1880s; those that were made by the French houses of Bru and Jumeau; and so-called character dolls. Even if you have a limited budget, you need not hesitate to start collecting dolls. A good collection can be created using dolls made from the 1930s onwards. Some nineteenth-century dolls are also quite modestly priced, notably those of wax and wax-over-composition, and the peg wooden dolls.

Gathering Information

When you acquire a doll, try to seek out as much information about it as you can: any known family history; who owned the doll before you and when; and if it has a name, either the maker's tradename or one given by a former owner. Anything that happens to a doll while it is in your care, for example having new clothing or receiving repairs, should also be noted.

~ Collecting dolls does require a certain investment, of time as well as money. However, you will find that dolls can open up several new avenues of interest – in fashion, architecture, interior design. Even after years of collecting and enjoying dolls, they will still be able to stir your imagination and bring you great pleasure.

store. As your knowledge increases, so will your ability to judge the quality, condition, and value of any doll you see. After a while, if you decide that you wish to refine your collection, it makes good sense to build up a network with other collectors, since many are willing to swap dolls instead of buying or selling them.

~ It is hard to give a definitive guide to dolls worth collecting: the market is changeable, and styles of doll seem to go in and out of fashion almost at random. In general, however, the most sought-after, and therefore the most expensive, dolls are the wooden ones made in the late seventeenth and early eighteenth centuries;

A SPECIALIST'S DELIGHT
(*RIGHT*) *Many people choose to specialize in their own collections, concentrating on dolls of one type or material, or those of one maker or one country. This Japanese boxed set, made in 1912, would be a real find for anyone focusing on oriental dolls: clothing and accessories accompany the figures (see page 133), and the whole is in excellent condition, with every piece intact. A set like this is likely to command a high price, not only because of its quality, but also because it may be of interest to those collecting other oriental artefacts.*

Caring For Your Collection

· Conservation and Restoration ·

IT IS CRUCIAL TO KEEP your doll collection in the right conditions. Most importantly, protect the dolls from sunlight, dust, and smoke from cigarettes or open fires. Dramatic changes in temperature cause major damage, so try to maintain the room at an even, but warmish, temperature, preferably somewhere between 18°C and 21°C (65–70°F), and keep the dolls away from hot-water pipes and radiators, or any source of direct heat.

You will not, of course, want to leave your dolls permanently on the shelf, but bear in mind that the less they are handled the better – not only to reduce the risk of damage, but also to prevent soiling from the natural oils in your skin. If you choose to wear cotton gloves when handling your dolls, wash them often to ensure that they are kept scrupulously clean.

Check your dolls regularly for signs of wear and tear; this will give you a better chance of arresting any problem – such as an attack of woodworm – before it becomes serious. If your dolls do need some form of repair, be guided by the expert advice of a professional doll restorer: inappropriate replacement parts or badly done work may ruin a doll, and even reduce its value.

Paint has begun to flake at the crown of the head, exposing the bare wood

Crudely finished joints wear badly, becoming loose or breaking

Hole in chest made by woodworm

Paint applied directly to the wood has no sound base and quickly begins to deteriorate

Damaged leg caused by rough and careless handling

WOODEN HEAD DETAIL

(ABOVE) *Flaking paint can be a major problem with old wooden dolls. In the 18th century, the wood was given a gesso base before it was painted; but later, in order to cut costs, the paint was applied directly to the wood. A slight knock can start the flaking process which, if unchecked, will continue until all the paint has disappeared.*

WOOD (LEFT)

THE QUALITY of wooden dolls deteriorated in the 19th and 20th centuries. Such dolls were rather crudely crafted and painted, and were not expected to become "antiques". Among the parts commonly damaged are the pegs in the joints: these are very small wooden pins, which snap extremely easily. The tenons of the joints may wear, too, or may even break off altogether.

RAG WITH COMPOSITION (BELOW)

ALL RAG DOLLS HAVE SIMILAR problems, many of which are caused by the way their owners handle them, rather than by any flaw in the construction of the doll. Soft rag dolls tend to be hugged and played with a good deal, especially by younger children. The areas most likely to be damaged are the parts that stick out – the nose and toes – and those that are pulled – the arms and the legs. With the example below, perhaps the doll's saving grace is that it has not suffered from "restoration", which can inflict as much damage as it attempts to repair.

Painted surface of the composition head is badly crazed and chipped

Tip of the nose is chipped, exposing the composition beneath

Fabric of the body is soiled, especially on the arms and legs

Left arm is split just above the wrist and stuffing is leaking

Soles of the feet are worn, revealing inner card stiffening

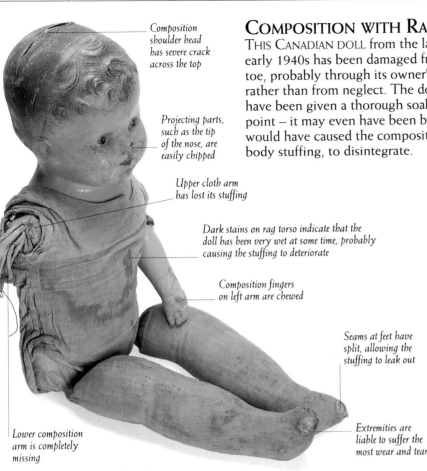

Composition shoulder head has severe crack across the top

Projecting parts, such as the tip of the nose, are easily chipped

Upper cloth arm has lost its stuffing

Dark stains on rag torso indicate that the doll has been very wet at some time, probably causing the stuffing to deteriorate

Composition fingers on left arm are chewed

Seams at feet have split, allowing the stuffing to leak out

Lower composition arm is completely missing

Extremities are liable to suffer the most wear and tear

COMPOSITION WITH RAG (*LEFT*)

THIS CANADIAN DOLL from the late 1930s or early 1940s has been damaged from head to toe, probably through its owner's enthusiasm rather than from neglect. The doll appears to have been given a thorough soaking at some point – it may even have been bathed. This would have caused the composition, and the body stuffing, to disintegrate.

Parts of the thick outer coating of wax have broken away, leaving features such as the nose vulnerable to damage

Composition base has shrunk away from its wax coating

WAX-OVER-COMPOSITION (*ABOVE*)

THE TECHNIQUE of using wax over moulded composition developed as a means of making heads with the look of expensive poured wax, at a fraction of the cost. A major problem of this combination, however, is the different rates at which the two materials expand and contract. As this occurs, the wax cracks and, in severe cases, large sections may fall away.

Inset hair has been damaged: overly vigorous brushing, insect infestation, or shaving are the most obvious causes

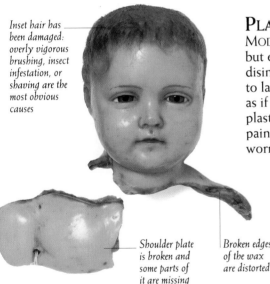

Shoulder plate is broken and some parts of it are missing

Broken edges of the wax are distorted

PLASTIC (*RIGHT*)

MODERN PLASTICS are durable materials, but earlier types, such as celluloid, slowly disintegrate as they age. If a plastic doll is to last, it must be looked after as carefully as if it were made of bisque or wax. Hard plastics are brittle and liable to break; if painted, the surface may chip away; and worn or pitted plastic is not easily cleaned.

Nylon wig is tangled and matted

Dirt has become ingrained in the plastic, especially on the face and in the crevices in the hands and feet

Neck is split on one side, along the mould line

Belly has caved in, probably under the weight of a child, or a chair

CELLULOID ARM DETAIL (*ABOVE*) *Repairing plastics that have split along a seam is possible; but if the crack occurs elsewhere, for example on the lower arm, as in the detail shown above, there is little that you can do. It is not a good idea to use glue, as this may cause a chemical reaction between the glue and elements in the plastic.*

POURED WAX (*ABOVE*)

THE MOST EASILY DAMAGED PART of a poured wax head is the neck, where the wax is thinnest, so never grasp a doll only by its neck. Dropping or knocking it on a hard surface will cause the wax to break. If the break is a clean one, an expert restorer may be able to repair it. However, as in this late 19th-century shoulder head, sometimes the wax twists and becomes slightly misshapen so that the edges will not fit exactly together.

Bisque with Composition (RIGHT)

THE WAY IN WHICH A DOLL IS STRUNG can be the cause of major problems. Ideally, the stringing ought to be tight enough to stop the head lolling about, but loose enough to allow the joints to move freely. In the case of this doll, made in France c.1900, too-tight stringing has caused friction at the joints of the torso and limbs, whose surfaces are badly worn. In general, the painted finish on later composition doll bodies like this one is poorer than on earlier models. The doll's bisque socket head also needs some skilled care and attention: a crack runs from the hairline through the right eyebrow and down the side of the nose; and the sleeping glass eyes have fallen or been pushed into the head itself.

Sleeping Eyes Mechanism

(RIGHT) Dabs of plaster hold the mechanism to the head. If the doll is stored on its back, the weight of the mechanism weakens the plaster fixing, and the eyes fall backwards.

Blown glass paperweight eyes set in bisque surround

Human hair lashes glued to the tops of the eyes

Lead weight hangs between the eyes and controls their movement

Mohair wig is matted and sparse in places

Bisque is cracked from hairline to side of nose

Eyes have fallen inside head; dolls with lead-weighted sleeping eyes should be stored face-down, on suitable padding to prevent rubbing

Teeth are missing from the mouth

Head has been broken from body, but has remained in one piece

Loose stringing causes joints to collapse

Hardened glue from an earlier repair; trying to remove it could damage the head further

Left and right arms have broken off and are missing

Composition is exposed and will gradually deteriorate

Paint on fingers is cracked and flaking

Too-tight stringing has resulted in an elongated hole, as torso and leg have rubbed together

Friction at the joint has caused varnish and paint to wear away, exposing the bare composition

Ball joint has come loose

Paintwork is subject to damage around ball joints at knees, wrists, and elbows, as well as at strung body parts

Paint on feet is damaged, and toes are worn away

Composition Fingers

(BELOW) Composition fingers are vulnerable to damage, especially if moulded separately, since they snap off easily. Repairs are hard to make, because the fingers are so small and have no internal support on which replacement parts could be built.

Composition Lower Legs

(BELOW) Composition toes tend to suffer the same kind of damage as fingers, although the toes are easier to repair because they are usually moulded together. Shoes normally offer some protection; but the doll shown here has only moulded and painted footwear, and the end of one foot has completely broken away.

All-Bisque (ABOVE) By far

the greatest harm that can befall a bisque doll is to drop it on or knock it against any hard surface: the bisque may fracture or shatter, or parts may be broken off altogether, as with this untinted bisque boy, made in Germany towards the end of the 19th century. Repairs are possible, but only with the use of special glues. Take great care when handling the pieces, as the broken edges may be jagged and sharp.

STUFFED KID (BELOW & RIGHT)

KID DOLLS SUFFER MOST when kept in hot, dry conditions, as the skin loses its natural oils, becoming brittle and crazed. Eventually the kid will split, usually at a seam since it is here that the strain is greatest. This in turn allows the stuffing to seep out, which can eventually spoil the shape of the whole doll. Very damp conditions also affect kid, causing mould growth or mildew; and both the kid and its stuffing are also vulnerable to attack by pests, such as insects and mice.

KID LEGS (LEFT) Ankle joints on kid dolls are usually formed by inserting an additional piece of kid between the leg and the foot. In this case, the ankle piece has come unstitched and the foot is breaking off, allowing the sawdust stuffing to leak out. Any repair like this is best left to a professional, to ensure that the kid is securely replaced and the shape of the doll is fully restored.

KID HANDS (RIGHT) A stuffed kid doll often has a wire armature providing the basic form. Over time, as the joints are bent, the metal breaks and may burst through the stuffing and puncture the skin. This tends to happen most at the smallest, narrowest parts of the body, such as the wrists. The wire may also rust and twist, damaging the kid skin.

KID JOINTS (LEFT) In a pinned joint, such as this shoulder, the pins often work loose. As this happens, the kid around the pin tends to split. In this case, the damage has been compounded by covering the hole with a sticky bandage, which it is impossible to remove without causing further harm.

Wire armature has broken through the kid covering

Kid has become crazed and brittle through being kept in hot, dry conditions

CLOTHING (BELOW & RIGHT)

THE CLOTHING OF DOLLS that are used as toys will, inevitably, be subject to general wear and tear. But even the clothes of display dolls can deteriorate if they are not kept in the right conditions. All fabrics have a natural rate of degeneration, but this can be exacerbated by excessive heat and damp; by the effect of the ultraviolet rays of the sun; and by attacks by mice or insects such as moths, beetles, and woodworm (which eat sawdust and straw stuffing as well as wood). Establishing a routine for checking your dolls will give you the best chance of remedying a problem before it gets out of hand.

MOULD (LEFT) Mould thrives in damp conditions and the "spotting" that results can ruin clothing made of natural fibres such as silk. In the case of wax dolls, similar damage is sometimes caused by a chemical in the dye that was used to colour the wax adversely affecting the fabric.

SILK (LEFT) Chemicals used in the manufacture of silk may hasten the natural deterioration of the fabric. The most common result of this is "laddering", the threaded effect as the fibres disintegrate; at worst, the silk will literally turn to dust.

MOTHS (LEFT) Dolls and their clothing seem particularly attractive to insects and rodents, which can do irreparable harm. Examine your dolls regularly for signs of attack, but seek advice from a doll expert before carrying out any treatment.

LEATHER (LEFT) Like any other natural material, leather begins to deteriorate after some time, getting dry and brittle so that the surface cracks and breaks up. Oiling the leather will help to keep it supple and also improve its appearance.

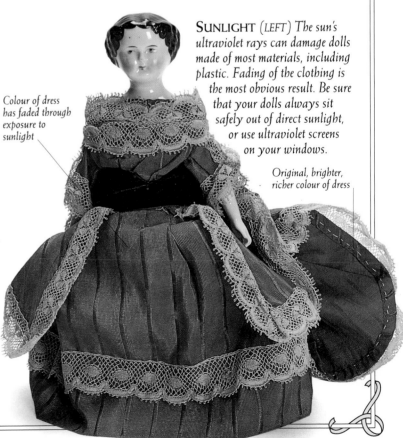

SUNLIGHT (LEFT) The sun's ultraviolet rays can damage dolls made of most materials, including plastic. Fading of the clothing is the most obvious result. Be sure that your dolls always sit safely out of direct sunlight, or use ultraviolet screens on your windows.

Colour of dress has faded through exposure to sunlight

Original, brighter, richer colour of dress

~ Addresses ~

MUSEUMS

BETHNAL GREEN MUSEUM OF CHILDHOOD
(A branch of the Victoria & Albert Museum)
Cambridge Heath Road
London E2 9PA
Telephone 081 980 3204

~

MARGARET WOODBURY STRONG MUSEUM
1 Manhattan Square
Rochester, N.Y. 14607, U.S.A.
Telephone 0101 716 263 2700

~

MUSEUM OF CHILDHOOD
42 High Street
Edinburgh EH1 1TG
Telephone 031 225 2424

~

MUSEUM OF DOLL ART
1116 108th Avenue North East
Bellevue, WA 98006, U.S.A.
Telephone 0101 206 455 1116

~

POLLOCK'S TOY MUSEUM
1 Scala Street
London W1P 1LT
Telephone 071 636 3452

~

WARWICK DOLL MUSEUM
Okens House
Castle Street
Warwick, Warwickshire CV34 4BP
Telephone 0926 495546/412500

WENHAM HISTORICAL ASSOCIATION
AND MUSEUM
132 Main Street
Wenham, MA 01984, U.S.A.
Telephone 0101 508 468 2377

~

WORTHING MUSEUM & ART GALLERY
Chapel Road
Worthing, West Sussex BN11 1HP
Telephone 0903 239999

CLUBS

THE DOLL CLUB OF GREAT BRITAIN
Mrs. Jane Dunne
Unity Cottage
Pishill Bank
Henley-on-Thames, Oxfordshire RG9 6HJ

~

DOLL COLLECTORS OF AMERICA
c/o Diane Buck
Wenham Historical Association
and Museum
see address above

~

DOLLOLOGY
affiliated to United Federation of Doll Clubs
see address below

~

UNITED FEDERATION OF DOLL CLUBS
10920 North Ambassador Drive
Kansas City, MO 64153, U.S.A.
Telephone 0101 816 891 7040

MAGAZINES

AUSTRALIAN DOLL DIGEST
Box 680
Goulburn, N.S.W. 2580, Australia
Telephone 010 48 213660

~

BRITISH DOLL COLLECTORS NEWS
The Anchorage
Wrotham Road, Colverston
Meopham, Kent DA13 0QW

~

DOLL CRAFTER
30595 Eight Mile
Livonia, MI 48152, U.S.A.

~

DOLL READER
Cumberland Publishing, Inc.
900 Frederick Street
Cumberland, MD 21502, U.S.A.
Telephone 0101 301 759 3770

~

DOLLS – THE COLLECTOR'S MAGAZINE
Collector Communications, Inc.
170 Fifth Avenue
New York, N.Y. 10010, U.S.A.
Telephone 0101 212 989 8700

~

U.K. DOLL DIRECTORY
Hugglets
P.O. Box 290
Brighton, East Sussex BN2 1DR
Telephone 0273 697974

Further Reading

1850S' ENGLISH WAX GIRL *This doll has a shoulder head of poured wax, with inset human hair and glass eyes. Its leather lower arms and calico body are all stuffed with cowhair. Ht: 46cm (18in)*

Anderton, Johana Gast *Twentieth Century Dolls, From Bisque to Vinyl*, Trojan Press, North Kansas City 1971
Cieslik, Jürgen and Marianne *Dolls, European Dolls 1800–1930*, Christie's South Kensington Collectors' Guides, Studio Vista, London 1979

Cieslik, Jürgen and Marianne *German Doll Encyclopedia 1800–1939*, Hobby House Press, Cumberland 1985
Coleman, Dorothy S., Elizabeth A., and Evelyn J. *The Collector's Encyclopedia of Dolls, Vols I and II*, Crown Publishers, Inc., New York 1968 and 1986
Eaton, Faith *Care & Repair of Antique & Modern Dolls*, B.T. Batsford Limited, London 1985
Eaton, Faith *Dolls in Colour*, Blandford Press, Poole 1975
Goodfellow, Caroline G. *Understanding Dolls*, Antique Collectors' Club, Woodbridge 1983
Mansell, Colette *The Collector's Guide to British Dolls Since 1920*, Robert Hale Ltd., London 1983

Glossary

AMERICAN CLOTH/OILCLOTH Heavy woven cotton or linen painted with oil-based paints.

BALL AND SOCKET JOINT Made by fitting a rounded ball into a concave socket. Usually seen on composition and plastic bodies.

BENT LIMBS Curved arms and legs, moulded as complete units, seen on baby doll bodies.

BISQUE Unglazed **porcelain**.

CELLULOID A synthetic material based on vegetable fibres mixed with nitric and sulphuric acids and additives; inflammable.

CLOSED MOUTH Lips are joined and moulded together, with no open space in-between.

CLOTH Common term for any linen or cotton fabric.

COMPOSITION Wood and/or paper pulp mixed with additives. Includes papier mâché.

ERZGEBIRGE Region of eastern Germany south of Dresden on the Czech border, producing carved wooden toys and dolls in the 19th and 20th centuries.

FELT Matted wool fibre fabric.

FLANGE NECK HEAD Neck edge of head curves outward. Usually seen on stuffed cloth bodies.

FLIRTY EYES Combination of **sleeping eyes** and eyes that move to the side or from side to side.

GESSO Fine mix of plaster and water or **size** applied over wood as a base for paint finishes.

GLAZED CHINA Porcelain with a shiny, high-gloss overglaze.

GOFUN Japanese material made from crushed oyster shells and additives; has a pearl-like finish.

GOOGLY EYES Eyes that glance to only one side; sometimes combined with **sleeping eyes**. Also known as roguish eyes.

GRÖDENER TAL Region on the borders of Austria, Germany, and Italy; now part of Italy. Produced carved wooden dolls in the 19th and early 20th centuries.

MOTORING MISS A German bisque doll models this c.1900 costume for London's Marshall & Snelgrove store. Ht: 30cm (12in)

GROMMET Metal eyelet. Usually seen only on poured wax dolls.

GUSSETED JOINT Made by inserting a V-shaped panel at elbow, thigh, and knee joints. Usually seen on kid and **rag** dolls.

INSET EYES Glass eyes set into the eye sockets; cannot move.

INTAGLIO EYES Moulded or carved, concave eyes, with painted pupils and irises.

KAPOK Plant material similar to cotton wool, used for stuffing.

LOWER ARM From elbow to wrist; usually includes hand.

LOWER LEG From knee to ankle; usually includes foot.

MORTISE AND TENON JOINT Made by fitting tongues from one part into grooves in another. Usually seen on wooden bodies.

OPEN MOUTH Lips are cut open after moulding. May include teeth and/or a moulded tongue.

OPEN/CLOSED MOUTH Lips are moulded open but not cut. May include a moulded tongue.

PARIAN *See* **untinted bisque**.

PEGGED JOINT Simple **mortise and tenon joint**, held by a peg. Usually seen on early wooden dolls and later cheap models.

PLASTIC Any synthetic material that is malleable when soft and can be moulded into set forms.

PORCELAIN Fine-grade ceramic material, fired at not less than 1300°C (2372°F).

RAG Any fabric material.

REVERSE SOCKET HEAD Head ends below chin. Jointed to a torso that extends upwards from the shoulders to form the neck. Usually made of composition. *See also* **socket head**.

SHOULDER HEAD Head, neck, shoulders, and front and back chest plates are built as one unit; head cannot turn. May be made of any material, in particular poured wax or **porcelain**, but generally not **rag**. *See also* **shoulder plates**.

SHOULDER PLATES Front and back chest parts of a **shoulder head**. *See also* **swivel head**.

SIZE Thin, gelatinous mix, often including glue, used as a surface sealer. Component of **gesso**.

SLEEPING EYES Glass eyes that open and shut mechanically so that the doll appears to sleep.

SOCKET HEAD Head is moulded to include the neck, shaped at the end as a ball. Jointed to a torso with a cup-shaped socket between the shoulders, into which the head fits. Usually made of **bisque** or **composition**. *See also* **reverse socket head**.

SONNEBERG Principal town of **Thuringia** in Germany. Trading centre of the doll industry until the end of the 1930s.

STOCKINET Machine-knitted silk or cotton fabric; usually stretchy.

SWIVEL HEAD Combination of a **shoulder** and **socket** head. Neck is included as part of the head, which fits into separately cast **shoulder plates**; head can turn. Usually made of **glazed china** or **bisque**.

THURINGIA *Thüringen* Region of Germany to the north of Bavaria. Location of most of the **porcelain** factories that produced doll heads and limbs in the 19th and 20th centuries.

TUCKCOMB/COMB High, carved ornament on the crown of early 19th-century wooden doll heads, resembling a small mantilla.

UNTINTED BISQUE Matt-finish porcelain, usually white. Also known as parian, particularly in the United States.

UPPER ARM From the elbow to the shoulder or shoulder joint.

UPPER LEG From the knee to the hip or hip joint.

VELVET Woven silk fabric, with a close, soft texture, short, dense pile, and lustrous sheen.

VELVETEEN Similar to **velvet**, but made of cotton rather than silk, and lacking the lustrous sheen.

VINYL Post-1945 **plastic**; when set, may be hard or soft.

WAX-OVER-COMPOSITION Moulded **composition**, coated with a thin layer of wax to create the appearance of poured wax. Used for limbs as well as heads.

WORSTED Woven fabric made of long-staple wool, with a close, hard texture and no pile.

~ Index ~

DAVY CROCKETT *Vogue Dolls, Inc. created this American folk-hero figure in 1955. Ht: 20cm (8in)* Vogue Dolls® is a registered trademark of Dakin, Inc. All Vogue Dolls designs © 1993 Dakin, Inc., Woodland Hills, California, USA, reproduced here courtesy of Dakin.

CHINESE BOY *This pressed felt doll with painted facial features, thought to be the work of Lenci or Chad Valley, was made in Europe in the 1930s. The fine black mohair stitched to its head extends to form a long braid. Ht: 65cm (26in)*

DOLLY FACE GIRL *The bisque socket head and jointed composition body of this doll are typical of those made by the* Société Française de Fabrication de Bébés et Jouets *in the early years of the 20th century. Ht: 38cm (15in)*

GEBRÜDER HEUBACH GIRL
*Best known for its character babies,
the German company of Gebrüder
Heubach also created many other
lines, including this c.1920s' girl
with dolly face. Ht: 40cm (16in)*

QUEEN ELIZABETH II *This bisque shoulder head was modelled in 1970 by Martha Thompson, a doll artist in the United States. The doll's lower arms and legs are also made of bisque, attached to a stuffed calico body. Doll ht: 35cm (14in)*

ORIENTAL GIRL *The bisque socket head of this late 19th-century German doll bears the mark of Schoenau & Hoffmeister. Ht: 35cm (14in)*

Acknowledgments

AUTHOR'S ACKNOWLEDGMENTS

My very grateful thanks to the Wenham Historical Association and Museum, Worthing Museum & Art Gallery, Christie's South Kensington, and Bethnal Green Museum of Childhood for their valuable assistance and cooperation; also Diane Buck, Sally White, Olivia Bristol, Christine Jeffery, Noreen Marshall, Betty Ridley, William Birnbaum, and Josephine Goodfellow. I especially thank Faith Eaton, for allowing the use of her wonderful dolls and for commenting on the text. Likewise, Dorothy and Evelyn Jane Coleman, my American family, deserve special thanks for sharing their vital knowledge as well as their beautiful dolls.
I am indebted to everyone at Dorling Kindersley for all their help, in particular Gillian Roberts, my good-humoured editor, and Kevin Ryan, who has designed a magnificent book. Many thanks also to Matthew Ward in England and Lynton Gardiner in the United States for their inspired photographs. Finally, to Tiber and Miss Polly, thank you for being so patient.

PUBLISHER'S ACKNOWLEDGMENTS

Dorling Kindersley acknowledges the generous help of those individuals without whom this book could not have been produced. Special thanks to Catherine Sidwell at Bethnal Green Museum of Childhood; Katherine Higgins at Christie's South Kensington; and Linda Stiles and Sally White at Worthing Museum & Art Gallery. Polly Boyd and Lesley Riley worked diligently and with great patience to complete the text pages, supported by Constance Novis; Alex Corrin compiled the index; Charlotte Davies, Alison Edmonds, Chris Legee, and Alison Shackleton provided the team with creature comforts; Sharon Moore helped to prepare pages for final film; Julia Pashley researched the archive picture material; Mel Roberts explained the ins and outs of the English language; Ann Thompson gave design assistance; Alastair Wardle contributed his computer expertise.

PUBLIC AND PRIVATE DOLL COLLECTIONS

Abbreviations indicate position on page:

t=top; b=bottom; c=centre; l=left; r=right

All the dolls photographed for this book belong to the private collection of **Faith Eaton**, except: **Bethnal Green Museum of Childhood** *A branch of the Victoria & Albert Museum* 2, 7 (r); 12 (l, r), 13 (tl, bl, br), 16, 17 (three dolls bl), 30 (l), 33 (tl, cr), 36, 37, 38, 39 (except bl, br), 40, 41, 57 (two dolls tr), 60, 65 (bl), 70 (l, r), 71 (br), 79 (br), 84, 85 (tr), 96, 107 (bl), 115 (br), 119 (except tc), 124, 125, 129 (b), 131 (b), 136, 139 (two dolls tl), 143 (br). **Christie's South Kensington** 61 (tl, tr, bl), 101 (br), 148 (br), 149 (tr), 150 (br). **Coleman Collection** 3, 42 (br), 43 (bl), 44, 45 (except tl), 46, 47 (except br), 48, 49 (tl, bl, bc, br), 50, 51 (tr, tc, c, br), 93 (tr), 97, 99 (tr), 101 (tl, tr). **Courtesy of the Wenham Museum, Wenham, MA.** 1, 6 (br), 9 (tl), 14, 15 (tl, bl), 17 (br), 22, 23 (c, br), 26, 27 (tl, tc, b), 32, 74 (r), 75, 88, 90, 91 (tl, bl, br), 92 (bc), 93 (five dolls b), 104 (br), 105 (br), 106, 107 (tr, r), 111 (tl, tc), 112, 113 (tl, tc, bl, br), 122 (cl), 127 (tr), 138, 139 (br), 156, 157 (tl). **Worthing Museum & Art Gallery** 3, 11 (tr), 15 (br), 21 (bl, br), 33 (bl), 35 (tr, br), 53 (tr), 54 (bl), 55 (bl, tl), 56, 57 (tl, bl), 59 (tl, tc, bl, br), 61 (cr), 62, 63, 65 (br), 69 (tc, bl), 71 (tr), 81 (bl), 87 (br), 128, 139 (tr), 142, 145 (tr), 154. **Other individuals** who kindly lent us either their own dolls or doll-associated items: Chris Dawson 126 (tl); Lucinda and Emma Ganderton 17 (tr), 89 (tl), 121 (br); Hilary Kennelly 120 (tl); exhibit on loan to Worthing

Museum by a former Worthing resident 59 (tl, tc); Carol Wagner Merriman 113 (c); Lynne and Michael Roche 81 (cl), 128; Gunilla Rosengren 101 (bl); Kevin Ryan 9 (bl), 137 (b); E.J. Taylor 30 (br), 146, 147; Matthew Ward 126.

The author and publisher also thank the **following manufacturers** for permission to reproduce their dolls in this book: A.C. Fincken, *Sunny Jim* 95 (tl); Alexander Doll Co., *Dionne Quintuplet Baby* and *Toddler Dolls, Dr. Allan Roy Dafoe* and *Nurse Louise De Kirilene* 26–27; Chad Valley Toys – exclusive to Woolworths', *Dwarfs* from Walt Disney's film *Snow White and the Seven Dwarfs* 99 (b); Dakin, Inc., *Vogue Dolls Girl Scout* 9 (tl), *Waac-ette* and *Wave-ette* 111 (t), *Skater* 112, *Jill and Jeff, Ginny's Pup, Miss 2000, Ginnette* all 113, *Sunshine Baby* 123 (lc), *Jimmy Cowboy* 127 (tr), *Davy Crockett* 156. Vogue Dolls® is a registered trademark of Dakin, Inc. All Vogue Dolls designs © 1993 Dakin, Inc., Woodland Hills, California, USA, reproduced by courtesy of Dakin; DC Comics, SUPERMAN, BATMAN and ROBIN ™ & © 1993 DC Comics. All rights reserved. Used by permission of DC Comics, 111; Johnny Gruelle's *Raggedy Ann*, copyright © Johnny B. Gruelle, Playskool/Hasbro, Inc., exclusive manufacturer 89; Hasbro International Inc., *Sindy* 120, 121 (tl, tr, bl), *Patch* 121 (c, br), *Action Man* 126, 127 (tl); Ideal UK, 1960s' *Shirley Temple* 114, 1982 *Shirley Temple* 115 (tl), 1930s' *Shirley Temple* 115 (tr); Jesco, *Bisque Kewpie* 86, *Celluloid Kewpies* 104 (br). "The KEWPIE® Trademark and KEWPIE® characters are protected by U.S. Trademark and Copyright Registrations, exclusively licensed to Jesco and reprinted under permission from Jesco"; Mattel UK Ltd., *Barbie* 116, 117, *Ken* 127 (bl, bc), *Heart Family* 128 (b); Merrythought Ltd., Two *Dwarfs* from Walt Disney's film *Snow White and the Seven Dwarfs* 99 (c); Villy Nielsen A/S, *Judith Mother and Baby* 129 (tc); Royal Doulton Limited, 124, 125: these items are no longer made by the Company, having been discontinued in 1985.

THE COMMISSIONED PHOTOGRAPHS

All photographs by **Matthew Ward**, except: **Lynton Gardiner** 1 (c), 3 (c), 6 (l, r), 9 (tl), 14, 15 (tl, bl), 22, 23 (c, br), 26, 27, 32, 33, 42 (br), 43, 44, 45 (except tl), 46, 47 (except br), 48, 49 (except c), 50, 51 (except tl, bl), 74 (r), 75, 88, 90, 91 (except tr), 92, 93 (except tl), 97, 99 (tr), 101 (tl, tr), 104 (br), 105 (br), 106, 107 (tr), 138 (cl), 139 (br), 156 (bl), 157 (tl); **Tony Sandin** 101 (bl).

THE COMMISSIONED ILLUSTRATIONS

The decorative watercolour, gouache, and airbrush on paper illustrations are the work of **Marc Adams**.
The decorative line devices and the drawing of a hand, used to indicate doll height, are the work of **Stephen Dew**.

ARCHIVE PICTURE CREDITS

Ashmolean Museum, Oxford 11 (br); Bridgeman Art Library 7 (bl); by kind permission of the Chairman, Mr. Mohamed Al Fayed, Harrods Ltd./Reuters 110 (b); Ursula Gander-Bonet 53; The Hulton Picture Company 31; Japan National Tourist Organization 131 (tl); Oscar and Peter Johnson 8 (c); Maidstone Museum and Art Gallery 43; Mary Evans Picture Library 89; Retrograph Archive 104 (l); Sotheby's, London 52 (bl); by courtesy of the Board of Trustees of the Victoria & Albert Museum 11 (tl).

NOVELTY HAT-DOFFER *Made in England at the end of the 19th century, this sprightly fellow has a ceramic head, with moulded and painted hair, and wooden arms and legs. A squeeze of the bellows, housed inside the wire body, activates the doll's arm. Ht: 20cm (8in)*